An English Arcadia
1600–1990

An English Arcadia

1600–1990

Designs for Gardens
and Garden Buildings in the Care of
the National Trust

Compiled and with an introduction by
Gervase Jackson-Stops

The American Institute of Architects Press
Washington D.C.

Published in association with
The British National Trust

For James and Alvilde Lees-Milne
who combine architecture and gardening and know
the meaning of Arcadia

The publication of this book has been made possible by a generous grant
from Mrs Henry J. Heinz II.

© The National Trust, 1991
All rights reserved
Designed by James Shurmer
Production by Bob Towell
Phototypeset in Monotype Lasercomp Garamond Series 156
by Southern Positives and Negatives (SPAN), Lingfield, Surrey (7782)
Printed and bound in Hong Kong

Published by
The American Institute of Architects Press
1735 New York Avenue, N.W., Washington, D.C. 20006

Jacket illustrations
(*Front*) Stourhead, Wiltshire, by Coplestone Warre Bampfylde

Frontispiece
Stowe, Buckinghamshire: The Temple of British Worthies and
the Palladian Bridge

PHOTOGRAPHIC ACKNOWLEDGEMENTS

Numerals refer to page numbers except where indicated
Aerofilms 51 (bottom); Bodleian Library, Oxford 13; British Library
catalogue numbers 32–3; British Museum 12 (bottom), 14 (top); *Country
Life* 20, 55 (bottom), 76; Courtauld Institute of Art 88 (bottom), catalogue
number 19; Henry E. Huntingdon Library and Art Gallery, San Marino,
California 15; National Trust Photographic Library 121; NTPL/James
Barfoot 21; NTPL/John Blake 28 (bottom); NTPL/Vera Collingwood 17
(bottom right); NTPL/John Hammond catalogue numbers 7, 23, 29, 60,
61, 62–4, 70–1, 78–84, 102–4, 113–18, 124; NTPL/Jerry Harpur
frontispiece; NTPL/Angelo Hornak catalogue numbers 1, 3, 4–6, 8–18,
20–2, 24–8, 30–1, 35–59, 65–9, 72–3, 77, 85–101, 105, 107–22, 125;
NTPL/M. W. Keen 16; NTPL/P. Lacey 154 (bottom); NTPL/Erik
Pelham 32 (bottom); NTPL/Martin Trelawny 10, 11, 12 (top), 14
(bottom); NTPL/Mike Williams 17 (bottom left), 18 (bottom left);
NTPL/Jeremy Whitaker 17 (top), 101 (bottom); Royal Institute of British
Architects, Drawings Collection 18 (top) and catalogue numbers 2, 34, 106;
Trustees of Sir John Soane's Museum 19; Quinlan Terry Esq catalogue
number 123; Victoria and Albert Museum catalogue numbers 74–5.

Library of Congress Cataloging-in-Publication Data

An English arcadia 1600–1990: designs for gardens and garden
    buildings in the care of the British National Trust/
    compiled and with an introduction by Gervase Jackson-Stops.
        p.   cm.
    "Published in association with the British National Trust."
    Includes bibliographical references and index.
    1. Gardens—Great Britain—History—Sources—Catalogs.
    2. Gardens—Great Britain—Designs and plans—Catalogs. 3. Parks—
    Great Britain—History—Sources—Catalogs. 4. Parks—Great
    Britain—Designs and plans—Catalogs. 5. Garden structures—Great
    Britain—History—Sources—Catalogs. 6. Garden structures—Great
    Britain—Designs and plans—Catalogs. 7. National Trust (Great
    Britain)—Art collections—Catalogs. I. Jackson-Stops, Gervase.
    II. National Trust (Great Britain)
    SB466.G7E54   1991   90—47109
    712'.5'0941—dc20   CIP

ISBN 1-55835-032-2 (hardcover)
ISBN 1-55835-033-0 (paperback)

First AIA Press paperback edition, 1992

Contents

A garden seat at Ascott, Wing, Buckinghamshire, designed by Walter Godfrey, c.1914 (RIBA Drawings Collection)

Foreword

On 12 July 1989 Dame Jennifer Jenkins, Chairman of the National Trust, stood on the steps of the Temple of Concord and Victory at Stowe in Buckinghamshire to announce the Trust's acquisition of the 562-acre landscape, the largest and arguably the finest surviving eighteenth-century garden in Britain. This historic statement was made thanks to the initiative of an anonymous benefactor, who gave £2 million, and further generous support from the National Heritage Memorial Fund and other grant-giving bodies. Nevertheless, the repair and future maintenance of 38 surviving temples, the dredging of lakes, the carving of missing statues and vases, the replanting of trees and shrubs, the laying of paths and the opening of vistas – all based on a close study of the surviving physical and documentary evidence – leaves the Trust with a considerable amount of money still to raise. An appeal for £1 million was launched in October 1989, and it is expected that individual projects within the gardens will need further sponsorship over the next ten years.

The idea of mounting an exhibition in support of the Stowe Landscape Gardens Appeal stemmed directly from the success of its predecessor, *Robert Adam and Kedleston*. A selection of the unrivalled architectural drawings from that house was shown in London in 1987, and subsequently travelled to a number of American cities including Washington, DC, New York, Chicago, Boston and Philadelphia, helping to raise funds for the Trust's Kedleston Appeal through the Royal Oak Foundation. As on that occasion, we are grateful to the American Institute of Architects for undertaking the circulation of this exhibition, and in particular to Judith Nyquist, formerly Director of the Octagon House and now Consulting Curator, Marilyn Montgomery, Director of Development, Nancy Davis, the present Director of the Octagon, and Linnea Hamer, Associate Curator.

To gather together the best designs for gardens and garden buildings from the Trust's properties all over England, Wales and Northern Ireland seemed a worthwhile exercise on various counts. To begin with, there could be no more appropriate way of celebrating Stowe than to show its central place in the history of British landscape gardening, with Rigaud's engravings and Nattes's watercolours of Stowe itself at the very

heart of the exhibition (Nos 35–45), preceded by the formal layouts which influenced Sir Richard Temple and Lord Cobham, and succeeded by the picturesque landscapes which Cobham and his successors in turn influenced.

The beauty, and relative obscurity, of the drawings selected – many of them published for the first time – were also good reasons for re-examining the Trust's holdings in this field. Pen-and-ink and watercolour sketches are, of course, extremely sensitive to the light. Few of them can therefore be on permanent display in our houses, and many are best kept in the folio cases or solander boxes where they were placed by previous owners, and where they can be examined by scholars. Others, framed and glazed for years, but protected by baize covers or hung in dark corners to avoid fading, are often overlooked by visitors. To bring them to the attention of a wide public on both sides of the Atlantic, if only for a short time, is likely to stimulate discussion about the gardens they depict, and to illuminate some of the lesser known byways of British garden history.

Another important justification for a show of this kind is the conservation work carried out to the exhibits, and here we must express our deep sense of gratitude for a generous grant from Mrs Paul Mellon, which almost entirely covered the necessary costs. The Trust's Adviser on Paper Conservation, Mary Goodwin, handled the huge extra workload with unfailing efficiency and good humour, and thanks should also go to the Registrar, Joanna Rickards, and the independent conservators who worked on the drawings: Peter Arris, Stephen Daly, Sheila Fairbrass, Claire Gaskell, Roy Graf, Kim Leyshon and Gillian Wood. The Trust's Advisor on Book Conservation, Dr Nicholas Pickwoad, also prepared book cradles and special cases for the three items on vellum.

We are also immensely grateful to Niall Hobhouse and Hazlitt Gooden and Fox Ltd in London and New York for their support of the exhibition throughout. We must also acknowledge the generous contribution of Arnold Wiggins and Sons, and its directors Pippa Mason and Michael Gregory, in providing frames for the exhibition.

Many of the larger plans and surveys of gardens made in the seventeenth and eighteenth centuries were drawn on vellum, partly perhaps because they could then be consulted indoors and out. That unfortunately creates a problem for travel today, since the medium is

(Opposite) The Temple of Concord at Stowe

7

notoriously affected by changes in relative humidity. Large-scale drawings on paper, like Capability Brown's famous design for Petworth, can present a different problem, in that damage from frequent use has rendered them barely legible. However, important examples in both these categories are illustrated in the Introduction, and these help to complete the picture. It was also felt impractical to include Humphry Repton's Attingham or Sheringham 'Red Books', when only one page could be shown at a time (with the flaps either up or down). They, too, are illustrated in the Introduction, while the exhibition contains several framed sheets from Repton's disbound Red Book for Wimpole (Nos 86–88).

Strictly speaking, not all the drawings in the show are designs. Some, like Robert Smythson's drawing of Ham (No. 2), are surveys, showing the appearance of a garden soon after its creation or after major alterations. Others, like Moses Griffith's watercolours of Shugborough (Nos. 62–63), are topographical views used, in the absence of the architect's lost drawings, to show the garden buildings in their original form and setting. Just a few, like Cyril Farey's wonderful perspective of Castle Drogo (No. 118), are included primarily to explain the other drawings in their group: in this case Lutyens's designs for the 'hanging gardens' originally intended immediately below its walls.

The large majority of the drawings is the property of the National Trust, but some collections still belong to the families concerned, and the Trust is particularly grateful to Viscount Astor and Sir Francis Dashwood, Bt, for loans from Cliveden and West Wycombe respectively. Other lenders include the Marquess of Anglesey, Mr Mark Blathwayt, Buckinghamshire County Museum, Aylesbury, the Governors of Claremont Fan Court School, Lord McAlpine, Mr Anthony Mitchell, Lady Margaret Myddelton, Mrs G. F. Pettit, the Trustees of the Powis Estate, the Drawings Collection of the Royal Institute of British Architects, Lord St Oswald, the Governors of Stowe School, Surrey Libraries, Mr Quinlan Terry, the Victoria and Albert Museum and the National Library of Wales.

The permanent legacy of an exhibition is its catalogue: in this case a book which we hope will reach a far wider audience than the show itself, appealing to the informed layman as much as the garden historian. The book could not have been published in its present form, with every drawing illustrated – and many of them in colour – without the very generous support of Mrs Henry J. Heinz II, a long-standing benefactor of the National Trust through the Royal Oak Foundation. As so often, her encouragement has been a crucial element in the whole venture.

For help over the catalogue entries, I would like to thank Alastair Laing, the Trust's Adviser on Paintings and Sculpture, John Sales, Chief Gardens Adviser, and John and Eileen Harris. Judy Egerton kindly checked many references, and helped with the research, while Edward Diestelkamp made valuable observations on the designs for conservatories. The Trust's Historic Buildings Representatives in the regions were also of great assistance: David Adshead (East Anglia), Andrew Barber (East Midlands), John Chesshyre (Kent & East Sussex), Belinda Cousens (Mercia), Susan Denyer (North West), Hugh Dixon (Northumbria), Jeffrey Haworth (Severn), John Maddison (East Anglia), Peter Marlow (Northern Ireland), Jonathan Marsden (North Wales), Hugh Meller (Devon), Anthony Mitchell (Wessex), Christopher Rowell (Southern), Christopher Wall (Thames & Chilterns) and Roger Whitworth (Yorkshire).

Jill Lever, Jane Preger and Andrew Norris of the RIBA Drawings Collection answered many queries, and others who generously helped in a variety of ways include Mme J. Barrier, John Baskett, Camilla Beresford, Michael Bevington, George Clarke, Antony Cleminson, John Cornforth, Martin Drury, Charlotte Fisher, John Fuggles, Leslie Harris, Sarah Lang, Richard Wheeler and James Yorke.

I am also deeply grateful to Margaret Willes, Samantha Wyndham and Anthony Lambert for ensuring the smooth production of the catalogue, despite fast-disappearing deadlines.

Last but not least, Maggie Grieve typed the entire manuscript, did the picture research and undertook much of the administration of the whole project. Neither the book nor the exhibition could have happened without her.

GERVASE JACKSON-STOPS
December 1990

A design for a sundial at Ascott, Wing, Buckinghamshire, from the office of George Devey (RIBA Drawings Collection)

8

Introduction

In almost a hundred years of existence, the British National Trust has never consciously set out to acquire a portfolio of property, whether of open spaces, country houses, parks or gardens. Unlike the National Gallery in London, which has always in some way attempted to tell the whole history of art, buying pictures consciously to fill gaps, the Trust has acted only to preserve properties which were under serious threat: houses that would otherwise have lost their contents; coastline that would otherwise have fallen to the developer; wind- and water-mills faced with demolition; archaeological sites threatened by the plough. At the same time, the Trust has been able to take on a property only where funds for its endowment can be found. It can gather the golden apples as they fall, but not go out and pick them off the tree.

This essentially passive role, becoming somewhat more active only since the foundation of the National Heritage Memorial Fund in 1979, could have led to a very unbalanced list. On the other hand, one of the chief criteria for acceptance has always been the rarity of a place, and this in itself has ensured the widest range of properties. If more by chance than design, the Trust now holds an unparalleled succession of historic houses and gardens with remarkably few periods and styles unrepresented.

Naturally, chance has played rather more of a part in the selection of gardens than of houses. Some of the best known, like Hidcote, Sissinghurst, Bodnant and most recently Biddulph Grange, have come on their own undisputed merits, but many others, of almost equal importance, have come only as an adjunct to a house. Masterpieces like Powis and Stourhead must always have been recognised as the equals of the medieval castles or Palladian villas to which they belonged, but others like Erddig, Wimpole, Calke and Canons Ashby have achieved independent stature virtually as afterthoughts – restoration having been carried out on the basis of surviving documents.

The fact that trees and flowers are so much more ephemeral than bricks and mortar underlines the importance of documents for the study of garden history. While the architectural historian can often piece together the development of a building from purely visual evidence, no amount of tree-dating, water-divining or even excavation, is going to re-establish the rapidly changing appearance of a garden over two or three centuries. The only way to do that is to study the nurserymen's accounts, the labourers' bills, painstakingly listed by some devoted steward, and above all, the drawings, engravings and surveyor's maps which record the comings and goings of avenues and ha-has, canals and lakes, paths and parterres.

Many of the Trust's most important restorations of gardens would have been impossible without such documentation. The detailed depiction of Westbury Court in Kip's bird's-eye view (No. 4), accompanied by Maynard Colchester's contemporary lists of bulbs and fruit trees, made the reconstruction of this Dutch Baroque garden worthwhile – although only the bare bones of its original layout survived. The more recent replanting of the seventeenth-century garden at Ham would equally have been unthinkable, had there not been the evidence of Slezer's survey (No. 3), supplemented by the painting of the Duke and Duchess of Lauderdale promenading in the 'wilderness', attributed to Danckerts and to be seen in the White Closet at Ham House (page 27).

Designs for gardens and garden buildings may be of more practical use in this way than designs for houses, but they also tend to be more interesting on a theoretical basis. Freed from the utilitarian needs of country-house planning, and the regimen of everyday life, they were in a better position to express ideas, often by mixing pleasure with instruction. They could also afford to take risks. It is no accident that the earliest Neo-classical buildings in England were garden pavilions, like the Grecian Temple at Stowe (No. 45), afterwards renamed Concord and Victory, which anticipated the Greek Revival churches and town halls of the Regency period by a clear half century. Gibbs's Gothic Temple at Stowe, built in the early 1740s, was similarly years ahead of its time, and immensely influential, not only in terms of style but also in its thinking. The deliberate asymmetry and the use of dark ironstone to suggest rude native traditions and liberties, with the proud inscription *Je rends graces aux dieux de nestre pas Romain*, looked forward to Pugin's rejection of classicism as an imported foreign currency.

Other buildings that experimented with novel ideas include Robert Adam's hermitage at Kedleston, with its rough tree-trunk columns, following Laugier's theories about the origins of primitive architecture and anticipating Soane's 'primitive' farm buildings at Wimpole. Experimentation could of course be in the structural rather than the stylistic field. The cast-iron frames of the Wyatt family's conservatories, like Lewis's at Tatton and Jeffry Wyatville's at Belton (Nos 89–91), led to the widespread use of the material in Victorian architecture, while the buildings were also among the pioneers of underfloor heating.

In contrast to domestic architecture, garden and garden building design could also be freer in its relation to the other arts. There are times, as at Stourhead, when it can seem almost a branch of landscape painting, with buildings erected purely for their incidental effect on the landscape, emulating the pictures of Claude and Poussin. But there are other times, at earlier and later periods, when parterres and knot gardens are conceived in the same spirit as inlaid floors and carpets, or derive their form from the ornamental pattern-books used by metalworkers and cabinet-makers.

Tempting as it is to separate house and garden in terms of design, the interaction of the two is a crucial element in their development. Long galleries, where exercise was taken on rainy days, were clearly seen in the sixteenth century as indoor garden walks. At Knole, the Cartoon Gallery is not only placed above an open arcade looking on to the garden (used for the same purpose in warmer weather), but has a ceiling decorated with plaster flowers within a rippling trellis pattern; more flowers as well as arabesques are painted on the walls. The effect is rather like walking under a pergola. Equally, some of the rare depictions of gardens known from this period show covered walks like corridors, formed of thick hedges and with

'windows' cut in them – wholly architectural and giving the feeling of an outdoor long gallery.

This exchange of roles between indoor and outdoor rooms survived throughout the eighteenth century. Thus, the Gobelins tapestries in the Ante Room at Osterley create the effect of a bower, ornamented for a festival with garlands and vases of flowers, while exotic birds fly freely against the pink foliage, supposed to represent a cut hedge. In the adjoining chamber, Adam's eight-post state bed is conceived almost as a complete garden building in its own right: a Temple of Venus, garlanded with swags of artificial flowers in coloured silks, and set against green velvet wall-hangings to represent a bosky woodland setting.

The opposite idea – garden pavilions having all the attributes of indoor rooms – can be seen at Stowe in the Ladies' Temple and Temple of Friendship, both designed by Gibbs, and looking at each other across Hawkwell Field. In effect these were extra drawing-rooms for use in the summer, as an alternative to those in the house: the first intended for Lady Cobham and her friends, and filled with the needlework and shell pictures they produced; the second for her husband and his Pitt and Grenville nephews, furnished with busts of their political heroes, and the scene of much gambling and drinking as well as philosophical debate.

Mark Girouard has shown how the roof turrets of Elizabethan houses like Longleat and Hardwick were used as banqueting rooms, to which the family and their guests would repair for desserts after the main courses had been served in the state rooms below.

A view across the lake at Stourhead in Wiltshire, showing the Palladian bridge in the foreground and the Pantheon on the far shore, both designed by Henry Flitcroft

Another view across the lake at Stourhead, showing the Temple of Flora on the left, and the Palladian bridge, the Bristol Cross and Stourton parish church on the right. These two views can be compared with the watercolours by Coplestone Warre Bampfylde (Nos 46 and 47)

Garden buildings at this period tended to have similar functions, and that may be why they are so closely related in design. Robert Smythson's two little banqueting rooms in the garden at Hardwick are decorated with strapwork parapets very like those on the towers that crown the house; the octagonal gazebo built against the garden wall at Melford Hall in Suffolk reminds one of the lantern room on the roof of Melbury in Dorset; while the twin pavilions flanking the entrance to the forecourt at Montacute, with their ogee roofs and 'compass' windows, echo the oriels of the long gallery and look almost as if they have flown down from the parapet.

The idea of walking on the leads was not only to enjoy the view, but also to watch the progress of the hunt down the long rides radiating from the house. This was particularly true of lodges like Ashdown, explaining their height and prominent cupolas, but it also accounts for the popularity of hunting towers as adjuncts to larger country houses, often seen on the

hillsides above, as at Chatsworth and at Lyme, where the building has long been called the Cage. This tradition was surprisingly long-lived, and can be traced through to belvederes like Vanbrugh's at Claremont (No. 32) and Adam's projected 'Viewing Tower' at Kedleston (No. 71).

The hunting grounds themselves were increasingly treated as woodland gardens, vastly extending the area previously considered within the park and, as John Evelyn had advocated in his *Sylva*, published in 1664, combining pleasure with profit. The rebuilding of London after the Great Fire, and continuous naval wars with the Dutch, had, after all, made forestry a lucrative business. The scale of such planting can be judged from the 1739 engraving of Stowe (No. 36), where the woodland garden dwarfs the pleasure grounds around the house, although the latter amounted to over 500 acres. In some particularly feudal parts of the country, surrounding landowners like the Duke of Beaufort's neighbours at Badminton were induced to continue his system of avenues and rides on their own land out of deference, transforming the look of the whole area.

The bird's-eye view was particularly popular at this period, because it could show the huge extent of these planned landscapes, not visible on the ground. But it also suited the geometry of the knot garden and the *broderie* parterre, intended to be seen from above, whether from the roof of the house, the principal apartments (still often on the upper floors) or from a tall gazebo. Mounts were also useful in this respect, and could sometimes be formed out of the old motte-and-bailey of an earlier castle, as at Dunham Massey. Sir Thomas Tresham's fascinating garden at Lyveden New Bield, only rediscovered comparatively recently below dense undergrowth and fallen trees, had no less than four mounts, two pyramidal and two spiral,

overlooking a system of canals forming a large square. Tresham described the square as 'my moated orchard'.

Terraces fulfilled the same function and could, like mounts, have had a military origin. It is no accident that Isaac de Caux and William Winde were both military engineers before they turned their attention to gardens, and Winde's terraces at Cliveden and Powis still have the feeling of ramparts, where you might expect to see soldiers marching up and down on sentry duty. Vanbrugh's admiration for the fortresses of Vauban, which he had seen as a prisoner of war in

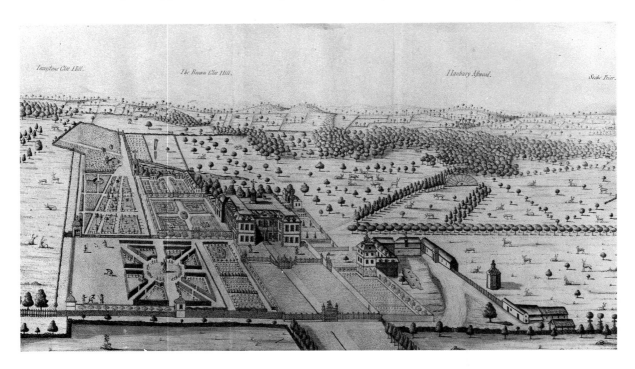

(*Above*) *Survey drawing of Hanbury Hall, Worcestershire, and its gardens, by Joseph Dougharty, 1732 (Worcestershire Record Office)*

(*Right*) '*Hanbury Hall from ye Bowlingreen', by Sir James Thornhill, c.1710 (British Museum)*

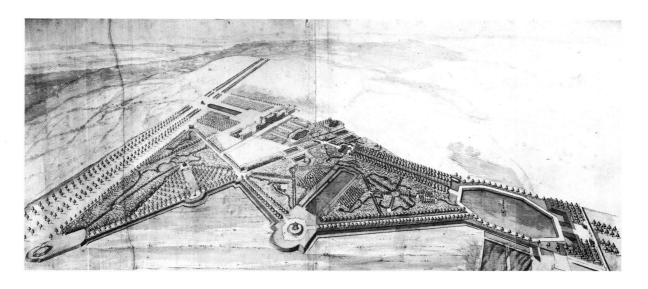

Bird's-eye view of Stowe, Buckinghamshire, attributed to Charles Bridgeman, c.1720 (Bodleian Library, Oxford)

France, was to encourage this trend still further in the early eighteenth century, and in the gardens where he collaborated with Charles Bridgeman – including Stowe and Claremont – the crucial development of the ha-ha appears to have been inspired by trench warfare, with circular 'bastions' at the junctions between the straight sections (see No. 35).

The strictly axial approach to garden design introduced in France under Le Nôtre rarely suited the topography of English parkland, and, although it became more popular with the increasing symmetry of the house itself, never wholly caught on. It is interesting, for instance, that despite William Talman's Francophile tendencies, the cascades at Chatsworth and Dyrham were not aligned on his façades – unlike the one at Marly, which was his probable source of inspiration. Badeslade's bird's-eye view of Knole shows that old houses which were not particularly symmetrical continued with their compartmented gardens – in this case echoing the seven courtyards of the house itself. Westbury, too, was entirely non-axial, though obviously influenced by ties with Holland rather than France.

A more typical compromise between French and Dutch taste can be seen in the garden at Hanbury, laid out by George London about 1700 and portrayed in Joseph Dougharty's bird's-eye view of 1732 (page 12). The entrance forecourt has a thoroughly symmetrical approach by way of a double avenue with two wrought-iron gatescreens. But the gardens on the west form a series of walled enclosures bearing little or no relation to the side elevation of the house. There are no less than six gazebos or pavilions terminating walks, or flanking vistas. Yet, despite the avenues marching out across the park to the east, one of them leading to a curious amphitheatre (which London intended as a platform to view various local landmarks), the feeling is one of introspection.

Charles Bridgeman's celebrated, and much more accomplished, bird's-eye view of Stowe (above) is a masterpiece of Baroque planning, comparable with Nicholas Hawksmoor's schemes for the rebuilding of Oxford and Cambridge. A persistent problem here had been the awkward angle at which the 'Great Cross Walk', running from the bastion on the far left (originally a public right of way leading to the parish church) met the main vista from the house to the Octagon Lake, and the spire of Buckingham church beyond. Bridgeman made a virtue of this irregularity with his complex system of diagonal *allées* and *pattes d'oie*, contrasted with serpentine walks and 'garden cabinets' in the woodland areas between.

Bird's-eye views, like John Harris's famous series of Dunham Massey, continued to be painted right through the 1750s by old-fashioned travelling artists and topographers. But it is interesting to find that the great divide between formal and picturesque gardening is reflected in a totally changed style of draughtsmanship, developed by the designers. William Kent's drawings for the Elysian Fields at Stowe, which must have been made almost at the same time as Bridgeman's bird's-eye, have sadly not survived, but his contemporary sketches for Claremont show this new technique for the first time. Important viewpoints, one from the windows of the house itself, another showing Vanbrugh's temple and belvedere framed by new 'naturalistic' planting (page 14), are depicted using an artist's eye to compose effects of light and shadow, depth and perspective, in place of the conventional surveyor's plan. There is a sense of theatre in the arrangement of groups of trees, placed like stage 'flats', which lead the eye inwards – perhaps inspired by the masque designs of Kent's hero, Inigo Jones.

Obviously plans were still necessary, and continued to be produced, but, like Robert Adam's for the pleasure ground at Kedleston (No. 70), now tended to accompany and explain a series of picturesque water-colours showing proposed viewpoints (below). The same applies to engravings, like Rocque's composite views of Chiswick and Claremont (No. 32), where the vignettes of individual buildings within their settings become more important than the plan itself.

Indeed, as straight lines vanished from the *jardin anglais*, to be replaced by serpentines and curves, plans became altogether harder to read. This was especially true because of the increasing importance of contours – the vertical curves represented by hills and valleys, as opposed to the horizontal curves of a lake shore, a clump of trees or a ha-ha. Thus F. M. Piper's plan of Stourhead, fascinating as it is in showing the sight-lines between the different garden buildings, wholly fails to give an idea of the lie of the land, or the character of the place. The series of three-dimensional 'pictures' in the manner of Claude and Poussin that unfold in the course of the visitor's promenade, can only properly be understood from the watercolours of artists like C. W. Bampfylde (Nos 46–47). The same could be said of Jolivet's plan of West Wycombe as compared with the paintings of William Hannan.

The inclusion of people in these views was nothing new. The Lauderdales' stately progress through the wilderness at Ham was recorded as early as the 1690s, while Thornhill's charming sketch of a game of bowls at Hanbury (page 12) reveals a less formal side to the Baroque garden. On the other hand, the clothes and the pose of those depicted underwent a change in the mid-eighteenth century, showing a different attitude to gardens and their uses. A drawing of Claremont, attributed to George Lambert (page 15), shows not only the *ferme ornée* brought into the garden, with cattle, horses and deer grazing beyond the ha-ha, but also groups of figures enjoying a rustic idyll: dairy-maids with aprons and pails, and shepherds with

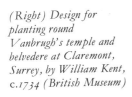

(*Above*) *Design for the landscape at Kedleston Hall, Derbyshire, including a new stable block, by Robert Adam, 1759 (National Trust)*

(*Right*) *Design for planting round Vanbrugh's temple and belvedere at Claremont, Surrey, by William Kent, c.1734 (British Museum)*

View of the ha-ha and lake at Claremont, Surrey, showing the grotto and Kent's island pavilion, attributed to George Lambert, c.1750 (Huntington Library, San Marino, California)

crooks, conversing in the foreground. The vogue for dairymaids, working away in ornamental milking parlours, was to continue well into the nineteenth century, and the chatelaines of at least two great houses – Uppark and Burghley – started life in this humble role.

Horace Walpole, describing a visit to Claremont in 1763, exactly captures the kind of rococo spirit in which the landscape garden was used: 'From thence [the Belvedere] we passed into the wood, and the ladies formed a circle of chairs before the mouth of the cave, which was overhung to a vast height with woodbines, lilacs and laburnums, and dignified with tall stately cypresses. On the descent of the hill were placed French horns; the abigails, servants and neighbours wandering below by the river; in short it was Parnassus, as Watteau would have painted it.'

Sir Francis Dashwood, something of an actor *manqué*, organised rather more studied *fêtes champêtres* at West Wycombe, like the one held in September 1771 to dedicate Nicholas Revett's west portico. The portico was in fact treated more as a garden building than as part of the house, and was actually known as the Temple of Bacchus, after its prototype at Telos on the coast of Asia Minor. On this occasion a procession was formed of 'Bacchanals, Priests, Priestesses, Pan, Fauns, Satyrs, Silenus &c. all in proper habits & skins wreathed with vine leaves', a sacrifice was made to the statue of Bacchus, and then the company repaired to the lake for more 'Paeans and libations' and 'discharges of Cannon' from several boats. The *fêtes champêtres* recently held by the National Trust at West Wycombe, Osterley, Stourhead and other gardens, are thus revivals of a well-established tradition. Performances of plays and operas were also held in gardens. On

1 August 1740 the amphitheatre at Cliveden was the scene of the first performance of Thomas Arne's *Alfred*, written for Frederick, Prince of Wales, and including the famous aria 'Rule Britannia'. Similar spectacles must have been given in the much larger amphitheatre at Claremont, which covers acres in eight steep terraces.

Lakes were regularly used in the eighteenth century for mock naval battles, and once again the best account comes from West Wycombe, where a fleet of four vessels was kept for the purpose – perhaps also a reminder that the Dashwoods owed their wealth to the ships of the Turkey and India trades. These boats, shown in Hannan's paintings (page 16), were described by a visitor, Thomas Phillibrown, in 1754. The largest was 'a snow, Burthen about 60 tun; it is compleately rigg'd and carries several brass carriage guns which were taken out of a French privateer and a sailor constantly is kept who lives aboard this snow to keep it in proper order'; there was also 'another smaller 2 mast vessel, a little in the Venetian manner, also a 1 mast vessel like a sloop, and also a barge'. In the mock battle which Phillibrown witnessed, 'a battery of guns in form of a fort was erected on the side of the canal in order to make a sham-fight between it and the little fleet, but in the engagement a Capt. who commanded the Snow coming too near the battery, received damage from the wadding of a gun which occasion'd him to spit blood and so put an end to the battle.'

Very similar engagements are recorded on the lake at Kedleston, where Lord Scarsdale also had large-scale models of men-of-war in glazed cases inside the house. On Rothley Lake at Wallington, and on the banks of the River Plym at Saltram, were batteries with cannon set into them for similar occasions, and another battery

View of the landscape at West Wycombe Park, Buckingham-shire, by William Hannan, c.1751–3 (Sir Francis Dashwood, Bt)

can still be seen on the shore of the lake at Clumber. The Duke of Newcastle's yacht, the *Lincoln*, built in 1817, was regularly used here right up to the Second World War, after which it was unfortunately sunk, and there are also records of a schooner named the *Salamanca*. British naval victories in the Seven Years War (which Lord Scarsdale planned to commemorate in his drawing-room at Kedleston) may have encouraged this fashion, and the growth of the Empire is also recorded in many garden buildings, from the Blenheim Pavilion at Cliveden (No. 14) to the Wolfe obelisk, the Grenville Column and the monument to Captain Cook, all at Stowe. One or two failures also received their due, like the colony of Vandalia, which a syndicate of English backers tried to set up in western Virginia in 1770. One enthusiastic member, Sir Matthew Fetherstonhaugh of Uppark, commissioned Henry Keene to design the Vandalian Tower on the highest point of his park (page 17) to mark the colony's foundation. But the government concession had still not been granted by 1775, when the War of Independence finally sealed its fate.

Of all these commemorative buildings, one of the most influential was the Chinese House at Shugborough (page 17), built by Thomas Anson about 1747 to celebrate his brother Admiral George Anson's circumnavigation, including his visit to Canton in 1743. According to Thomas Pennant, the Chinese House was based on drawings of an actual building there, recorded 'by the skilful pencil of Sir Piercy Brett', the Admiral's second-in-command: 'a true pattern of the architecture of that nation, not a mongrel invention of British carpenters.' Pre-dating Chambers's Chinese pagoda at Kew, it was the progenitor of countless *chinoiserie* buildings in English gardens, right up to the one at Cliveden (page 17), surprisingly made for the Paris Exhibition of 1867 and only bought by the Astors in the 1890s.

Voyages to different parts of the world not only resulted in a vast new range of plants being made available to nurserymen and gardeners, but also increased the fashion for private aviaries and menageries. Natural history often appealed as much as botany to the enquiring mind of the eighteenth-century landowner, and the observation of rare species brought back to this country was a matter of scientific interest, beyond mere love of the exotic. Most large country houses had collections of birds or animals at some time in their history, though few of the original buildings that housed them now remain. The memory of the one at Wimpole is kept alive only by the pub known as the *Tiger* at Arrington, which backed on to the section of park where the animals were kept. Nostell Priory has a building (altered by Adam) which is still known as the Menagerie, but no evidence of the original cages, while the same applies to the Aviary at Knole, as depicted by Hendrik de Cort. Once the home of the golden pheasants brought back from China by the 4th Duke of Dorset's brother-in-law, Lord Amherst (who gave his name to the species), this was sadly burnt out only recently, and has been virtually rebuilt.

One of the most elaborate menageries was the one just below the Belvedere at Claremont, originally built by the Duke of Newcastle and later re-stocked with animals by Lord Clive, including a zebra and foal, various breeds of deer, an 'African Bull' and seven goats, the last 'very troublesome'. Another large menagerie is shown in a wooded enclosure just behind the house on a plan of Uppark, which can be attributed to Capability Brown on stylistic grounds, but which was sadly destroyed by the fire in 1989. A late example, but consciously looking back to eighteenth-century precedents, is the magnificent aviary at Waddesdon built by Baron Ferdinand de Rothschild in 1888, and probably designed by Destailleur, the architect of the house.

The Chinese House at Shugborough, Staffordshire, built about 1747 in imitation of a house at Canton, sketched three years earlier by Sir Piercy Brett, second-in-command during the course of Admiral Anson's circumnavigation

The Pagoda at Cliveden, Buckinghamshire, made for the Paris Exhibition of 1867

(Left) Design for the Vandalian Tower at Uppark, Sussex, by Henry Keene, c.1774. The drawing was destroyed in the Uppark fire of 1989.

Scene near the Temple, with a hint of the house on the Site proposed: distant about 3/4 of a Mile.

A view of Sheringham Park in Norfolk from Humphry Repton's Red Book of 1812 (National Trust)

The quest for nature, inspired by the writings of Rousseau and Voltaire, provoked an interest in geology as well as zoology. Porous tufa, stalactites and stalagmites, shells, fossils, flints and petrified bark, were all used to decorate garden buildings so as to make them appear organic – as if they had almost grown out of the surrounding rock. The engravings in Thomas Wright's *Book of Arbours* (1755) and *Book of Grottoes* (1758) show buildings of this kind for the first time in wholly naturalistic surroundings: some are made of tree trunks which are actually sprouting; others are hollowed out of the steep hillside. The word 'artificial', earlier used as a term of praise, began instead to condemn those buildings where the hand of man was too much in evidence.

As already suggested, this move towards extreme naturalism had literary and political sources, like Addison's famous essay in the *Spectator*, now thought to be the iconographical source for Kent's Elysian Fields at Stowe. Increasingly, individual buildings could be endowed with different associations (or even emotions) depending on their style, their form and their setting. Sometimes the message could be almost painfully obvious, as with the ruinous Temple of Modern Virtue at Stowe, complete with its headless

The Mausoleum at Blickling, Norfolk, designed by Joseph Bonomi, in memory of the 2nd Earl of Buckinghamshire, in 1794

Design for a Gothick conservatory at Plas Newydd, Anglesey, from Repton's Observations, *published in 1803 (Sir John Soane Museum)*

statue of Sir Robert Walpole – deliberately contrasted with the classical perfection of the Temples of Ancient Virtue and British Worthies. At other times, it could be obscure and possibly even mistaken, like the triangular plans of the Gothic Temple by Gibbs, and King Alfred's Tower at Stourhead – then thought to be Saxon in origin, but probably only deriving from Elizabethan buildings like Sir Thomas Tresham's Triangular Lodge at Rushton.

The cult of the solitary and the melancholic, another Elizabethan phenomenon which came back into fashion in the Georgian period, was easily expressed in gardening terms by evergreen glades, arbours for contemplation equipped with books and writing tables, hermitages and even mausolea. Until the building of Hawksmoor's monumental mausoleum at Castle Howard, most families continued to be buried in the local parish church along with their ancestors, but such a major architectural statement was bound to have followers. What is perhaps more surprising is the preference for Classical rather than Gothic dress, both for mausolea – like James Wyatt's *tempietto* at Brocklesby or Joseph Bonomi's pyramid at Blickling (page 18) – and for churches, on the rare occasions they were built within a landscape setting – like James Paine's at Gibside, and 'Athenian' Stuart's at Nuneham Park. The reason may be that the Gothic style was still associated with superstition, allowable in the play-acting ambience of hermitages and magician's huts, but not to be put on a par with the 'Temple of Reason', where the average Church of England landowner chose to worship, and be buried.

One of the first Gothic mausolea appears to have been the one at Claremont designed by J. B. Papworth

and A. C. Pugin in 1817; but even this was originally designed as a tea house for the Prince Regent's daughter, Princess Charlotte, and only became a shrine to her memory after the Princess's death in childbirth the same year. By contrast, when someone suggested turning the Temple of the Winds at Mount Stewart into a mausoleum after Castlereagh's death in 1822, his brother, Lord Londonderry, wrote in answer 'I am entirely against the Idea... I have no Taste for Turning a Temple built for Mirth & Jollity into a Sepulchre – The place is solely appropriate for a Junketing Retreat in the Grounds.'

By the end of the eighteenth century, the pendulum of picturesque taste had swung to its fullest extent, and a picture like Thomas Daniell's view of West Wycombe shows the house itself disguised as a series of independent garden buildings, screened from each other by trees, and thus entirely subservient to the landscape. The watercolours in Humphry Repton's justly famous Red Books mark a culmination of the style in one sense, and in another the beginnings of its rejection. At Sheringham, one of his own favourite commissions, the site of the 'appropriate gentlemanlike residence', and its form, were entirely dictated by its landscape setting (page 18), and it would be hard to equal the mastery with which the hills and valleys are clothed and different glimpses of the sea contrived. Yet at Wimpole (No. 86) the railings proposed on the north front of the house mark the beginnings of a return to formality, which gradually restored the primacy of the 'mansion' over its surroundings.

One aspect of this trend was the increasing importance of greenhouses and conservatories. In the late seventeenth century, orangeries, like those at Dyrham

A garden party in the grounds of the old castle at Crom, County Fermanagh, by an unknown artist, 1850

and Felbrigg, were such a novelty that they could be built immediately adjoining the house, and there was no question of hiding them away. But the early disciples of the picturesque generally found them too 'artificial', both in construction and in the type of potted plants they contained, removing them to walled gardens or other secluded spots. However, the arrival of increasingly rare tropical plants towards the end of the century coincided with technical advances in the heating apparatus available, and in the provision of glazed roofs. So it soon became the fashion to build a conservatory or winter garden on to the end of a house – particularly at a time when asymmetry was coming to be accepted for villas and country houses. Repton himself recommended that the conservatory should adjoin the library – then the general living-room of the house – and form a natural transition between the interior and exterior. It could be built in almost any style to suit the house, and his ingenious proposal for an octagonal Gothic conservatory at Plas Newydd, 'terminating a magnificent enfilade through a long line of principal apartments', was designed so that 'the side window frames might be removed entirely in summer'. In the lost sketch from the Red Book, fortunately engraved for his *Observations* of 1803, he imagines it 'seen from the library on one of those warm summer evenings, when such a pavilion wd tempt us to walk out by moonlight, to enjoy the murmur of the waves, & the perfume of those plants which are most fragrant at that time.'

Just as the nineteenth century was the great age of public buildings rather than private houses, it could be

argued that the municipal parks laid out by designers like J. C. Loudon were more ambitious and innovative than what was happening in the country-house world. But there were important exceptions. William Sawrey Gilpin's work, at Scotney Castle in Kent and at Crom Castle in Northern Ireland, represents a culmination of picturesque composition on the one hand, and on the other a new historical sense, preserving the ruins of earlier houses on the site and making them key elements in the new garden layout. At Crom (above), the lawn of the old castle with its ancient yews (supposedly the oldest in Ireland) was laid out as a formal garden in a conscious reconstruction of an earlier period. A little later on, Charles Barry and W. A. Nesfield revived a still more formal Italianate style of gardening, with strong architectural 'bones' in the form of balustraded terraces, staircases, fountains and statues. Huge greenhouses were now able to produce bedding-out plants on a gigantic scale, and the Duke of Sutherland's head gardener at Cliveden, John Fleming, is credited with introducing the biannual replanting of parterres in polychrome hues as strong as contemporary encaustic tiles.

Records of such gardens are far from perfect, however. Professionals like Fleming – and even Paxton, his opposite number at Chatsworth – did not need to make presentation drawings for their clients in the same way as outsiders not on the payroll. Architects like Barry also developed an unfortunate tendency to use tracing paper, now discoloured and brittle if it has survived at all. There is another problem: from James Bateman at Biddulph Grange to Laurence Johnston at Hidcote and V. Sackville-West at Sissinghurst, there has been a tradition of the gifted horticulturist owner, who created a garden gradually, by eye and by touch, without having to be guided by elaborate designs.

Virtually the only early representations of Biddulph are the plans of the garden reproduced by Edward Kemp in his articles for the *Gardener's Chronicle* of 1862 (below). But this is enough to show the ingenuity of its 'circuit', arranged on old-fashioned picturesque lines, and thus offering a series of totally different scenes and experiences along the route, yet at the same time novel in its planting, with a scholarly attempt to provide the right kind of terrain for the right kind of plant: rhododendrons and azaleas in rocky dells bringing a taste of the Himalayas to suburban Staffordshire; golden larches, mahonias and variegated bamboos among the willow-pattern prettiness of 'China' with its pond, pagoda and sacred cow; sitkas, Douglas firs and rarer conifers in the pinetum, recalling the Norway of trolls and fjords. There is an earthy Victorian humour, too, as you pass the gloomy portals of 'Egypt', a set for *Aida* in clipped yew, only to emerge from a 'Tudorbethan' Cheshire cottage. The age of the Great Exhibition, encouraging an intense curiosity about other nations and their customs, can be seen here at its most eclectic.

Alongside the scientific knowledge of country-house owners like George Maw, the tile manufacturer and botanist, of Benthall Hall, there was an increasing interest in the history of native gardening traditions in

Plan of the garden at Biddulph Grange, Staffordshire, from the Gardener's Chronicle, *1862*

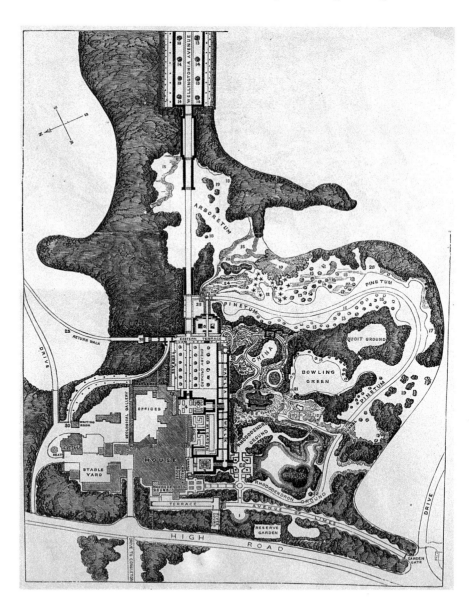

the later Victorian period. Early pattern books had already been plundered for the re-creation of parterres in the Baroque taste – for instance at Oxburgh in the 1840s, using a plate from d'Argenville's *Theory and Practice of Gardening*, published in England by John James in 1709. At Belton, the Dutch Garden was laid out in 1879, copying part of the *Vitruvius Britannicus* engraving of the garden published in 1727, though on a smaller scale and on a different side of the house. But the literature on British garden history, including books like Inigo Triggs's *Formal Gardens in England and Scotland* (1902) also encouraged direct imitations of places often thought to be older than they were. The famous topiary garden at Levens, in fact mostly replanted in the 1830s, or the 'Elizabethan' walled garden at Canons Ashby, actually dating from the early 1700s, were to be the inspiration for many Edwardians, as the cult of 'old-world charm' gathered pace.

Any danger that gardening might become merely an art of the pastiche at this period was dispelled by the formidable partnership between Edwin Lutyens and Gertrude Jekyll. Brought up in the same Arts and Crafts world as Beatrix Potter and Kate Greenaway, Gertrude Jekyll's original inspiration was the profusion of the cottage garden and its essential Englishness, as cosy and unpretentious as a snug, chintz sitting-room. Her application of its principles (no visible earth, carefully scaled planting, native species preferred over exotics) to the broader canvas of the country-house garden, was achieved also with a sure taste in the use of colour. Rejecting the polychrome hues of the 'bedding-out' school, she was the first to plan herbaceous borders in the subtler, more controlled combinations later taken up at Hidcote and Sissinghurst. Whether consciously or not, her white gardens (with touches of blue and silver) use the same palette as some of Whistler's *Nocturnes*.

Lutyens's contribution was just as important, bringing back architectural features like pergolas, brick and stone paths set in patterns, reflecting ponds and a sense of outdoor 'rooms' linked by axial vistas or 'corridors'. Their combined garden plans, like those for Lindisfarne Castle, now at the University of Berkeley, California, show how the partnership worked: in this case Lutyens sketched the outline, in tapering perspec-tive so as to make the small walled garden seem larger when seen from the ramparts of the castle high above; and then Gertrude Jekyll filled in the planting with rapid annotations. Recently reconstructed to match these plans (and old photographs), the garden is simple but wonderfully effective in its wild, exposed setting. Other garden designers like Charles Wade and his mentor, C. H. Baillie Scott, were also influential in the development of gardens whose compartments were treated architecturally, continuing and elaborating the ground plan of the house itself (see No. 113), and Wade's influence on the creation of Hidcote, only a few miles away from Snowshill, deserves further exploration.

Another important development which Lutyens and Jekyll championed was the use of 'antiques' in a garden: urns and vases, old lead statues and wrought-iron gates for grander houses, and well-heads, mill-stones and oak benches outside simpler cottages. This extension of the collecting instinct, already well developed indoors, can be seen at William Waldorf Astor's Cliveden, at Lord Fairhaven's Anglesey Abbey, and at Lord Aberconway's Bodnant – where the Pin Mill is a genuine eighteenth-century building bought, like a piece of furniture, to decorate the Canal Terrace in the 1930s. In a sense, this use of old sculpture and architectural features continued the tradition begun by William John Bankes's Egyptian obelisk, erected on the lawn at Kingston Lacy a hundred years earlier.

The lack of drawings and designs for so many of the National Trust's most important twentieth-century gardens is in many ways mitigated by the development of photography. In the case of Waddesdon, a truly remarkable collection of hand-tinted stereoscopic transparencies dating from 1910 document the garden in vivid detail, while gardens like Mount Stewart, Nymans and Sissinghurst were endlessly photographed for gardening magazines and journals in their heyday. There is, however, no substitute for the beauty of a good drawing, whether by a garden designer or an architect, and Quinlan Terry's beautifully rendered designs for recent follies at West Green (Nos. 123–124) are a welcome reminder that the art is not dead – and that Arcadian visions can still be realised.

An English Arcadia

Note to the Reader

In the dimensions for drawings, height is given before width. Short references within the text, and under the heading *Literature*, are given in full in the Bibliography on page 157. Unless a reference is provided in the text, sources for all quotations will be found in the literature listed at the end of the entry. No references to National Trust old-style guide books have been included in the bibliographical references. To avoid the constant repetition of county names, the location of all gardens and houses is given in the index on page 159.

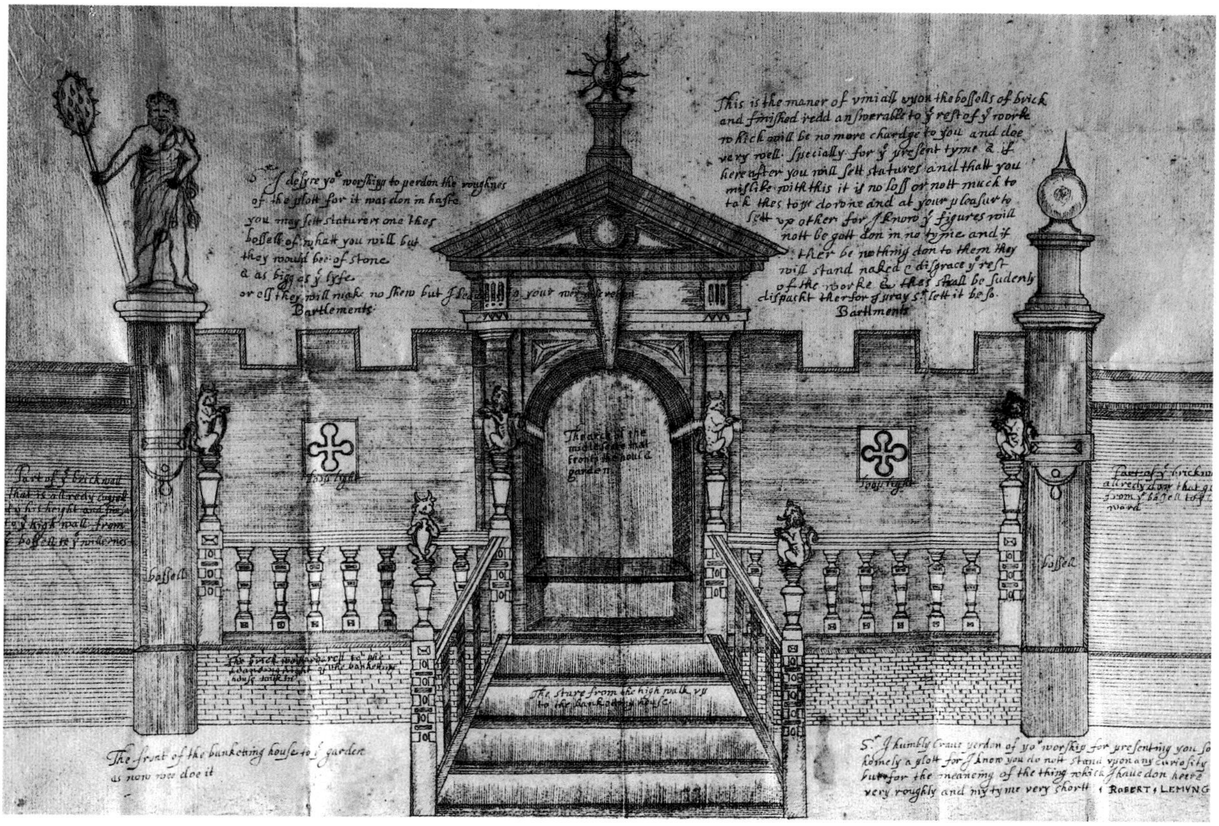

1

1 Design for a banqueting house in the garden at Blickling Hall, Norfolk, *c.*1620

Robert Lyminge (d.1623)

Pen and sepia ink, and pencil (statue of Hercules)

Inscribed bottom left: 'The front of the banketting house to ye garden/as now wee doe it'; [on wall at left] 'Part of ye brick wall/that is already coped/to his height and finised/to ye high wall from/ye bossell to ye willernes'; [on terrace wall to left of central stair] 'The brickwork reared to the Leaneing hight of the banketting house within'; [top left] 'Sr. I desyre yor Worshipp to perdon the roughnes/of the plott for it was don in haste/you may sett staturers one thes/bossells of whatt you will but/they would bee of stone/& as bigg as ye lyfe/or els they will make no shew but I leave it to your wor discretion'; [in central arch] 'The arch of the/midle seate that/fronts the hous &/garden'; [on stairs below] 'The stare from the high walk up/to the banketting house'; [top right] 'This is the maner of viniall upon the bossells of brick/and finished redd answerable to ye rest of ye worke/which will be no more chardge to you and doe/very well. Specially for ye present tyme & if/here after you will sett statures and that you/mislike with this it is no loss or nott much to/tak thes tops downe and at your pleasur to/sett up other for I know ye figures will/nott be gott don in no tyme and if/they be nothing don to them they/will stand naked & disgrace ye rest/of the worke & thes shall be sudenly/dispacht therfor I pray Sr lett it be so.' [on wall at right] 'Part of ye brickwall/allredy don that goeth/from ye bossell to y church/ward.' [bottom right] 'Sr. I humbly Crave perdon of yor Worship for presenting you so/homely a plott for I know you do nott stand upon any curiosity/but for the meaneing of the thing which I have don heere/very roughly and my tyme very shortt/ ROBERT LEMYNG'

Watermark: Shield, Star M

370 × 478mm ($14\frac{1}{2}$ × $18\frac{3}{4}$in)

The National Trust (Lothian Collection), Blickling Hall, Norfolk

This is the only known drawing by Robert Lyminge, the architect of Hatfield House and Blickling, and proves that he also had a hand in the Jacobean garden at Blickling. This garden was laid out by Sir Henry Hobart on the east side of the house, which he had begun to remodel in 1619 and which was only completed after his death in 1626. The banqueting house, like those surviving at Hardwick and Montacute, would have been used for serving desserts and sweetmeats in summer, after the company had finished the main courses served in the great chamber or parlour of the main house.

The annotations tell us that the building was to be set into a wall, on a terrace or 'high walk' parallel with the east front. This wall would have formed one side of a formal garden whose centrepiece was probably the white marble fountain supplied by Thomas Larger in 1620. The 'high walk' led north to a wilderness, which was no doubt a second rectangular enclosure with a geometrical layout of walks and hedges.

Lyminge's design is of particular interest for its mock-medieval features, such as the castellated parapet, the quatrefoil arrow-loops (which also recur on the entrance bridge at Blickling) and the flaming grenade crowning the central pediment. Similar ornaments can be found in some of Inigo Jones's contemporary masque designs, but in the case of Blickling they may have been suggested by the surviving north and west ranges of the old castle, built by Sir Nicholas Dagworth in the 1390s and later owned by Sir Thomas Erpingham, Sir John Fastolfe and the Boleyn family. With no wish to appear *nouveau riche*, the Hobarts may have been stressing the ancient origins of their seat, and, if so, foreshadowing the more scholarly antiquarianism of Gothick garden buildings in the eighteenth century.

Literature: Newman & Maddison, 1987, pp. 23–4, 56.

2 Survey plan of Ham House, Surrey, and its garden, 1609

Robert Smythson (*c*.1536–1614)

Pen and sepia ink, with pencil shading
Watermark: small bunch of grapes
195 × 185mm (7¾ × 7⅜in)
Drawings Collection, Royal Institute of British Architects, London

The original house at Ham was built by Sir Thomas Vavasour, who was a minor official at the court of James I. This drawing is thought to date from 1609, when Robert Smythson made a visit to London, drawing a number of survey plans of houses, apparently as a personal record for himself,

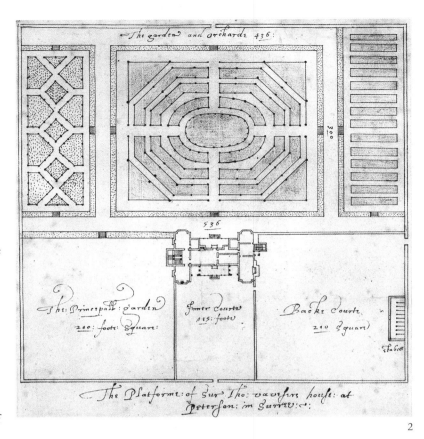

2

though possibly with the idea of eventual publication. Roy Strong has suggested that the striking, axial garden plan, novel for England, was based on a knowledge of Claude Mollet I's garden at St Germain-en-Laye, made for Henri IV. However, the main parterre, not drawn out in detail by Smythson, still lay to the north-east of the house (to the left of the forecourt on this plan), and not aligned on it in any way.

The area with rectangular strips on the right was evidently a kitchen garden, as it still remained in 1739 when included in Badeslade and Rocque's engraving for the fourth volume of *Vitruvius Britannicus*. The corresponding area on the left with its diamond-shaped plots may well have been planted with espalier fruit trees, to judge by their close planting. This later became a longer but simpler plantation of

trees in rows (see No. 3), while the central 'Wilderness' was moved farther south and replaced by eight square 'plotts' of grass. How the original wilderness was planted remains a mystery, but fruit trees might again be possible, their linking branches giving the oval and octagonal paths the feeling of a maze. The raised terraces would have given views over all four gardens, increasing the sense of neat geometry.

Literature: Girouard, 1962, p. 70, cat. no. I/7; Strong, 1979, p. 117, fig. 68; Brown, 1989, p. 32, cat. no. 6.

3 Survey plan of the garden at Ham House, Surrey, c.1671

John Abraham Slezer (d.1714), with figures attributed to Jan Wyck (c.1640–1702)

Pen, ink and watercolour

Scale: 1in to 50ft

507 × 395mm (19¾ × 15⅜in)

Victoria and Albert Museum (on loan to the National Trust, Ham House, Surrey)

John Evelyn, not usually given to superlatives, recorded walking to Ham after dinner one summer's evening in 1678 'to see the House and Garden of the Duke of Lauderdale, which is indeed inferior to few of the best Villas in Italy itself; the house furnished like a great Prince's, the Parterres, Flower Gardens, Orangeries, Groves, Avenues, Courts, Statues, Perspectives, Fountains, Aviaries, & all this at the banks of the Sweetest River in the World, must needs be surprising.'

The overall design of the garden can be judged from this plan by the German military engineer and surveyor John Slezer, who made similar drawings for the Lauderdales' Scottish houses and who regularly employed the young Jan Wyck 'for filling up [his drawings] with little figures'. A painting attributed to Henry Danckerts, still in the house, shows the Duke and Duchess walking in the oval clearing at the centre of the wilderness, and closely conforms with the Slezer drawing.

The surviving accounts prove that this garden was being made between 1672 and 1675, at the same time as the Lauderdales' remodelling of the house, and that Sir Thomas Vavasour's earlier layout (see No. 2) was almost entirely swept away in the process.

(Bottom right) View of the garden at Ham House, with the Duke and Duchess of Lauderdale walking, attributed to Hendrick Danckerts, c.1675 (National Trust)

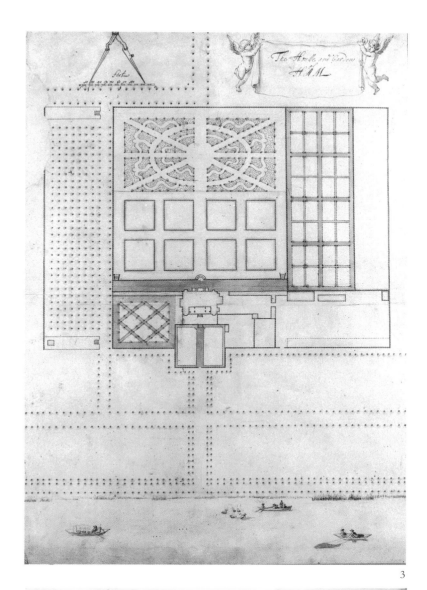

3

However, Slezer's drawing does not show the closets added at each end of the south front in these years, and thus probably dates from about 1671. A slightly later drawing of the façade with the added closets has been less plausibly attributed to him, but is of interest in showing the wilderness in the foreground densely planted with firs, obscuring its geometrical lines.

The wiggly paths between the main axial ones recall Sir William Temple's experiments with 'Shara-wadgi' (the informal style of garden practised by the Chinese) at Moor Park in the same decade, and are equally important precursors of the Picturesque movement later in the eighteenth century. Since 1975, the garden at Ham has been restored by the National Trust, as far as possible to its appearance in the late seventeenth century.

Literature: Jackson-Stops, 1975, p. 902, fig. 3; ed. Dixon Hunt & de Jong, 1988, pp. 255–8, cat. no. 105a.

4 View of Westbury Court, Gloucestershire, 1712

Johannes Kip (d. 1722)

Engraving

Inscribed: 'Westbury Court the Seat of Maynard Colchester Esqr/J. Kip delin et Sculp.'

350 × 440mm (13¾ × 17¼in)

Anthony Mitchell, Esq.

The creation of the garden at Westbury was largely the work of one man, Maynard Colchester (1665–1715), whose grandfather had bought the Elizabethan house and its estate on the banks of the River Severn. Kip's view of the gardens was first published in Sir Robert Atkyns's *Ancient and Present State of Gloucestershire* in 1712. It shows a layout essentially similar to that which still exists, and Kip's

(Bottom right) View of the garden at Westbury Court, Gloucestershire, showing the pavilion, canals and statue of Neptune

accuracy is confirmed by entries in Colchester's personal account book from 1696 to 1705, which also help to date much of the work precisely.

The canal with the tall summer-house at one end was begun in 1696; in 1699, 1,000 yews and 1,000 hollies of three years' growth were planted (almost certainly the hedges and topiary flanking the canal); and in 1700 came the parterre to the south of the house and the orchard beyond the canal. The summer-house itself is of 1702–3, and markedly Dutch in character – as is the whole plan.

Rather than the French ideal of a unified, architecturally conceived design with long vistas and *broderie* parterres centred on the house, Westbury is flat, small in scale, divided into little compartments, and above all horticultural in emphasis. The account book shows the purchase of hundreds of bulbs, not only tulips, but also irises,

crocuses, jonquils, hyacinths, double narcissus, anemone and ranunculus, and shrubs such as syringa, laurestinus, mezereon and phillyrea.

The Elizabethan manor was rebuilt in 1745–8, but this house was in turn demolished in 1805, and the family returned to Westbury only in 1895, when a new mansion was built attached to the summer-house. In 1960 the property was sold to a speculator who obtained planning permission for ten bungalows in the garden, and who demolished the house and the great wall running the whole length of the canal. The summer-house was left in a condition almost past repair, and the canals, stagnant and completely overgrown, were saved only at the last moment from being filled with rubble.

In 1967 the National Trust acquired the garden and, with the help of the local authorities and

many other benefactors and volunteers, embarked on a full-scale restoration programme, returning it to its former glory.

Literature: Jackson-Stops, 1973, pp. 864–6.

5 View of Dyrham Park, Avon, from the west, 1712

Johannes Kip (d. 1722)

Engraving
Signed: J. Kip Delin et Sculp.
347 × 428mm ($13\frac{5}{8}$ × $16\frac{7}{8}$in)
Anthony Mitchell, Esq.

Kip's well-known engraving of Dyrham also first appeared in Atkyns's *Ancient and Present State of Gloucestershire* in 1712. For a long time it was thought that the gardens depicted were too elaborate and ambitious ever to have been carried out. But a detailed description of the layout by Stephen Switzer was then

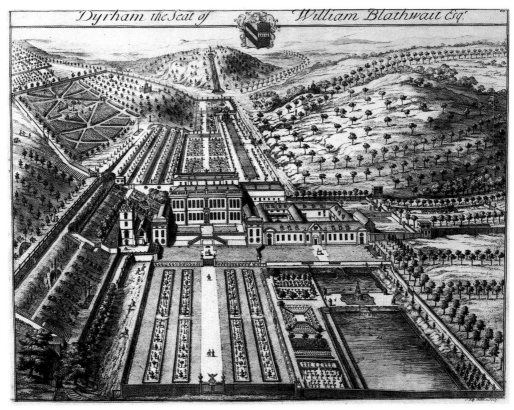

5

rediscovered, printed as an appendix to the third volume of his rare *Ichnographia Rustica* in 1718. This description, and subsequent research in the Blathwayt family papers, has now confirmed practically every square inch of the engraving, and greatly expanded our knowledge of the whole garden.

William Blathwayt, who created the layout between 1691 and about 1704, was one of William III's most trusted ministers, and it is no surprise that he should have employed William Talman, Comptroller of the King's Works, as his architect, together with the Royal gardener George London. However, the west front seen here (with the medieval parish church to the left of it) pre-dates Talman's arrival on the scene, and was designed by the Huguenot Samuel Hauduroy, before 1694.

The garden was conceived in the Franco-Dutch style, influenced by Daniel Marot's layout at Het Loo, William III's Dutch palace, which Blathwayt regularly visited. However, two important modifications were made. First, the available flat ground was small, and although it was extended by levelling, full use was also made of the surrounding hills, 'cut out into the utmost Variety of Walks', as Switzer put it. Second, the ample water supply from the springs in the park was used to create a cascade of 224 steps, flowing down the hillside and into the canal on an axis with Talman's orangery. At first this cascade, described by Dudley Ryder in 1716 as 'the finest in England except the Duke of Devonshire's', was headed by a jet of water 20 feet high, but some time after 1700 this was replaced by the Neptune fountain carved by John Harvey of Bath.

From a horticultural standpoint, the garden at Dyrham was equally remarkable. Hurnall, the head gardener, was constantly going over to Longleat to meet George

6

London and procure packets of rare seeds. There exist bills for evergreens, for lemons, pyracantha, phillyrea, and laurustinus ('to plant against the wall of ye upper parterre'), and from the colonies Blathwayt obtained exotic trees such as Virginia pine, sassafras, tulip trees and Virginian oak.

Literature: Mitchell, 1977–8, pp. 83–108, figs 4, 22–30.

6 View of Dyrham Park, Avon, from the west, c.1790

Anonymous

Pen, ink and watercolour
440 × 570mm (17⅞ × 22½in)
Mark Blathwayt, Esq.

Writing about Dyrham in 1779, the county historian Samuel Rudder recorded that 'the curious waterworks, which were made at great expense, are much neglected and going to decay', while twelve years later Ralph Bigland commented that Kip's engraving (No. 5) 'is the more valuable as exhibiting a Bird's Eye View of the Pleasure Ground, now reconciled to modern Taste'. It is not known who exactly swept away William Blathwayt's formal gardens

between these two dates, although the Bath surveyor Charles Harcourt-Masters was responsible for moving quantities of earth, and re-routing the drive, in 1798–9; and Humphry Repton was also called in to give advice between 1800 and 1803 (see No. 85).

This anonymous drawing, evidently made before that date, shows the extraordinary transformation of the landscape already achieved. The long terrace walk shown on the left, and the two square ponds in front of the stables, remain practically the only survivors from William Blathwayt's formal gardens, though the statue of Neptune from the head of the cascade still survives above Harcourt-Masters's new drive, and various other features can be traced on the ground in times of drought.

Literature: Mitchell, 1977–8, fig. 13.

7 Three designs for *trompe-l'oeil* paintings in the garden of a house in Bloomsbury Square, London, *c.*1712

Sir James Thornhill (1675–1734)

(a) Pen, ink and wash;
(b) red chalk and wash;
(c) pen, ink and wash over red chalk

Watermarks: (b) Pro Patria (lion with sword and sheaf of arrows in paling etc.); (c) IV

(a) Inscribed at top left 'Mr Mellor in Bloomsbury.'; above diagram '7 clear ye Pict:'; in right-hand margin '9ftt high ye Pictr: without ye real work'; below, 'I propose something of this kind/-Mellor-' ('I propose something of this kinde' also written in faint pencil under); and on verso with apparently unrelated calculations in pencil; (b) inscribed on verso 'Sketches for ye Garden in Bloomsbury Square'

(a) 148 × 190mm (15¾ × 17½in);
(b) 205 × 328mm (18 × 12⅞in);
(c) 186 × 310mm (17¼ × 12⅛in)

The National Trust (Yorke Collection), Erddig, Clwyd (on loan to Clwyd Record Office)

The idea of outdoor decorative paintings, used to add length and space to city gardens by a subtle play of illusionistic tricks, was popular in the Italian Renaissance, inspired in turn by the discovery of similar features in the gardens of antique Roman villas. The fashion spread to France in the seventeenth century, and the painter Jacques Rousseau (1630–93) particularly specialised in the genre, having first studied to be an architect in Paris. His 'perspectives' at the Hotel Fieubet on the Quai des Celestins, and the Hotel Dangeau in the Place des Vosges, were both engraved by Perelle, and he later painted similar murals on a massive scale for the orangery at St Cloud, and for the 'offices' at Marly. As a Huguenot, Rousseau fled from France in 1685, coming to London soon afterwards, where he worked on the saloon and staircase at Montagu House in Bloomsbury.

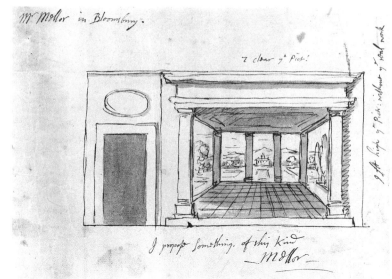

7a

7b

7c

Thornhill was a particular admirer of Rousseau, citing his work at Montagu House in a memorandum to the Greenwich Commissioners in 1717, and owning Rousseau's huge design for the St Cloud orangery (over 5 feet long), now in the Victoria and Albert Museum. The three drawings shown here, all attributable to Thornhill, were made for a house on the east side of Bloomsbury Square, only a stone's throw from the Duke of Montagu's. This was owned by a prosperous London lawyer named John Meller, who lived there full time until 1716, when he purchased Erddig in North Wales; the lease was eventually assigned to a Mrs Elizabeth Stewart in 1726.

The first design may represent a working up of an initial pencil sketch by Meller himself. The inscription suggests that the pilasters and entablature were intended to be three-dimensional (like the colonnades at Marly and the Hotel Dangeau), with the wall-painting recessed behind them. The other two more fully developed designs are very French in character: the one with the fountain is particularly close to Rousseau's St Cloud vignettes, while the one with the balustrade and loggia recalls the contemporary work of Isaac de Moucheron, which Thornhill could have seen on his visit to Holland in 1711.

Literature: Evans, 1972, vol. 22, no. 2, pp. 142–61.

8 Plan of the garden at Clandon Park, Surrey, c.1730

Anonymous

Pen, ink and watercolour

Scale: 1in to 40ft

990 × 720mm (39 × 28⅜in)

The National Trust (Onslow Collection), Clandon Park, Surrey

Sir Richard Onslow bought the Clandon estate in 1641 from the Weston family, but it was not until about 1731 that his great-grandson Thomas finally rebuilt the Westons' early seventeenth-century house. A large oil painting by Leonard Knyff, still at Clandon, shows the old house surrounded by elaborate formal gardens. These were evidently laid out by Sir Richard Onslow, 2nd Bt, who had succeeded in 1688, and who became Speaker of the House of Commons in 1708, the year the picture was painted. As a partisan of William III, becoming Lord of the Admiralty in 1691, it is possible that he patronised the royal gardeners, George London and Henry Wise, though no documents have yet been found to shed light on the work.

This large-scale drawing of the gardens must be considerably later than the Knyff picture since it includes the outline 'Plan of the new house', built by the Venetian architect Giacomo Leoni some time between 1729 and 1733. A great many of the features shown by Knyff can still be seen, however. These include the raised terrace south (right) of the house with a small circular pond on axis with the south front; the avenue beyond, leading to a mount where the plan talks of 'a design'd Belvidere'; the wood to the left of the main approach with straight rides cut through it; and the canal here, which Knyff shows ending in a large trefoil pond.

On the other hand there are some important differences: notably the 'Gravel Garden' just beyond the house where previously there had been an intricate parterre; the forming of turfed banks like the 'bastions' Charles Bridgeman and Stephen Switzer had already made popular at Eastbury Park and Claremont (see No. 32); and the rearrangement of the wilderness to the right of the main approach, with a central vista aligned on the terrace already mentioned. The Gothic script suggests the hand of a surveyor rather than a garden

(Opposite page, bottom) Bird's-eye view of Clandon Park, Surrey, by Leonard Knyff, 1708 (National Trust)

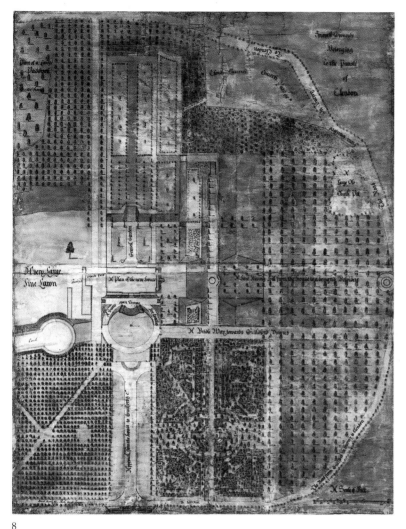

8

designer, and that may also account for the survival of so many strictly formal features at such a comparatively late date.

Hardly any of these features now survive, for the process of 'naturalising' the garden at Clandon was probably begun shortly after the completion of Leoni's new house. A painting of the forecourt by James Seymour, thought to date from the early 1750s, already shows a more informal landscape with a rockwork grotto facing the south front, although many of the old straight paths and avenues still appear in a survey map of 1776, now in Surrey Record Office. The process was finally completed by Capability Brown, who demolished the old stable block near the house, building a new range much further west, and who converted the canal and ponds into a serpentine lake, after 1781.

Literature: Harris, 1979, p. 119, cat. no. 114 (for the Knyff painting).

9 Two alternative designs for a parterre at Cliveden, Buckinghamshire, *c.*1713

Claude Desgots (d. 1732)

Pen and ink, heightened with green wash

Both inscribed with measurements and endorsed 'fait par Desgotz architecte et Controlleur general/Des Battiments du Roy/a Versaille ce 10 Juillet 1713'

Scale: 1in to 10 'toise[?]'

Both 160 × 415mm (6¼ × 16⅜in)

The Viscount Astor

Claude Desgots, the nephew of Le Nôtre and his successor as Louis XIV's chief garden designer, paid a brief visit to England in 1700 when he designed the Maestricht Garden at Windsor for William III, later abandoned because of constant flooding. His commission to make these designs for Cliveden thirteen years later may be explained both by its proximity to Windsor, and by the fact that its owner, the 1st

Earl of Orkney, having married William III's only English mistress, Elizabeth Villiers, was at that time within the King's immediate circle – where he could easily have met Desgots.

These two alternative proposals, close to Desgots's contemporary schemes for the Luxembourg Palace and for a garden for the Duchess of Orléans (both in the Tessin Collection, Stockholm), are interesting examples of the direct influence of French on English garden design in the early eighteenth century. Another less finished plan for the whole layout, showing a remodelled entrance courtyard as well as a parterre with 'bosquets' and intersecting paths, could also be by him, while from a long memorandum, again in Desgots's hand, it appears that he may have sent yet other designs including elevations for two 'cabinets de treillage'. In addition the memorandum gives much fascinating advice about the planting of oaks, elms and chestnuts, and the bordering of the parterre beds (or 'plattes bandes'), not with the usual yews alternating with hollies, but with flowering shrubs (including honeysuckle, syringa and lilac) between each evergreen.

Lord Orkney's main intention at this time seems to have been the enlarging of an earlier and much simpler parterre, probably designed by Henry Wise about 1706.

Literature: Jackson-Stops, 1976–7, pp. 100, 103, figs. 4 and 5, cat. nos 2 and 3 (see also fig. 3 for parterre design attributed to Wise).

10 Design for a parterre at Cliveden, Buckinghamshire, c.1720
Anonymous

Pen, ink and wash, heightened in red and green watercolour
Inscribed in sepia ink 'A Design for the Parterre at Cliffden'
Scale indistinct: approx. 1in to 43ft
700 × 505mm (27½ × 21¾in)
The Viscount Astor

This is the most elaborate of a group of three anonymous designs formerly in the Cliveden album, suggesting alternative treatments for the main parterre. These depict the site far more accurately than Desgots's drawings (No. 9) – in this instance showing the River Thames in the top right corner – and probably date from later in the same decade.

They are evidently in a French hand too, since they are related to a fourth 'plan du bout du Parterre' showing a complicated system of draining the far end of the parterre as eventually laid out. The author of these drawings remains a mystery. The complicated mound – perhaps derived from Vauban's forts – at the far end of the parterre (on which Lord Orkney has pencilled the word 'ugly'), is close to the turf 'ramparts' favoured by Charles Bridgeman, who is also known to have been involved with the garden at Cliveden in 1723 (see No. 11). So it is possible that this French draughtsman was either employed by Bridgeman, or working in collaboration with him.

After all these ambitious schemes, Lord Orkney finally settled on a far simpler solution – a perfectly plain lawn (in place of parterre beds) with raised terrace walks either side, planted with a double row of elms, and a circular platform at the far end with the elms continuing round it. Lord Ronald Gower, remembering Cliveden as his father first bought it in 1849, recalled this 'circus of

turf at the end of the lawn, where in old Lord Orkney's time horses were exercised – an open air *manège*'. An 'Account of ye charge of making ye Parter', formerly in the Cliveden album, is unfortunately unsigned and undated, but two further letters in the National Library of Scotland show that this is likely to have taken place in the winter of 1723–4. On 5 December, Lord Orkney reported to his brother that he had been 'this fortnight att Cleifden struling with rain and wind to get my trees planted', continuing: 'I call it a quaker parter for it is very plain and yet I believe you will think it noble'.

Literature: Jackson-Stops, 1976–7, pp. 105–6, fig. 9, cat. no. 8.

11 Design for part of the gardens at Cliveden, Buckinghamshire, including the Amphitheatre, c.1723
Anonymous (French hand)

Pen, ink and wash, heightened with yellow and green wash
Inscribed at bottom: 'Walks on the Side of the Hill at Cliffden'
Scale: 1in to 30 'pieds'
497 × 720mm (19⅝ × 28⅜in)
The Viscount Astor

This plan shows part of the layout on the steep hillside above the Thames north-west of the house, with a grass amphitheatre on the same site as (though far larger than) the present one. In a letter of 2 October 1723 (now in the National Library of Scotland) Lord Orkney reported to his brother that 'the Amphitheatre is quite struck out' – probably meaning that the site had been staked preparatory to excavation. Moreover the letter goes on to reveal the probable author of this singular feature. As well as the problem of 'wher to get turfe and trees for la grand machine', Lord Orkney continues: '. . . besides ther is great difficulty

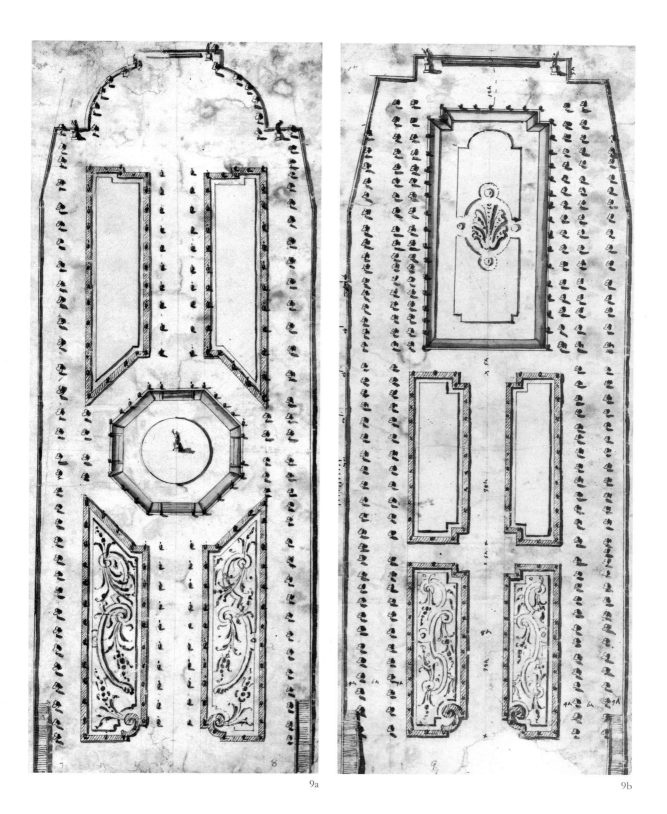

9a

9b

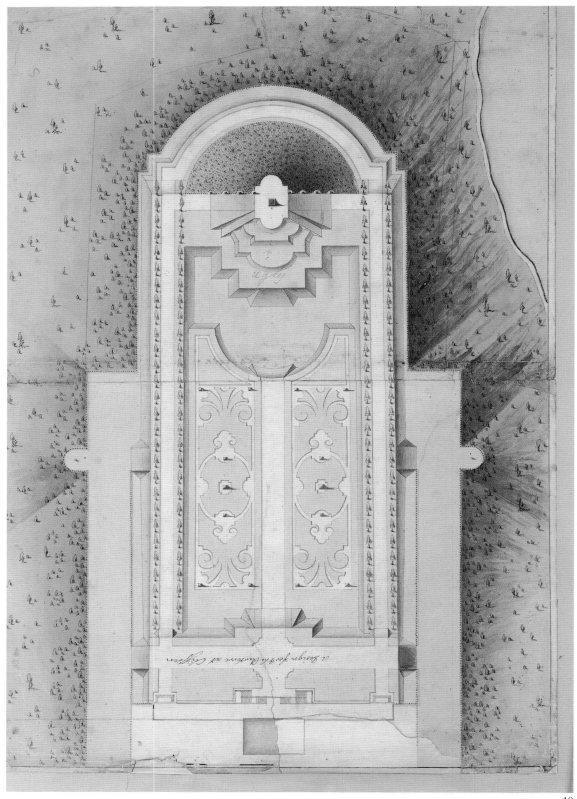

10

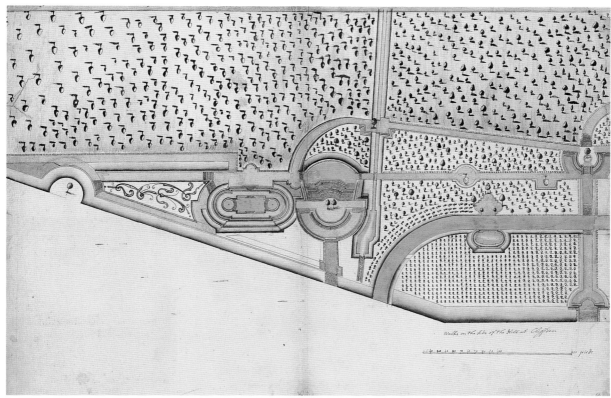

Walks on the side of the Hill at Clifden

11

to get the slope all that side of the Hill where the precipice was, but Bridgeman mackes difficultys of nothing. I told him if I thought it to had been the one Halfe of what I see it will cost I believe I never had done it, he says the beginning is the worst...'.

The Cliveden amphitheatre is extremely similar to those made by Charles Bridgeman and William Kent at Claremont and Rousham House in Oxfordshire, and to Alexander Pope's description of his 'little Bridgemannick theatre' at Twickenham, turfed in 1726. The rather naive technique of this drawing and the fact that its scale is marked in 'pieds', could be explained either by Bridgeman employing a French draughtsman, or by the anonymous designer of the parterre schemes (including No. 10) co-operating with him; the slightly absurd trees placed everywhere at different angles

could well be a later addition. What is particularly interesting about the drawing (and again suggests that it emanated from a leading designer like Bridgeman) is the way in which the amphitheatre is placed next to a sunken enclosure shaped like a Roman circus: an unusually early example of classical town-planning applied to eighteenth-century garden design. There is no evidence that the 'circus' was ever executed, although the paths shown running almost parallel along the hillside may well be those which still exist bordered by yews, once perhaps cut as hedges, but now grown to enormous size. In 1743 this part of the garden was described by Jeremiah Milles as 'a hanging wood... wch is cutt out very agreably in walks and *vistos* that present the most beautiful prospects of ye river'. On 1 August 1740 the Amphitheatre was the scene of the first performance of

Thomas Arne's masque *Alfred*, written for Frederick, Prince of Wales (who leased Cliveden from 1739 to 1751), and including the famous aria 'Rule Britannia'.

Literature: Jackson-Stops, 1976–7, pp. 106–7, fig. 11, cat. no. 10.

12 Design for ten different forms of elaborate topiary, Cliveden, Buckinghamshire, *c.*1705

Alexander Edward (1651–1708)

Sepia pen and ink with green wash
Inscribed 'Yews at Versails'; 'Spruce Firrs at Versails'; 'Silver Firrs'; 'Broome or furze'; 'Syprefss'; 'Hollies'; 'A Hollie at Aloa'
Scale: 1in to approx. 3ft 2in
185 × 310mm (7¼ × 12¼in)
The Viscount Astor

The very individual style and calligraphy are closely comparable to other signed drawings by the

37

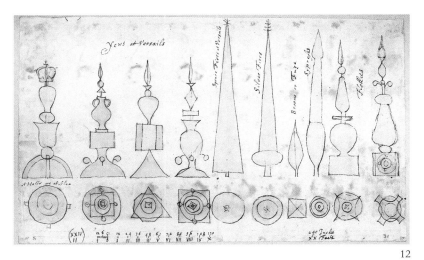

Yews at Versails

12

Scotsman Alexander Edward, who acted as Sir William Bruce's draughtsman at Kinross in 1684, and later at Melville and Hopetoun. The researches of Mr John Dunbar have revealed that Edward was sent abroad to England, France and the Low Countries by a circle of Scottish noblemen headed by his chief patron, James, 4th Earl of Panmure, in 1701. This drawing with its depiction of 'yews at Versails' must obviously post-date this journey, and have therefore been executed between 1701 and his death in 1708. Among other clients for whom Edward executed commissions on his tour was the 23rd Earl of Mar, and the 'Hollie at Aloa' here obviously refers to Lord Mar's house, Alloa in Clackmannan, for which Edward is known to have supplied trees and to have advised on garden and possibly architectural matters.

In the year of his death, Edward prepared an ambitious layout for the policies of Hamilton Palace at the request of the Duchess of Hamilton, mother of the 1st Earl of Orkney, so it may have been through this connection that his advice was also sought for Cliveden. The crazy shapes of Edward's topiary confections, shown here in elevation and cross-section, give a fascinating sidelight on the elaboration and artificiality of Baroque garden design.

Literature: Jackson-Stops, 1976–7, pp. 107–8, fig. 14, cat. no. 13.

13 Design for topiary in five different shapes, Cliveden, Buckinghamshire, *c*.1720

Anonymous (French hand)

Pen, ink and wash
Inscribed in sepia ink with height of each example in French, eg 'dix pieds hauteur', etc.
Scale: 1in to approx. 6 'pieds'
685 × 190mm (27 × 7½in)
The Viscount Astor

This design for topiary may be in the same hand as a group of parterre designs (including No. 10), a related survey plan showing the lower end of the parterre at Cliveden, and a long anonymous memorandum in French explaining its system of drainage. The internal evidence is that these are likely to date from between 1720 and 1723, when Lord Orkney was busy completing this part of the garden. Why the drawing on the left-hand half of the sheet is repeated in reverse on the right remains something of a mystery.

Literature: Jackson-Stops, 1976–7, p. 107, fig. 15 (detail), cat. no. 14.

14 Design for the Blenheim Pavilion, Cliveden, Buckinghamshire, *c*.1727

Giacomo Leoni (*c*.1686–1746)

Pen, ink and pencil
Inscribed: (in room with semicircular apse at centre back) '*Bagno*'; (in small room at back on left) '*water closet*'
Scale: 1in to approx. 3ft 9in
480 × 320mm (18⅞ × 12⅝in)
The Viscount Astor

In 1727, the 1st Earl of Orkney commissioned designs from the Venetian architect Giacomo Leoni for a complete rebuilding of his house at Cliveden, along Palladian lines. This scheme was never executed, but probably about the same time Leoni made this elevation and ground plan for the Blenheim Pavilion, still to be found at the north-western end of the gardens (together with a companion cross-section and ceiling design). The Pavilion is shown almost exactly as built, though the 'Bagno' and water-closet at the back are no longer there, and may never have existed.

The military trophies which decorate the façade suggest that the building may always have gone under this name, given also Lord Orkney's prominent role at Blenheim where he commanded a brigade, and the fact that an early nineteenth-century writer credited him with 'figuring the battle of Blenheim, by plantations of trees, now in full vigour' (Lewis, 1831, p. 300). The design is more Baroque in feeling than Leoni's proposals for the Octagon Temple (No. 15), probably made slightly later; the obelisks resting on cannon-balls on the parapet may even derive from Vanbrugh's at King's Weston.

Literature: Jackson-Stops, 1977, pp. 8–9, fig. 6a; Jackson-Stops, 1977a, p. 441, fig. 11.

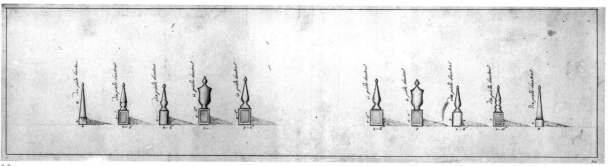

13

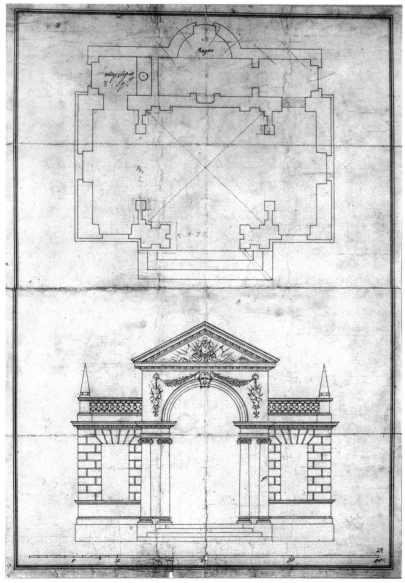

14

15 Two alternative designs for the Octagon Temple at Cliveden, Buckinghamshire, c.1735

Giacomo Leoni (c.1686–1746)

Pen, ink and wash, with red colouring for walls of cross-section

Inscribed: 'Prospect of the Opposite side of the Temple letter A/Front of the Temple letter A/Front of the Temple letter B/Section of the Temple letter B'; (on ground plan A) 'Plan of a plain Octagon Temple'; (on ground plan B) 'Plan of An Octagon Temple with Ionick Pillars on the Coins'

Scale: 1in to 8ft

330 × 465mm (13 × 18¼in)

The Viscount Astor

The Octagon Temple at Cliveden was built on the very edge of the cliff above the Thames, to the right of the parterre seen from the garden front. Apart from Leoni's contract drawing (signed by Lord Orkney and the contractor Edward Vickers), which shows the building much as it is today, there are no fewer than four preliminary designs by him: two shown in this drawing, and two with ogee domes in another. An alternative proposal was also made by James Gibbs, whose *Book of Architecture*, published in 1728, contains very similar 'summer houses in form of Temples'.

Leoni refers to the construction of the Temple in a letter to Lord Orkney dated 20 June 1735, only two years before the latter's death, hoping he has given the carpenter 'suficently direction for ye framing

Prospect of the Opposite side of the Temple Letter A

Front of the Temple Letter A

Front of the Temple Letter B

Section of the Temple Letter B

A
16 Feet

B
16 Feet

Plan of a plain Octagon Temple

Plan of the Octagon Temple with Ionick Pillars on the Coins

of ye Cupollo'. The upper part originally contained a 'Prospect-Room' described by Jeremiah Milles in 1743 as having a 'ceiling... prettily done in fretwork', while the rusticated basement (visible only on the river side) was 'a little cool room by way of grotto'. In 1893 the floor between the two was taken out by the 1st Viscount Astor, and the building converted into a chapel. Leoni's pedimented doorcase on the side facing the parterre was also removed at the same time.

Literature: Jackson-Stops, 1977, pp. 9–10, fig. 8a; Jackson-Stops, 1977a, pp. 440–1, fig. 6.

16 Design for a large vase at Cliveden, Buckinghamshire, 1725

Thomas Greenaway (fl. 1707–20)

Pen, ink and wash

Scale: 1in to 1ft

200 × 310mm ($7\frac{7}{8}$ × $12\frac{1}{4}$in)

The Viscount Astor.

This design corresponds exactly with a pair of large stone vases on pedestals, now flanking Leoni's Octagon Temple at Cliveden (see No. 15). However, these pre-date the building by at least ten years, for the design was accompanied (in the Cliveden album) by an explanatory note from the sculptor, Thomas Greenaway, dated 'Bath Octobere ye 20, 1725./The prise of a Pedestal and Vause upon it according to the draft with the Scale an inch to the foot for

Honble. Lord Orkney the Vause carv'd as in the draft but the carving of the pedestal excepted the base of the Pedestal to be in one Stone and the body in one Stone and the capital in two with the Vause that finish it. All this above mentioned good stone and well wrought and set up in London for Fifteen Pounds by me.' Wood's *Description of Bath*, published in 1729, commends Greenaway's 'small ornaments in freestone', sold from his house in St John's Court. He was probably the father of Benjamin and Daniel Greenaway, who later worked for Wood as masons and sculptors on the building of the Bristol Exchange in 1745.

Literature: Jackson-Stops, 1976–7, pp. 108–9, fig. 16, cat. no. 15.

Wimple in the County of Cambridge the Seat of ye Rt Honble Charles Bodville Lord Robartes Baron of Truro Viscount Bodmyn and Earl of Radnor Ld Lt & Custos Rotulorum of ye County of Cornwall

17 View of Wimpole Hall, Cambridgeshire, 1707

Johannes Kip (1653–1722) after
Leonard Knyff (1650–1721)

Engraving
Inscribed 'Knyff Delin/Kip Sculp/
Wimpole in the County of Cambridge
the/Seat of Ye Rt Honble Charles
Bodville/Lord Robartes/Baron of
Truro/Viscount Bodmyn & Earl of
Radnor/ Ld Lt & Custos Rotulorum of
ye County of Cornwall'
342 × 486mm ($13\frac{1}{2}$ × $19\frac{1}{8}$in)
The National Trust (Bambridge
Collection), Wimpole Hall,
Cambridgeshire

In 1693, Wimpole was inherited by
Charles Robartes, 2nd Earl of
Radnor, from his father-in-law, Sir
John Cutler. A kinsman, writing in
1713, estimated that Lord Radnor
spent £20,000 on the house and
gardens, and Knyff's view shows
the extent of his achievement,
which included the building of a
detached orangery and service wing
to the left and right of the house,
and a stable block to the south-east,
set at right angles.

Although the engraving shows a
remodelling of the old 1640
'double-pile' house that was never
in fact carried out, a comparison
with Charles Bridgeman's later
drawings suggests that the gardens
were very accurately depicted.
Work on them must have been
completed by 1701 when the
antiquary Peter le Neve called the
'fine gardens lately made... worth
riding 20 miles out of the way to
see'.

One interesting detail is the
splendid wrought-iron gatescreen
shown by Knyff at the entrance to
the forecourt, which exactly
matches a design in Jean Tijou's
New Booke of Drawings, published in
1693. This was in existence in
Bridgeman's day, though it has
since disappeared. If Lord Radnor
employed the Royal blacksmith, he
may also (like the Duke of
Devonshire at Chatsworth and the
Duchess of Norfolk at Drayton)
have persuaded other members of
the Office of Works team to work
at Wimpole, notably the gardeners
George London and Henry Wise,
and the architect William Talman.
This would certainly confirm
Defoe's description of the garden
as containing 'all the most exquisite
Contrivances which the best Heads
cou'd invent'.

The only obvious survivors of
the layout today are the two

avenues on the cross-axis, either side of the parterre, though the original iron *clairvoyées* which separated them from the garden were replaced by ha-has in the 1750s. Unhappily both avenues suffered from Dutch elm disease, and have had to be replanted in recent years.

Literature: Jackson-Stops, 1979, p. 659, fig. 1.

18 Design for the 'Grand Parade' at Wimpole Hall, Cambridgeshire, c.1721

Charles Bridgeman (d.1738)

Pen, sepia ink and wash
Scale: 1in to 100ft
750 × 520mm (29½ × 20½in)
The National Trust (Bambridge Collection), Wimpole Hall, Cambridgeshire

In 1710 Lord Radnor sold Wimpole to the Duke of Newcastle, who died the following year leaving an only daughter, Henrietta, who married in 1713 Edward Harley, son of Robert, 1st Earl of Oxford, the great Tory statesman. Lord Harley soon commissioned James Gibbs to add wings joining the original 1640s house to Lord Radnor's orangery and service block, but it was not until 1721 that he turned his attention to the park and garden.

In March of that year a team of virtuosi – Gibbs, the painters Sir James Thornhill and John Wootton, and the landscape gardener Charles Bridgeman – made a joint expedition to Wimpole, during which the poet Matthew Prior wrote to Harley that he presumed 'Sir James has rather been speculating in the chapel he is to paint, than praying in the neighbouring church, and friend Bridgeman's devotion has consisted chiefly in contriving how the diagonal may take Whaddon steeple exactly in the middle'. Harley's bank account at Child's records payments of almost £3,000

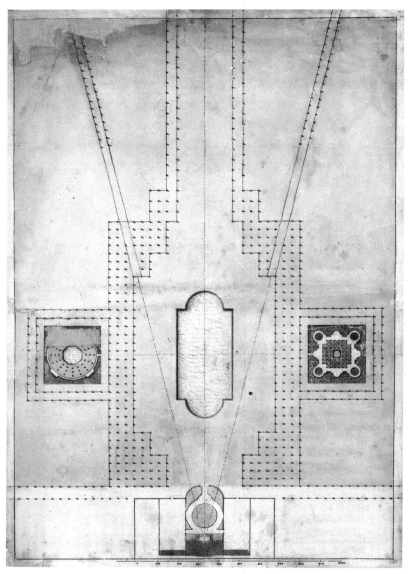

18

to Bridgeman between 1721 and
1726.

Prior's letter proves that
Bridgeman's first object was the
planning of the great south avenue
and its two subsidiary vistas, the
one on the left of this drawing
aligned on the tower of Whaddon
church. The main avenue, 250
yards wide and over 2½ miles long,
with a large 'Octangular Bason'
near the far end, survived until
recently and has now been
replanted. Nearer the house
Bridgeman intended a 'Grand
Parade' with a still larger central
pond, flanked by formal *bosquets* in
the French manner, as shown here,
and sweeping away Lord Radnor's
narrower double avenue and the
canals and groves on either side of
it. Harley's friends persuaded him
against this, however, and his old
tutor, Dr Stratford, wrote on 9
April 1721, that he was 'mightily
pleased to hear that my sweet grove
and the old avenue have got a
reprieve'.

Literature: Jackson-Stops, 1979,
pp. 659–60.

19 Design for one of a pair of hexagonal garden pavilions at Wimpole Hall, Cambridgeshire, c.1721

James Gibbs (1682–1754)

Pen, ink and wash

Scale: 1in to 3ft

438 × 265mm (17¼ × 10⅜in)

The National Trust (Bambridge
Collection), Wimpole Hall,
Cambridgeshire

Lord Radnor's parterre and
'wildernesses' on the north side of
Wimpole seem to have been
retained largely intact by
Bridgeman and Lord Harley.
However, the bowling green seen
at the far end in Knyff's view
(No. 17) was slightly enlarged, and
a pair of summer-houses built in
the far corners, flanking the vista to
Johnson's Hill. This drawing is one
of Gibbs's preliminary designs, but

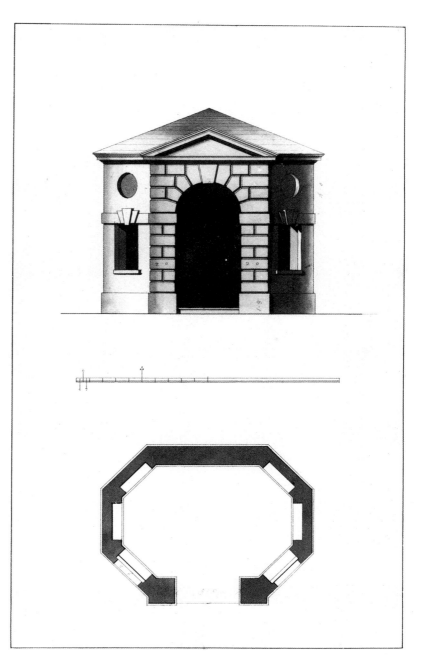

19

there is no record of their actual appearance, nor of their interiors which Sir Matthew Decker described in 1728 as being 'painted, and the best I ever saw done by Sir James Thornhill'.

Literature: Jackson-Stops, 1979, p.660, fig.9.

20 Design for the garden at Wimpole Hall, Cambridgeshire, c.1752

Robert Greening (d.1758)

Pen and ink

Inscribed: 'Wimple/the Seat of the Right Honourable/Philip Lord Hardwick/Lord High Chancellor/of/Great Brittain'

680 × 950mm (26¾ × 37⅜in)

The National Trust (Bambridge Collection), Wimpole Hall, Cambridgeshire

In 1740 Wimpole was bought by Philip Yorke, 1st Earl of Hardwicke, who employed Henry Flitcroft to make major changes to the house. The old formal parterre on the north side was finally brought up to date in 1752–3 under the direction of Robert Greening, whose father and uncle were Royal gardeners at Kensington and Hampton Court, and who had himself worked for Frederick, Prince of Wales, at Kew in the 1740s. Advice on landscaping was also given by the architect and antiquary Sanderson Miller (see No.59) and the poet George Shenstone.

Greening's large-scale plan proposed a more radical de-formalising of the north garden than was actually achieved. Another drawing shows the new 'Ah ha!' (or ha-ha) as executed, generally following the straight lines of the old walls shown in Knyff's view (No.17), but with the same sort of pleasure-ground inside it: a wide lawn surrounded by small island beds of laurels, laurestinus and other shrubs, intersected by serpentine paths. The earth dug out of the ha-ha was piled up against the east wall of the garden, and thickly planted so as to conceal the medieval barn as well as the old *potager* on this side, which Greening converted into a nursery with fruit trees trained against its walls.

Two sad losses at this time were Tijou's gatescreen, replaced by another ha-ha (at the bottom of the plan) and Gibbs's summer-houses (shown as squares at the top of the plan, flanking the vista from the house) which Shenstone recommended 'shd. be pulled

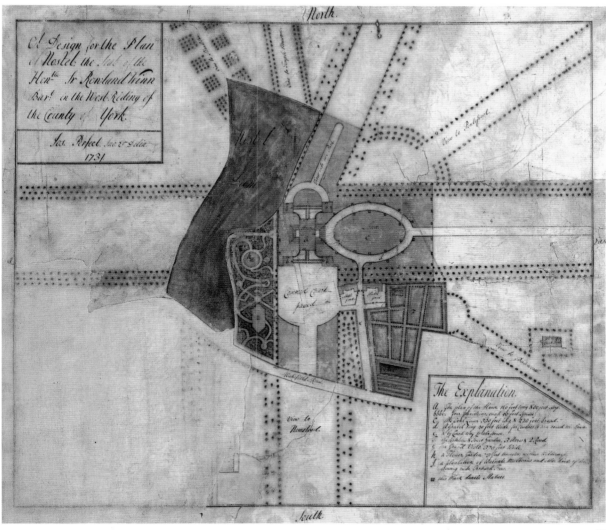

down'. But by way of
compensation a domed ice-house
was built in a circular clump of
trees at the northern end of the 'Fir
Walk' (top left on the plan). A
drawing for it, among the
Hardwicke papers in the British
Museum, may possibly be in
Flitcroft's hand.

Literature: Jackson-Stops, 1979,
p. 661, fig. 11.

21 Design for the park at Nostell Priory, Yorkshire, 1731

Joseph Perfect (fl. 1730s)

Pen and ink

Inscribed top left: 'A Design for the
Plan/of Nostel; the Seat of the/Honble
Sr Rowland Winn/Bart; in the West
Riding of/the County of York/Jos.
Perfect Inv & Delin/1731'; and at
bottom right 'The Explanation/A The
Plan of the House 160 foot long & 80
foot deep/bbbb Four Pavilions each 50
foot square/C An Oval Lawn 330 foot
long & 220 foot broad/d. A Gravel
Ring 40 foot wide for Coaches to run
round lawn/E a by Coach way to the
House/F the Kitchen & Fruit Garden 3
Acres & 2 Rood/G the Grand Vista
370 foot wide/h a Flower Garden 73
foot diameter, with a Wilderness/J a
Plantation of Walnuts, Mulberries and
other kinds of high/growing rude
Orchard Trees/■ This mark denote
Statues'

644×725 mm ($25\frac{3}{8} \times 28\frac{1}{2}$in)

The Lord St Oswald, Nostell Priory,
Yorkshire

Though badly damaged, this
drawing is of crucial importance in
showing the Palladian plan of the
new Nostell Priory already
developed, five years before James
Paine's arrival on the scene as

executant architect in 1736. The rectangular block, joined by quadrant wings to four square pavilions, clearly derives from Palladio's Villa Mocenigo, and seems to have been conceived by a Yorkshire gentleman-architect named Colonel James Moyser, who had connections both with Lord Burlington and Colen Campbell.

The dotted lines to the south of the new house, in the area marked 'Common Court paved', indicate the site of the old Augustinian priory which the Winns had occupied (and adapted) since purchasing the estate in 1650. The left hand of the two stable blocks, aligned on the old rather than the new house, was built by Sir Rowland Winn, 3rd Bt, just before his death in 1722.

Practically nothing is known of Joseph Perfect as a landscape gardener, though five generations of his family are recorded as nurserymen in Pontefract from 1722 until the business was sold in 1810 (Harvey, 1972, 30). For a local man, his scheme is surprisingly ambitious, with a series of 'Grand Vistos' or avenues radiating from the house, each planted differently in quincunxes, lines and squares. The flower garden and wilderness south-west of the house, on the steep bank above the lake, is also sophisticated, with serpentine paths linking the different clearings in the style of Charles Bridgeman. Perfect may indeed have known Bridgeman's designs for two other Yorkshire houses, Ledston Hall and Scampston Hall – the latter actually being laid out in the same year, 1731 (Willis, 1977, p. 61, figs. 48a, 48b). The lake to the west of the house is mentioned in charters of the medieval priory and appears to be a natural one, probably enlarged by the monks as a stewpond.

22 Design for the park at Nostell Priory, Yorkshire, c.1730–40

Stephen Switzer (?1682–1745)

Pen and ink on vellum

Inscribed top right: 'This View of the New House, Offices and Park at Nostell, Yorkshire, with ye improvements as made and to be made in ye Plantation and in ye Park and Wood as designed & drawn by Stephen Switzer'; and top left with key: 'A. The Plan of new Intended House/B. The Hall Front or main Access/to ye House/C. The Common Access or Approach/D, E. The Parterre & Slope to ye Lake/F. The Lake, Cont:g about 30 Acres/G. A Hermitage and Cascade out of the Old Quarry/H. A Menagerie and place for Fowls/I, J. The 2 old stables remov:ed/K. The Comon Court South/of the New Buildings/L. An Orangerie & Green House/M. An Amphitheatre & Mount/in ye wilderness Containing about 6 Acres/ N. A Grand Cabinet in Do/O.O.O. A Diagonal visto from ye/North Front Eastward/P. Another Diagonal from ye North/front Westwards/Q. A Reservoir in Foulby Wood/designed to be planted wth Beech & (?)/for Game, Containing about 14 Acres/R. Corn Field for benifitt of Game/S.S.S. The Mill dam Head and/the Ah. Ah. Terrass to Enclose Foulby/Wood for Game/ T.T.T. A Serpentine River coming/out of Foulby Field/U, The Segg Dam in full View from/the Ah. Ah. Terrass S./ W. A Grand Lawn in ye Park/660 feet wide, the sweep's 680, mall 1340/Feet wide, & 2100 Feet Long/X. A designed Belvidere/Y. Corn Fields for Hares/Z. The Potagerie, or Fruit and/Kitchen Garden/A. New Designed Road from Wragby/to Foulby/B. A New designed Bridge for Do/C. The Leys Yard/D. The Church Yard/E. A Park Gate to ye Grand Avenue/F. The New Slated Avenue/G. Wragby Wood Cull out into Walks/H. A Grand Lawn/I. Another Road designed to place ye/House in ye Middle of ye Park/K. The Road from Doncaster to Wakefield if yt succeeds.'

Scale: 1 in to 200 ft

910 × 695 mm (35$\frac{7}{8}$ × 27$\frac{3}{8}$ in)

The Lord St Oswald, Nostell Priory, Yorkshire

Stephen Switzer is best known today as the author of *The Nobleman, Gentleman, and Gardener's Recreation*, published in 1715, and expanded in 1718 as the first of the three-volume *Ichnographia Rustica* (see No. 5) – a second edition appearing in 1742. But besides being an influential writer on gardening, generally supporting Bridgeman but occasionally critical of his more grandiose projects, Switzer was himself a practising landscape designer, as well as a seedsman and nurseryman. In the *Ichnographia* he describes himself as 'Gardener, Several Years Servant to Mr. *London* and Mr. *Wise*', working for them at Brompton, Blenheim and St James's Park, and later on his own account at Grimsthorpe Castle, Cirencester Park and for other major private patrons.

In the *Ichnographia*, Switzer advocated a unified design for garden and park, bound together by one or two great axial lines in the French manner – he was indeed fond of referring to it as *la grande manière*. The avenues shown to the north, south and east on the Nostell plan conform to this general rule, though the first two are more fragmented in the style of Bridgeman's Grand Avenue at Blenheim, and the third, shown in identical form on Jospeh Perfect's design (No. 21) and used as the main approach, may already have been planted. For the rest, the design shows Switzer, late in his career, moving towards a less centralised and more informal scheme.

In the 1742 edition of *Ichnographia*, he recommends an 'Ambit, Circuit or Tour... such as in all large Designs can only be done on Horseback, or in a Chaise or Coach', and just such a perimeter drive can be seen round the whole northern section of the park in this design, anticipating a favourite device of Capability Brown. The main lake appears to

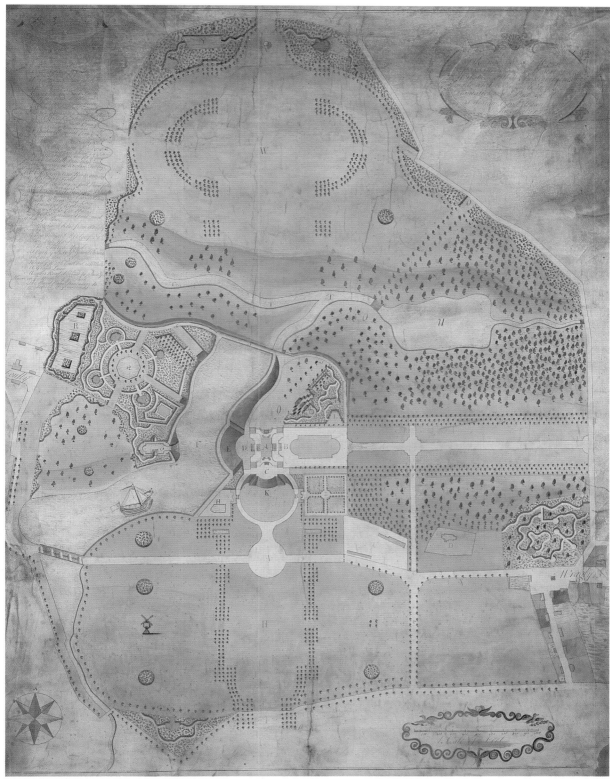

be the same shape as in Perfect's drawing, but the serpentine ha-ha across its northern end (marked 'The Mill Dam Head and Ah! Ah! terrass'), the lower lake with its undulating edges, fed by a winding stream, the uneven planting of trees round it, and the use of circular clumps, are all features which Brown would later adopt.

Some of Switzer's suggestions were probably adopted, given the reference to 'ye improvements as made and to be made' in the inscription. However, none of the garden buildings indicated, such as the Orangery, the Greenhouse, the 'designed Belvidere' or the 'Amphitheatre and Mount in ye Wilderness', has survived, and Switzer's menagerie is also quite differently planned and sited from the present Gothick pavilion, enlarged by Robert Adam.

23 Design for a formal garden at Erddig, Clwyd, c.1725

Attributed to Stephen Switzer (?1682–1745)

Pen and ink with green and sepia washes
Inscribed with letters referring to a key (now missing) and at bottom left 'A Scale of Five Yards'
Watermark: Fleur-de-lis above shield with double chevron, and IV
436×530mm ($17\frac{1}{8} \times 20\frac{7}{8}$in)
The National Trust (Yorke Collection), Erddig, Clwyd (on loan to Clwyd Record Office)

This hitherto unpublished drawing represents the eastern half of the formal garden at Erddig, near Wrexham, and can be attributed to Switzer on stylistic grounds, and because he worked on two other gardens in the neighbourhood: Leeswood and Rhual, both near Mold. Erddig was a late seventeenth-century house bought in 1716 by a successful London lawyer, John Meller (see No. 7) and subsequently enlarged. There was

already a walled garden enclosure adjoining the east front, and a list of its espaliered fruit trees is dated 1718.

Some time in the next decade Meller decided to double the size of this garden, creating a long canal on axis with the house, and a large rectangular pond to the north of it, later known as the menagerie pond. Both of these survive as shown on the plan, and on Badeslade's bird's-eye view engraving of 1739 (No. 24). The curious bite out of the north-eastern corner of the new garden was apparently to allow for a public road which could not be diverted. Badeslade confirms this and the odd pattern of niched yew hedges between this corner and the menagerie pond – possibly intended for beehives, or even animals' cages. A sundial bearing John Meller's arms now stands in the centre of this section, though the plan suggests it may have been intended to go between the canal and the pond.

On the west side of the canal, Badeslade shows a much simpler rectangular bowling green with two plantations of trees beyond it, instead of the elaborate wilderness shown here; nor does he show the mount at the far end of the canal. The wilderness, with its curving zig-zag paths, can be compared with the 'Plan of a Forest or Rural Garden' in Switzer's *Ichnographia Rustica* (1742 edition, vol. III, facing p. 44), while the mount is virtually identical with the lower part of Bridgeman's amphitheatre at Claremont (see No. 32), admired by Switzer and illustrated in his *Introduction to a General System of Hydrostaticks and Hydraulicks* (1729, plate 37).

24 The West Prospect of Erddig, Clwyd, 1739

Thomas Badeslade (c.1715–50) and William Henry Toms (d.c.1750)

Engraving
Inscribed: 'The West Prospect of Erthig in Denbighshire the Seat of Simon Yorke Esqr. . . .' and below 'NB The House extends 224 Feet in Front and stands about 20 Yards high above the River/The Gravel Walk in the Wood (AA) is betwixt 20 & 30 Yards high above the River, & overlooking ye country commands at both ends of it a very agreeable Prospect/W H Toms sculpt/Tho Badeslade delin'
445×565mm ($17\frac{1}{2} \times 22\frac{1}{4}$in)
The National Trust (Yorke Collection), Erddig, Clwyd, North Wales

Badeslade's bird's-eye view of Erddig, engraved by Toms, is one of those rare prints of houses in North Wales, including Chirk (No. 28) and Hawarden, perhaps intended for a sequel to the fourth volume of *Vitruvius Britannicus*, which he and John Rocque published in this same year. It shows the house built by Joshua Edisbury between 1684 and 1687, with wings added by John Meller in the 1720s. The original late seventeenth-century garden stretched only as far as the slight change in level, halfway to the canal. The rest, laid out between 1718 and 1732, probably to designs by Stephen Switzer (see No. 23), has been remarkably little changed since then, though the landscape gardener William Emes made a number of 'improvements' to the park between 1767 and 1789.

The little castellated tower on the hill to the left, used as a belvedere or summer-house, occupies the site of a Norman castle with a motte and bailey. The terrace walk just below it is reminiscent of Bridgeman's at Claremont (No. 32), a garden which Switzer praised – and illustrated – in his *System of Hydrostatics* (1727). The extensive use of conifers is of

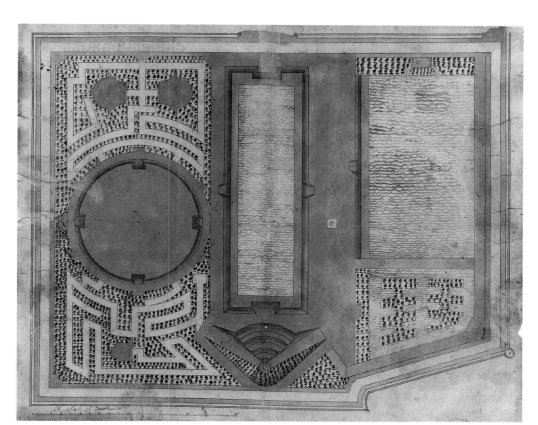

23

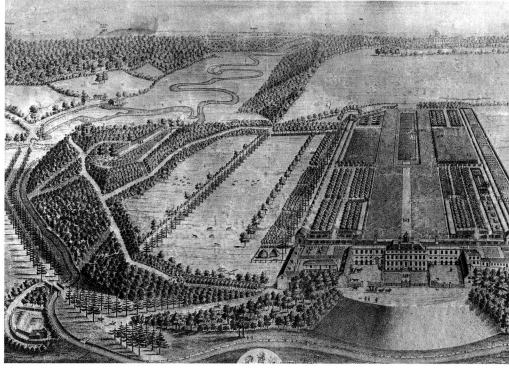

24

interest, as is the kitchen garden, consisting of one long strip down the right-hand side of the formal layout. The cupola on top of the house (later removed by James Wyatt) gave access to a platform on the roof, where John Meller's guests could stroll, admiring the geometrical lines of the garden below.

25 View of Powis Castle, Powys, seen across the Grand Lawn, 1742

Samuel (c.1696–1779) and Nathaniel Buck (d. before 1779)

Engraving

149 × 353mm (5⅞ × 13⅞in)

The National Library of Wales, Aberystwyth

Powis is one of the few places in Britain where the full grandeur of a baroque garden can still be appreciated. The great series of descending terraces on the south side of the medieval castle still survives, together with the orangery and the open arcade above it, even though the clipped yews have grown into fantastic shapes never envisaged when they were planted. This view is of particular importance, however, for it shows many original features of the formal garden swept away by the end of the eighteenth century.

The engraving forms part of a huge series of 'Views of the most remarkable Ruins of Abbeys and Castles now remaining', begun by Samuel Buck as early as 1721, and later continued in partnership with his brother Nathaniel. These prints appear to have been sold separately, or in batches by county, though the first collected edition (in three volumes) was only published in 1774 under the title *Buck's Antiquities*.

The design of the terraces and orangery is generally attributed to William Winde, who constructed a similar arcaded terrace at Cliveden, and who rebuilt the 1st Marquess

of Powis's London house in 1684–8. In 1697 he is recorded as travelling with the 2nd Marquess to Powis, but a few months later his patron, a staunch Jacobite, went into exile in Flanders, returning only in 1703.

When he did so, he was accompanied by one Adrian Duval of Rouen, whom Lady Powis had engaged as a gardener in Ghent. Duval, who was still employed at Powis in 1717, may well have been an expert on hydraulics, for two years after his arrival a visitor to the castle, John Bridgeman, praised 'the water-works and fountains that are finished there... much beyond anything I ever saw, whose streams play near twenty yards in height. The Cascade has two falls of water which concludes in a noble bason.'

The top of this cascade, with a *tempietto* crowned by a statue and two flanking fountains, can be seen in the left foreground of this view, though the chain of lead cisterns cut into the hillside below faced the castle, and thus remains invisible. The prodigal use of lead, not only for the cascade but also for the many statues and urns on the terraces and parterres, is explained by the lucrative Montgomeryshire lead mines owned by the family from 1692 until 1745. The huge equestrian group representing Fame, now in the courtyard, and the Hercules on the top terrace are both signed by Andries Carpentière, but others may well be by his master, Jan van Nost (d.1729).

(Opposite page, bottom) Aerial view of the gardens at Powis Castle, Powys

A Perspective View of POWES CASTLE *in the County of Montgomery.*

25

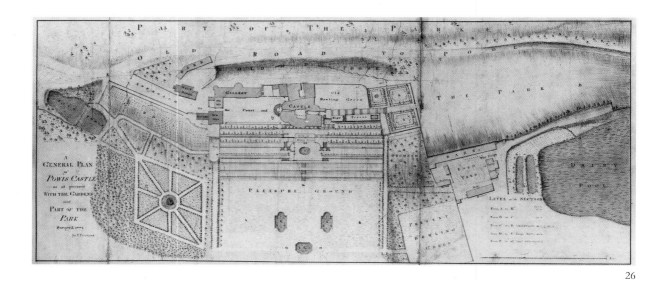

26 Survey plan of Powis Castle and gardens, 1771

Thomas Farnolls Pritchard (1723–77)

Pen, ink and wash

Signed and dated

Inscribed: 'A/General Plan/of/Powis Castle/as at present/With The Gardens/and/Part of the/Park/Survey'd 1771/by T. Pritchard'

Scale: 1in to approx. 52ft

425 × 950mm (16¾ × 37⅜in)

The Trustees of the Powis Estate

In 1771 the Shrewsbury architect Thomas Farnolls Pritchard was commissioned by the 2nd Earl of Powis to make a 'Plan of the present Castle and Buildings with a Plan and Section of the ground 60 yards round them... so as to enable His Lordship to have the whole further considered in London'. The Earl clearly intended considerable alterations inside and out, for at the same time he sent for the landscape gardener William Emes to make recommendations for the park and garden.

Pritchard's meticulous survey plan confirms many of the details seen in the earlier Buck engraving, and adds to our knowledge of the formal gardens laid out in the late seventeenth and early eighteenth centuries. The two large ponds in the middle of what is now the Grand Lawn can be seen complete with their statuary, though the surrounding *platte-bandes* planted with topiary have already disappeared. The third pond, near the bottom edge of the drawing, must be the 'noble bason' at the bottom of the cascade, with Andries Carpentière's lead equestrian group representing *Fame* in the centre – only later moved to the courtyard.

On the site of the present Upper Lawn, Pritchard shows a diamond-shaped wilderness, with paths converging on a central round pond, with another large fountain. He also shows an oval pond in the centre of the middle terrace, in front of the orangery – long since filled in; the so-called 'Apple Slope' below this consisting of three further terraces; and elaborate parterre beds flanking the approach from the east, between the Davies brothers' great wrought-iron gate and the foot of the long, open staircase leading up to the east front. The area marked 'Present Bowling Green' was made into a kitchen garden in the late nineteenth century, but the fish pond on the far left is almost exactly the same shape as the present pool.

Literature: Lawson and Waterson, 1975–6, p. 8.

27 View of the garden at Chirk Castle, Clwyd, from the east, c.1720

Peter Tillemans (1684–1734)

Watercolour with pencil (2 figures in foreground blocked out)

Watermark: Knight in armour, spear, in wheel/Pro Patria/P__

200 × 390mm (7⅞ × 15⅜in)

Lady Margaret Myddelton, Chirk Castle, Clwyd, North Wales

The Flemish-born artist Peter Tillemans was reimbursed 'for Cloth or Canvas bought by him and colours £2.3.6, for pencils and brushes 7s.' during a visit to Chirk in November 1720. This watercolour was almost certainly made at that time, probably as a preparatory sketch for an oil painting: either an alternative to, or a companion for, the large *North Prospect of Chirk* still owned by the Myddelton family (Harris, 1979, p. 232). Both views show the magnificent wrought-iron gatescreen (seen on the far right in the watercolour) made between 1712 and 1719 by the brothers Robert and John Davies of Bersham, near Wrexham.

27

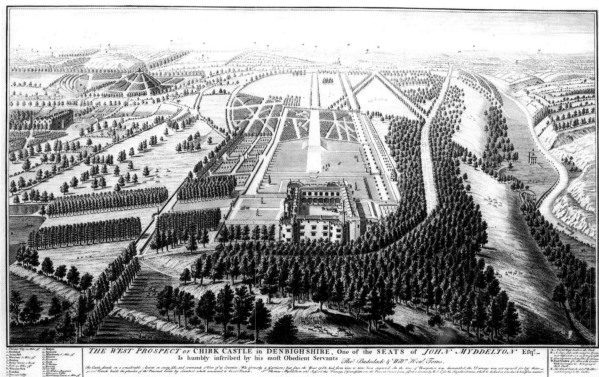

THE WEST PROSPECT OF CHIRK CASTLE in DENBIGHSHIRE, One of the SEATS of *JOHN. MYDDELTON* Esq.
Is humbly inscribed by his most Obedient Servants *Tho.ᵴ Badeslade & Will.ᵐ Hen.ʳ Toms.*

28

Though copying the form of the original Welsh border castle, begun in 1295, the east front, shown here, was almost entirely rebuilt by Sir Thomas Myddelton, 2nd Bt, between 1672 and 1678, after serious damage in the Civil War. However, a stone tablet in the garden, carved with a Latin inscription (*Horti/Voluptatis, amaenitatisque/Causa Parati/Thom. Myddelton/Milite/1653*) suggests that his father may have begun work on the garden at an earlier date. A new long gallery was formed after the Restoration on the upper floor overlooking the garden, and the large east window of the chapel, dating from about 1400, can be seen on the left. The three terraces with steps leading down to a sunken bowling green could be of the 1650s, though the two Dutch-looking gazebos on the middle terrace (one with a mullion window and the other a sash) look like late seventeenth-century additions. Some of the panelling inside the castle is close to designs by William Winde, who also worked nearby at Powis (No. 25), so it is possible that he was also consulted about the garden in the 1670s and '80s.

The seated figure of the artist in the foreground appears in many of Tillemans's drawings, though it is hard to see why his two companions have been blotted out.

28 The West Prospect of Chirk Castle, Clwyd, 1739

Thomas Badeslade (*c.*1715–50) and William Henry Toms (d.*c.*1750)

Engraving

Inscribed: 'The West Prospect of Chirk Castle in Denbighshire, One of the Seats of John Myddelton Esqr/Is humbly inscribed by his most Obedient Servants/Thos Badeslade & Willm Heny Toms'; and with two keys: one refers to mileages; the other 'A. A Cold Bath built in the Park/B. A Large Lake at the end of an Avenue near half a mile

seen in front of ye Castle/C.Ceven-y-Wern a Seat of this Gentlemans/D. Fruit Garden of 12-Acres with circular Walks & Terraces &c belonging to Chirk Castle./E. The Black Park stock'd with Red Deer and belonging to the Castle'

470 × 720mm (18$\frac{1}{2}$ × 28$\frac{3}{8}$in)
The National Trust (Myddelton Collection), Chirk Castle, Clwyd, North Wales

This engraving, from the same series as the bird's-eye view of Erddig (No. 23), shows the dramatic site of the medieval castle with a steep drop on the south to the River Ceiriog, which here forms the border between England and Wales. In the foreground is a section of Offa's Dyke, the great eighth-century earthwork intended to run from the Dee estuary to the Severn. The dovecote to the south-east of the castle is the one shown in Tillemans's drawing (No. 27), and the three descending terraces and the bowling green are also visible. However, the gazebos on the middle terrace seem to have disappeared and may already have been demolished. An extensive kitchen garden is shown to the left of the bowling green area, with a fir walk beyond.

The gabled house on the far left, identified as Cefn-y-Wern, also belonged to the Myddeltons but was burnt down earlier in this century – a sad loss. Beyond it is a hill planted to resemble an artificial mount, with walks round it at different levels, and also a 12-acre fruit garden with further curving terraces. All these formal features disappeared between 1761 and 1774 when William Emes was employed to create a landscaped pleasure-ground of lawns, shrubberies and woodland, the whole enclosed by a sunk deer fence. The Davies brothers' forecourt gatescreen was moved to the far edge of the park to form a new entrance, and the lead statues of Mars and Hercules were taken out of the forecourt and re-erected as distant eye-catchers in

the park. The latter still survives and has recently been returned to the garden on the east side of the castle, where it has been placed at the end of an *allée* of limes dated about 1720, among the only trees shown by Badeslade that still survive.

29 The Cascade at Belton House, Lincolnshire, 1749

Francis Vivares (1709–80) after Thomas Smith (d.1769)

Engraving

Dated 1749 on plate

Inscribed: 'A View of the New Waterworks &c at Belton in Lincolnshire to the Rt Honble the Lord Vist Tyrconnell/to whom this Plate is inscribed by his Lordships most dutiful and most huble Servt/T. Smith./T. Smith Pin. F. Vivares Scul:/Published Oct 1749'

390 × 540mm (15$\frac{3}{8}$ × 21$\frac{1}{4}$in)
The National Trust (Brownlow Collection), Belton House, Lincolnshire

In April 1745 Viscount Tyrconnel wrote to his nephew, John Cust: 'Belton never so Green and Pleasant; ye ponds and canal over-flowing full, a grand Rustick arch finished with vast Rough Stones over ye Cascade of ye River, and two Huge Artificial Rocks on each side, Design'd and executed, as I think, in a taste superior to anything that I have seen, either at Lord Gainsborough's or Lord Cobham's [ie at Exton, only a few miles away in Rutland, or Stowe in Buckinghamshire].'

Tyrconnel had begun building the cascade in May 1742, when the first payment was made to the mason, William Grey. Prior to that, the gardens at Belton lay on the east side of the house with four formally planned 'wildernesses' flanking a central vista. But at this point, he decided to exploit the 'capabilities' of the little River

(Opposite page, bottom) The cascade at Belton House, Lincolnshire, c.1890

A View of the New Waterworks &c at Belton in Lincolnshire, belonging to the Rt Honble the Lord Vis Tyrconnel
to whom this Plate is inscribd by his Lordships most dutiful and most humble Servt T. Smith

29

Witham to the west, planting its valley with trees and shrubs, laying out serpentine paths, and draining the stream to form an impressive waterfall. This new 'Wilderness', much more naturalistic than its predecessors, was conceived in the newly fashionable 'picturesque' taste, though its designer is still unknown.

A mock-Gothic ruin built above the cascade enhanced its scale and produced an effect of balanced asymmetry, even if the tiered fountains either side of the main cascade seem highly artificial to our eyes. Soon after its completion, Lord Tyrconnel commissioned the painter Thomas Smith of Derby, famous for his Peak District landscapes and his bird's-eye views of country houses in the Midlands, to record the appearance of the cascade, and it is this picture (perhaps the one now in the Breakfast Room at Belton, though this may be a copy) which Vivares afterwards engraved. The building seen on the left is the seventeenth-century stable block designed by the master-mason William Stanton.

After Tyrconnel's death, the cascade seems to have fallen into disrepair, and Lord Torrington on a visit to Belton in 1791 wrote that '... for the water works (now destroy'd) I repine, as they must have been curiously imagined'. About 1816, the cascade was restored by the nurseryman and landscape gardener William Pontet for the 1st Earl Brownlow, though lowered and further 'naturalised' in the process.

30 View of the Banqueting House and Rotonda, Studley Royal, Yorkshire, 1758

Anthony Walker (1726–65)

Inscribed: 'Drawn and Engraved by A. Walker 1758'; and handwritten below: 'A view of the Banqueting House and Round Temple at Studley, the Seat of William Aislabie Equire./ ANNO 1758.'

394 × 508mm (15½ × 20in)

Mrs G. F. Pettit (on loan to the National Trust, East Riddlesden Hall, Yorkshire)

John Aislabie was disgraced as Chancellor of the Exchequer at the time of the South Sea Bubble in 1720. He subsequently retired to his estate at Studley Royal near Ripon and set about creating the most magnificent formal water-garden in England – 'look'd upon as the Wonder of the North', according to John Tracy Atkyns's *Iter Boreale* of 1732. Instead of rebuilding the old Tudor house, which Atkyns thought still 'of the poorest appearance', he commissioned Colen Campbell (in association with Roger Morris) to design a new stable block and a number of garden buildings, which were erected by the Westminster mason Robert Doe between 1727 and 1730. These buildings included the Temple of Piety overlooking the Moon Ponds, the cascade, flanked by two little fishing pavilions, and the rotonda and banqueting house seen in this engraving, on the hill to the west.

The last of these is closely comparable to the 'Great Room' which Campbell built in the garden at Hall Barn, Buckinghamshire, for Aislabie's stepson, Harry Waller. Originally known as the 'greenhouse', it probably had windows in the side walls as well as the main elevation, and was used for keeping orange trees and other tender plants in the winter. The domed alcoves either side are likely to have been added after Aislabie's death in 1742, when his son converted it into a banqueting room with rococo plasterwork decoration. The plain parapet must have been replaced by a balustrade later on in the century. The Ionic rotonda, again very like the one at Hall Barn, was later moved to the other side of the valley, and its order changed to the Doric. Some of the early accounts refer to it as the Temple of Fame, perhaps

named after a statue placed in the centre, but afterwards removed.

Walker's engraving is of great interest in showing the original juxtaposition of the two buildings – too close by later eighteenth-century standards – and the formal terraces and clipped hedges since replaced by an oval lawn. The rotonda, standing on the edge of the hill, would have been as much of a landmark as Vanbrugh's at Stowe (No. 35).

This early hand-coloured copy of the engraving and its companion (No. 31) are rare in that they bear a date, next to Walker's name, and also because of the handwritten inscription below.

Literature: Hussey, 1967, pp. 132–7, fig. 182.

31 View of Fountains Abbey and Tent Hill from the gardens of Studley Royal, Yorkshire, 1758

Anthony Walker (1726–65)

Engraving

Inscribed: 'Drawn and Engraved by A. Walker 1758'; and handwritten below: 'A View of the Reservoir & Artificial Mount, in the Gardens of Studley the Seat of William Aislabie Esqr. with a Distant View of Fountains Abby./ANNO 1758.'

394 × 508mm (15½ × 20in)

Mrs G. F. Pettit (on loan to the National Trust, East Riddlesden Hall, Yorkshire)

Like Vanbrugh, who tried unsuccessfully to preserve the old manor house of Woodstock in view of the front of Blenheim in 1709, John Aislabie had an appreciation of old buildings far in advance of his time. In 1719, for instance, he and Vanbrugh both agreed that the old Holbein Gate in Whitehall 'ought not to be destroyed if other expedients can be found'. Although the ruins of the great Cistercian abbey of Fountains lay outside the boundaries of his estate at Studley Royal, the views of it from his

A View of the Banqueting House and Round Temple at Studley, the Seat of William Aislabie Esquire.
ANNO 1758.

30

A View of the Reservoir & Artificial Mound, in the Gardens of Studley the Seat of William Aislabie Esqr with a Distant View of Fountains Abby.

31

57

garden were considered of great importance from the beginning. Atkyns, who visited Studley in 1730, noted that 'the ruins of an old place called Fountain Abbey make a very pretty point of view one way'.

To begin with, the usual vantage point seems to have been Tent Hill, in the centre of this engraving, called after the tent which Aislabie had erected here in the summer months. This was later replaced by a domed octagonal pavilion, as shown in the engraving, but that in turn disappeared in the nineteenth century. By about 1750, the garden had been extended further across the valley, and an alcove seat built to give a more distant straight-on view of the abbey, with the canalised River Skell in the foreground, and the dam, with the arch leading to the grotto-cascade on the right.

Finally, ten years after this engraving was made, William Aislabie managed to buy the ruins of the abbey, which his father had so much coveted. According to William Gilpin this was a mixed blessing, for immediately 'his busy hands were let loose upon it... he has pared away all the bold roughness and freedom of the scene and given every part a trim polish... a *legal* right the proprietor unquestionably has to deform his ruin, as he pleases. But tho he fear no indictment in the king's bench, he must expect a very severe prosecution in the court of taste.' (Gilpin, 1786, pp. 184–8).

Literature: Hussey, 1967, pp. 133–4.

32 Survey plan of the garden at Claremont, Surrey, with views of the house and garden buildings, 1738

John Rocque (*c*.1704–62)

Engraving
Inscribed: '1. The House/2. Flower Garden/3. The Alcove/4. The terrass/ 5. Stables/6. Kitchen Garden/ 7. Obelisk/8. The Avenue/ 9. Mr. Greenings House/10. The Mount/11. The Bowling Green/12. The Thacht House/13. Nine Pin Alley/ 14. Amphitheater/15. The Temple/ PLAN/Du Jardin et parc de Claremount/a 15 Milles de Londres une des/Maisons du DUC de NEWCASTLE/tres Exatement levé et Gravé par/J. Rocque 1738'
Scale: 1in to approx. 190yd
1085 × 775mm (42¾ × 30½in)
The Governors of Claremont Fan Court School

Claremont began life as a small villa which Sir John Vanbrugh built for himself near Esher in 1708, and which he sold in 1711 to his friend Thomas Pelham-Holles, Earl of Clare (and later Duke of Newcastle). Over the next fifteen years, the house was hugely enlarged by Vanbrugh for its new owner, with a belvedere crowning the 'mount' to the west of the house, and elaborate semi-formal gardens laid out beyond it by Charles Bridgeman. An engraving by Colen Campbell, published in the third volume of *Vitruvius Britannicus*, shows its appearance in 1725, just before the construction of Bridgeman's great turf amphitheatre.

Vanbrugh died in 1726, and in the following decade the Duke employed William Kent to alter the layout and add a number of garden buildings. As Sir Thomas Robinson reported to Lord Carlisle in 1734, 'a general alteration of some of the most considerable gardens in the Kingdom is begun after Mr. Kent's notion, viz. to lay them out and work without level or line... the more agreeable as, when finished, it has the appearance of beautiful nature... The celebrated gardens of Claremont, Chiswick and Stowe are now full of labourers to modernize the expensive works finished in them even since everyone's memory.'

(Right) The amphitheatre at Claremont, Surrey

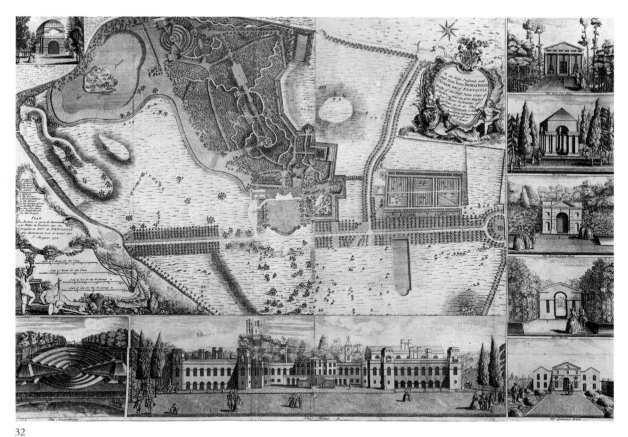

32

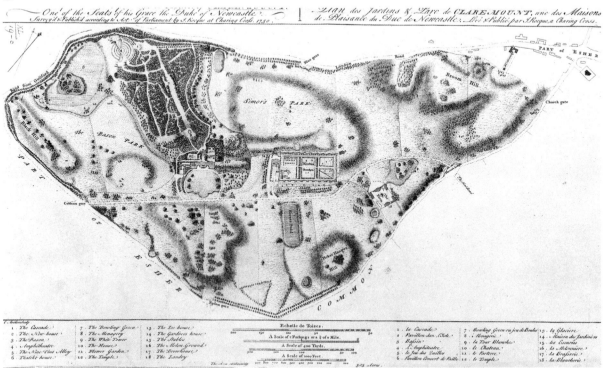

One of the Seats of his Grace the Duke of Newcastle.
Survey'd & Publish'd according to Act of Parliament by J. Rocque at Charing Cross. 1750.

PLAN des Jardins & Parc de CLAREMOUNT, une des Maisons de Plaisance du Duc de Newcastle. Levé & Publié par J. Rocque, a Charing Cross.

1. The Cascade	7. The Bowling Green	13. The Ice house
2. The New house	8. The Menagery	14. The Gardens house
3. The Bason	9. The White Tower	15. The Stables
4. Amphitheatre	10. The House	16. The Melon Ground
5. The Nine Vine Alley	11. Flower Garden	17. The Greenhouse
6. Thatcht house	12. The Temple	18. The Landry

Echelle de Toises.
A Scale of 2 Furlongs or a ¼ of a Mile.
A Scale of 400 Yards.
A Scale of 1000 Feet.

1. la Cascade	7. Bowling Green ou jeu de Boules	13. la Glaciere
2. Pavillon dans l'Isle	8. Menagerie	14. Maison du jardinier
3. Bassin	9. la Tour Blanche	15. les Ecuries
4. l'Amphitéatre	10. le Chateau	16. la Melonniere
5. le jeu des Quilles	11. le Parterre	17. la Brasserie
6. Pavillon Couvert de Paille	12. le Temple	18. la Blancherie

33

John Rocque's plan of Claremont made in 1738, bordered by vignettes of many of the garden buildings (like his Chiswick plan, made two years earlier), shows the extent of Kent's contribution. Bridgeman's eastern avenue, on the main axis of the house, has been split up into clumps; his straight 'ramparts' along the southern side of the garden have been replaced by a serpentine ha-ha; and his round pond on the western edge – a facsimile of the one in Kensington Gardens – has been made into an informal lake, with an island in the centre. On this island Kent built a pavilion called the New House, probably not complete at the time Rocque was making his survey, for the view of it, tucked away at the top left-hand corner, does not appear on early impressions of the engraving (eg Rorschach, 1983, p. 99), nor is the building mentioned in the key. The roof is also shown as a squared dome rather than a pyramid, as executed.

The Duke of Newcastle's house, shown at the bottom, was demolished by Lord Clive, who bought the estate in 1769, and who commissioned Capability Brown to build a new mansion slightly further north. Vanbrugh's Belvedere, still in existence, can be seen on the hill behind. To the left Rocque shows Bridgeman's amphitheatre, described in Batty Langley's *New Principles of Gardening* (1726) and Stephen Switzer's *System of Hydrostatics* (1727). Totally overgrown by rhododendrons in the late nineteenth century, this has recently been restored by the National Trust.

'Mr. Greening's House' (bottom right) also survives, though in a somewhat altered state, near the remains of the old walled garden. Both this building and the long-demolished 'Temple' (second from top, on right) are shown in the 1725 plan, and can be attributed to

Vanbrugh. The other three buildings shown, all attributable to Kent, have sadly disappeared. The 'Nine Pin Alley' pavilion, near the top of the amphitheatre, survived until about 1929, and the Trust hopes to rebuild it one day; the 'Bowling Green House' perished at some earlier date; while the 'Alcove' was presumably removed in the 1770s, since it was no longer on axis with Lord Clive's new house.

Literature: Stroud, 1976, pp. 32–7, fig. 8.

33 Survey plan of the garden at Claremont, Surrey, 1750

François Antoine Aveline (1727–62) after John Rocque (c.1704–62)

Engraving

Inscribed: 'A SURVEY of the House, Gardens & Park of CLAREMOUNT... Survey'd & Publish'd according to Act of Parliament by J. Rocque at Charing Cross. 1750/1. The Cascade/2. The New-house/3. The Bason/4. Amphitheatre/5. The Nine Pins Alley/6. Thatcht house/7. The Bowling Green/8. The Menagery/9. The White Tower/10. The House/11. Flower Garden/12. The Temple/13. The Ice house/14. The Gardiners house/15. The Stables/16. The Melon Ground/17. The Brewhouse/18. The Laundry'

Scale: 1in to approx. 115yd

312 × 516mm (12¼ × 20¼in)

Surrey Libraries

William Kent died in 1748, but a second plan of Claremont by Rocque, dated two years later, shows that the process of 'naturalising' the landscape had continued apace during that decade – long before Capability Brown's appearance on the scene. Bridgeman's great north and south avenues have now been removed, with only a few trees left in clumps; his ramparts on the northern border of the garden (retained during Kent's first phase of work) have also gone, with the line

softened by planting; while further informal planting has been carried out beyond the main pleasure grounds to the north, taking in Senior's Park and Broom Hill. The wiggly paths in the wilderness have been simplified, the sharp formality of the Bowling Green has been blurred with random planting of beech, and the earth bastions below the Belvedere swept away. A menagerie has also been created in the woodland south-east of the Bowling Green, and Lord Clive's later inventories describe the animals which he kept there, including a zebra and foal, various breeds of deer, an 'African Bull' 'and seven goats, the last 'very troublesome'.

This 1750 plan also shows the lake being fed from a cascade of three arches in the south-west corner. This was later turned into a grotto (seen in another drawing attributed to George Lambert, page 15), possibly by Joseph and Josiah Lane, whose famous Painshill grotto, only a few miles away, was completed by 1765.

Despite the sole initial 'A', the engraver cannot have been Antoine Aveline, who died in Paris in 1743, but could be his son François Antoine, who is known to have worked in London until his death in 1762. Later versions of this print were published by Robert Sayer of 53 Fleet Street, and his successor Richard Holmes Laurie – the latter as late as 1821.

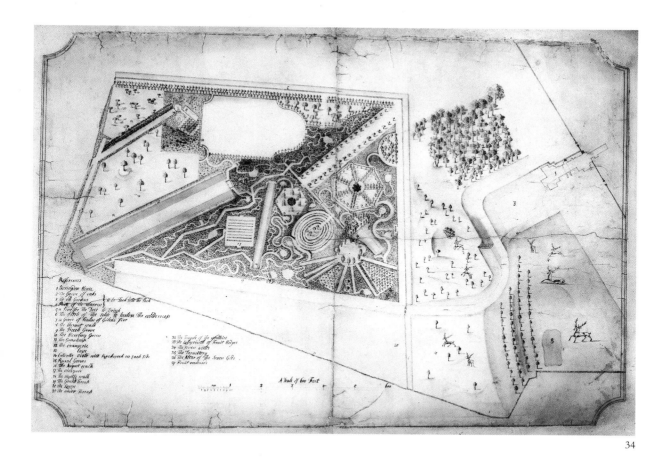

34 Survey drawing of the garden at Boringdon House, Devon, *c*.1735

Anonymous

Pen with sepia and grey ink, watercolour and pencil

Inscribed: 'References/1 Boringdon House/2 The Grove of Oaks/3 The old Gardens/4 Part of the warren [2–4 bracketed 'To be Took into the Park']/5 A Pond for the Deer to Drink/6 The Ditch of the ahh [ie ha-ha] to Inclose the wilderness/7 A Grove of Balm of Gilead firr/8 The Chestnut Walk/9 The Beech Grove/10 The Bowling Green/11 The Greenhouse/12 The Orangerie/13 Cave/14 Catwater Visto with Rockwork on Each Side/15 Rural Groves/16 The August walk/17 the Vineyard/18 The Myrtle Walk/19 The Grand Terrass/20 The Lawn/21 The under Terrass/22 The Temple of the Worthies/23 The Labyrinth of Fruit Hedges/24 The Seven Vistos/25 The Dormitory/26 The Altar of the Saxon Gods/27 Fruit Orchards'

Scale: 1in to 66ft

506 × 735mm (19$\frac{7}{8}$ × 29in)

The National Trust (Morley Collection), Saltram, Devon (on loan to the Drawings Collection, Royal Institute of British Architects, London)

John Parker married Frances Mayhew, the heiress to Boringdon in 1583, and the family continued to live there until 1743 when they moved to Saltram only a few miles to the south. This extraordinarily elaborate garden plan evidently dates from just before the move, when plans were also afoot to regularise the entrance front of the old Elizabethan and Jacobean house, and add flanking pavilions joined by curving quadrants – shown here faintly pencilled in. This Palladian solution could be associated with William Kent himself, who produced a design for a great house with similar quadrants that still survives among the Parker papers in the Devon Record Office (Cornforth, 1967, p. 998, fig. 2).

No vestiges of such a garden now remain at Boringdon, though the ha-ha shown at the top of the drawing is roughly in line with a field boundary on the high downs above the house. Furthermore, the precipitous nature of the site makes it unlikely that the design could have been achieved without considerable earth-moving. It is puzzling that the style of drawing looks more like a survey than a design, but that may simply be explained by the designer having trained as a surveyor.

The great interest of this layout is its mixture of formal and informal features crammed into a comparatively small space, and, still more, the appearance of a 'Temple of the Worthies', an 'Altar of the Saxon Gods' (with radiating walks evidently leading to their statues) and a 'Dormitory'. All these rare features are also found in the gardens at Stowe: the Dormitory or Temple of Sleep, designed by Vanbrugh before 1726; the Saxon Gods, carved before 1731 by Rysbrack to stand around a seven-sided altar; and Kent's Temple of British Worthies, built in 1735 (Nos 37 and 38). Another possible link is the mention of a 'Cave' in the key – with a blank space before it, as if the surveyor could not remember (or understand) its correct name – for it is tempting to compare this with Dido's Cave at Stowe, once again in existence by 1731.

Charles Bridgeman, who was so deeply involved with the creation of the Stowe landscape, may have had a hand in the garden at Castle Hill, not far from Boringdon, in the 1730s, for the turf 'ramparts' there are very much in his style. However, the Boringdon plan lacks the bold axial vistas and the essential unity of his designs, and is equally alien to the more flowing naturalism of Kent's Elysian Fields at Stowe, and his work at Rousham. One can only think that it represents a provincial response to one of the most influential gardens of its day, perhaps following a visit to Stowe either by the Parkers or by their unknown garden designer. Another source for the crowding together of different geometrical features might be Robert Castell's imaginary reconstruction of the gardens round the younger Pliny's villa at Tusculum, illustrated in his *Villas of the Ancients* in 1728 (Dixon Hunt and Willis, 1975, fig. 69).

Boringdon House, sold by the Parker family in 1920, has recently been rescued from dereliction, and converted into an hotel.

35 View of the Queen's Temple from the Rotonda, Stowe, Buckinghamshire, 1734

Jacques Rigaud (*c.*1681–1754) and Bernard Baron (*c.*1700–66)

Engraving
Inscribed: 'Published by S. Bridgeman May 12 1739/Rigaud & Baron del.& Sculp.'
Watermark: Spread eagle
364 × 514mm (14¼ × 20¼in)
The Governors of Stowe School

This is one of fifteen views of the garden at Stowe commissioned not by its owner, Lord Cobham, but by his landscape gardener Charles Bridgeman, who specially invited the French artist and engraver Jacques Rigaud over from Paris for the purpose. All of the drawings and most of the plates were completed by the end of 1734, but a quarrel over Rigaud's fee delayed publication until 1739, when the project was completed by the London engraver Bernard Baron.

Publish'd by S.Bridgeman May 12 1739.   Rigaud & Baron del. & sculp.

35

By this time Bridgeman himself was dead, and the series was published by his widow, Sarah, as an act of piety. There may also have been an element of propaganda, however, for the style of formal gardening depicted here was already being undermined by William Kent's more naturalistic layout of the Elysian Fields, and Kent's garden buildings – like the Temple of Venus and the Hermitage – are either studiously ignored, or relegated to the distant background.

According to George Vertue, all the drawings were by Rigaud ('most excellently performed'), and Baron only engraved five of the plates, although adding his name to Rigaud's on all the rest, including this one. In any case, the engravings remain among the earliest and finest sets of views devoted to a single English garden, with few competitors even in France. Their accuracy has been confirmed in almost every detail, and they are of particular interest in depicting a number of identifiable figures.

In this view Lord and Lady Cobham are seen, each with their attendants, and each seated in a mobile chair of state such as Louis XIV used at Versailles. The theme of the engravings, celebrating Vanbrugh at Kent's expense, is clear in Lord Cobham's attitude of melancholy: in George Clarke's words 'not the extreme form of the humour derided in *L'Allegro*, but the mood of serious reflection in *Il Penseroso*. As he contemplates Vanbrugh's perfect temple, he remembers how much his garden owes to his dead friend.'

Some artistic licence has been necessary, for the sight lines to Nelson's Seat (on the far left) and the fountain in the Octagon Lake (on the far right) would have been more than 120 degrees. But Rigaud has depicted the radiating vistas from the Rotunda with the greatest skill and the minimum of distortion. The Rotunda, built in 1721, is shown slightly larger than it really is, with Vanbrugh's original dome, lowered by Borra in the 1770s when the gilded statue of Venus was also removed. The house can be seen immediately to the right, and beyond it the King's Column (see No. 42), the tower of Stowe church, and Queen Caroline's Monument (later re-sited), with its turf terraces. On the far right can be seen part of Bridgeman's famous ha-ha, whose ditch and protruding stakes kept livestock out of the garden. 'Lady and cow gaze at each other across the ditch', as George Clarke observes, 'but Art and Nature are kept strictly apart.'

Literature: Clarke, 1987, introduction and note to plate 8.

36 Plan of the gardens, park and woodlands at Stowe, Buckinghamshire, 1739

Anonymous

Engraving

Inscribed: 'A General Plan/of the Woods, Park and Gardens of/Stowe/with several Perspective Views/in the Gardens/*Dedicated* to his Lordship/by his most humble and obedient/Servant *Sarah Bridgeman* 1739'; key at bottom left: 'A. The Park with the Aproach to the House/b. The House and Offices/c. The two Orangereys/d. The House Terras/e. The two Orangery Walks/f. The Upper River/g. Congreve's Monument/h. The Stone Bridge/i. The Entrance to ye Garden with ye Pavilions/k. The Octagon Bason/l. The Lower River/m. The Monument/n. The Elysian Fields/o. The Witch Wood/q. The Stone Temple/r. The Church/s. Part of the Kitchen Gardens/ t. The Grotto and Shell Temple/v. The Alder River/w. The Shell Bridge/x. The Cascade and Rocks/y. The Lake/z. The Hermitage'; key at bottom right: '1. Peggs Terras/2. Kent's Bastion and Building/3. Warden Hill Walk/4. Lake Walk/5. Gibbs' Building/6. Boycot & Speed's Building wth ye Entrance to ye Park/7. Nelson's Walk/8. The Pyramid/ 9. Lady Temple's Spinny/10. The Temple/11. Coucher's Obelisk/12. Nelson's Seat/13. Rogers's/14. Kitchen Gardens/15. The great cross Lime Walk/16. The Rotunda/17. The Queens Theatre/18. The King's Pillar/19. Gurness Walk/20. The Sleeping House and Wood/21. The Abeel Walk/22. The Perterre/23. The Home Park/24. Hawkwell Hill and Field'

Scale: 1in to 45oft

970 × 610mm (38$\frac{1}{8}$ × 24in)

The Governors of Stowe School

This large plan of the park and gardens at Stowe was commissioned by Charles Bridgeman's widow, Sarah, after his death in 1738, to accompany the series of fifteen views by Jacques Rigaud (see No. 35) – and to act as a title page. George Vertue noted that it was 'by another graver': ie not Rigaud or Bernard Baron, who engraved five of the views. The series was advertised early in 1740 at 4 guineas a set, but when Sarah herself died in 1744, the unsold prints were bought by four London booksellers who added a title page of their own and offered them for sale at a reduced price in 1746.

The plan is interesting in that the garden takes up such a small proportion of the whole, and suggests that Bridgeman may also have had a hand in laying out the 'forest garden': the great system of woodland rides stretching north towards Silverstone. Recent research suggests that these rides were mostly aligned on neighbouring parish churches – except for the great double avenue leading to Stowe Castle (a farmhouse disguised by mock-medieval curtain walls) at bottom right. This had only just been built in the previous year, 1738, probably to designs by Gibbs. Just to the left of the double avenue is the village of Lamport, not then belonging to the family.

So far as can be checked, the plan is highly accurate, even to the extent of showing a long canal on the north front, instead of the large round pond in Rigaud's view – either an unexecuted project or a

63

simple mistake. It is also fascinating in showing the garden at the moment when Kent's more informal style of landscape gardening, created 'without either level or line', was beginning to dissolve the formal lines of Bridgeman's axial layout. This can be clearly seen in the Elysian Fields, with its irregular chain of lakes and open, naturalistic tree planting, immediately to the right of the main vista from the house to the Octagon Pond.

However, the anti-Kent propaganda sensed in the views themselves may be continued by the keys to the plan, which do not give their correct names to any of Kent's major buildings: the Temple of British Worthies is merely 'The Monument'; Ancient Virtue (terminating Bridgeman's 'great cross Lime Walk') is called 'The Stone Temple'; and the Temple of Venus simply 'Kent's Bastion and Building'. All three are correctly described in Samuel Richardson's edition of Defoe's *Tour thro the Whole Island of Britain* published in 1742.

Literature: Willis, 1977, fig. 123; Clarke, 1987, introduction and note to plate 1.

37 Elevation and ground plan for the Temple of British Worthies at Stowe, Buckinghamshire, c.1735

William Kent (1685–1748)

Pen, ink and wash

Inscribed: behind the central section on the ground plan, 'You may hollow this backwards and make a/seat in it if thought fit'

Scale: approx. 1in to $4\frac{1}{2}$ft

325 × 375 mm ($12\frac{3}{4}$ × $14\frac{3}{4}$in)

The Governors of Stowe School

Kent's Temple of British Worthies, built about 1735, is one of the key elements in the complex symbolism of the Elysian Fields – the little valley south-east of the house and church at Stowe, whose informal, naturalistic landscape was so revolutionary for its time. The usual entrance to the Elysian Fields was by way of Kent's circular Temple of Ancient Virtue (based on the Temple of Vesta at Tivoli) at the end of Bridgeman's 'great cross walk'. This housed statues of four heroes of antiquity, and was juxtaposed to a Temple of Modern Virtue nearby, deliberately in ruins and containing a headless torso supposed to represent Lord Cobham's arch-enemy, Sir Robert Walpole.

Ancient Virtue also looked across the winding river, the upper part of it originally known as the Styx, to the Temple of British Worthies, containing busts (by Rysbrack and Scheemakers) of those Britons whose deeds could truly be compared to their classical counterparts. Eight of these busts – of Queen Elizabeth, Bacon, Shakespeare, Hampden, William III, Locke, Newton and Milton – were originally placed round Gibbs's Building on the west side of the gardens, but were subsequently moved here. The rest – Pope, Inigo Jones, Sir Thomas Gresham, King Alfred, the Black Prince, Ralegh, Drake and Sir John Barnard – were then added, with men of contemplation (poets, philosophers and artists) placed on the left, and men of action (kings, statesmen and military leaders) on the right.

Once again the choice represented an attack on Walpole, who regarded Barnard as his most dangerous opponent, and on George II, in favour of his estranged son Frederick, Prince of Wales, who was often identified with the Black Prince, and who was expected to restore the ancient, native liberties established by King Alfred. The inscription above the niches, some attributed to Pope, also voice the patriotic sentiments of Lord Cobham's Whig opposition. The niches in the central pyramid originally contained a bust of Mercury, who led the souls of heroes into the Elysian Fields. The curious object propped up against the wall below might at first be taken for a sundial. However, it is shown facing almost due north, and is more likely to represent an antique targe or shield, symbolising heroic deeds of valour.

Kent's inspiration for the Temple, first found in an unexecuted design for Chiswick, came from some of the Renaissance gardens he had seen in Italy, using the antique Roman exedra form particularly associated with funerary monuments. One of the best known was at the Villa Mattei, outside Rome, engraved by Falda, but similar examples could be found at the Villa Borghese and the Villa d'Este at Tivoli. A series of Roman emperors in pedimented niches, forming a circle, still exists at the Villa Brenzone on Lake Garda, and here the 'tabernacles' are hollowed out at the back rather in the manner Kent suggests in his inscription, behind the central pyramid. This niche turns out to be a typical Kentian joke, for, after the grandiloquence of the main façade, it contains a memorial to 'Signior Fido, an *Italian* of good Extraction; who came into *England*, not to bite us, like most of his Countrymen, but to gain an honest Livelyhood...' – ending after a long and fulsome epitaph, 'this stone is guiltless of Flattery, for he to whom it is inscrib'd was not a Man, but a Grey-Hound'.

Literature: Clarke, 1973, pp. 566–71; Burrell, 1983, *passim*; Dixon Hunt, 1987, pp. 53–4, cat. no. 109.

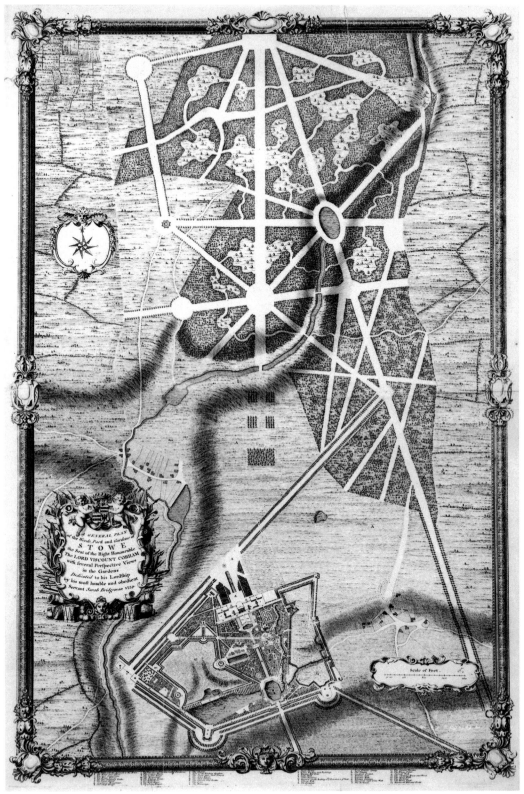

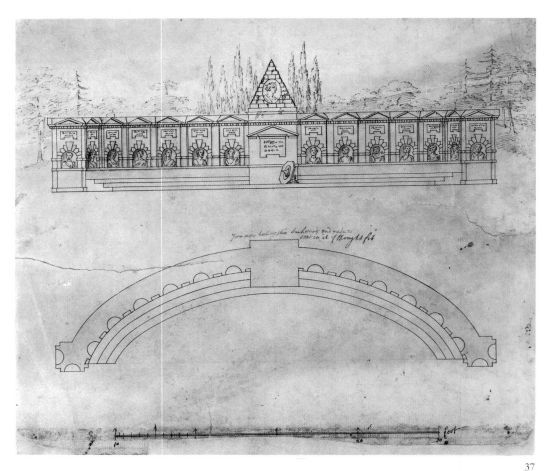

You may hall in this buthouse and nich a
see in it if thought fit

37

38

38 View of the Temple of British Worthies across the Elysian Fields, Stowe, Buckinghamshire, c.1805

Thomas Rowlandson (1756–1827)

Pen, ink and watercolour

280 × 430mm (11 × 17in)

The Governors of Stowe School

This is one of nine known drawings of Stowe by Rowlandson, eight of which derive from Seeley's 1797 edition of the Stowe guidebook, with engravings by Medland. The only major difference between the drawings and the engravings are the groups of sightseers and picnickers which have been added with Rowlandson's characteristic humour, omitting Medland's stiffer and more conventional figures. Six of the drawings (recently in the hands of Colnaghi's in London) are on two sheets – recto and verso – with accompanying text in the artist's hand, also selected from Seeley's guide, while one of them bears the watermark 'John Hall

1805'. The only drawing not based on Seeley is a highly imaginative (and inaccurate) representation of the Saxon Deities, in the Huntington Library, San Marino, California, which derives partly from an engraving in Bickham's earlier *Beauties of Stow* (1750, 1753 and 1756 editions).

What Rowlandson's intentions were is not altogether clear, but he may simply have been collecting authentic settings for a series of drawings of tourists visiting noblemen's country seats. There is no evidence that he actually visited the place. Yet his views admirably illustrate the character of Stowe in the Regency period, when visitors from all over Europe came to see it, staying at the New Inn on the edge of the park, and entering the gardens by the Bell Gate. In this instance, Kent's celebrated Temple of British Worthies (see No. 37) is shown in its setting on the banks of the 'Worthies River', with the Shell Bridge on the left. The seat below the central pyramid is shown in early photographs, and the

National Trust hopes to replace this shortly, together with the central bust of Mercury in the round niche.

39 The Gothic Temple and Queen's Temple, Stowe, Buckinghamshire, 1805

John Claude Nattes (c.1765–1822)

Signed and dated

Ink and wash over pencil

319 × 472mm (12½ × 18⅝in)

Buckinghamshire County Museum, Aylesbury

This is one of a series of over a hundred views of Stowe made by John Claude Nattes between 1805 and 1809 for George Grenville, 1st Marquess of Buckingham. The original intention may have been to engrave and publish the whole series but this was never done, and the drawings, bound in two albums, were sold with the library in January 1849, following the 2nd Duke of Buckingham's bankruptcy. Buckinghamshire County Museum

39

acquired 105 views in 1980, but a further fourteen, apparently from a small 'overflow' album, were presented to Stowe School in the 1920s.

Nattes's views may be of variable artistic quality, but they usually possess great charm. In addition, their wealth of detail is of inestimable value in recording the appearance of the gardens at their peak – with the trees planted by Bridgeman and Kent grown to full maturity, but the vistas between the many different temples and eye-catchers still carefully kept open.

The Gothic Temple, shown here, was designed by James Gibbs and begun in 1741, overlooking Hawkwell Field on the east side of the gardens. One of the major monuments of the early Gothic Revival, it was built of dark Northamptonshire ironstone and was deliberately uncouth: a reminder of the 'natural liberties' thought to have existed at the dawn of British history. Indeed, it was originally known as the Temple of Liberty, surrounded by Rysbrack's statues of the seven Saxon deities, who gave their names to the days of the week. By Nattes's day, these had long since been removed to another position (their third), and the planting softened and 'naturalised'. The building is now leased to the Landmark Trust and is available to the public for short-term holiday accommodation.

On the left can be seen a vista to the Queen's (originally the Ladies') Temple. This was also designed by Gibbs, between 1744 and 1748, though radically altered in the 1770s, and in 1789 re-dedicated to Queen Charlotte, who had just nursed George III back to sanity – thereby saving the Grenvilles and Pitts from political eclipse.

Literature: Gowing and Clarke, 1983, pp. 3–4, cat. no. 36, plate 14.

40 View of the Keeper's Lodge (later the Bourbon Tower), Stowe, Buckinghamshire, 1805

John Claude Nattes (*c*.1765–1822)

Signed and dated

Grey wash over pencil, with ink, heightened with pen and ink and some scratching out

Watermark: Blackwell & Jones 1801, and crowned fleur-de-lis with monogram AB below

278 × 372mm (10$\frac{7}{8}$ × 14$\frac{5}{8}$in)

Buckinghamshire County Museum, Aylesbury

Some of the Nattes's views of Stowe have particular value in showing garden buildings that are otherwise scarcely recorded. This is true of the Keeper's Lodge in the park at Stowe, some distance to the east of Hawkwell Field. The Lodge was being built in 1741–2 by the carpenter John Smallbones, who was employed on Gibbs's Gothic Temple at exactly the same moment. Constructed of the same dark ironstone as the Temple, it can be attributed to Gibbs not only on these grounds, but because of its similarity to his simpler Gothic Tower at Hartwell, near Aylesbury, dating from before 1738. The machicolated parapet supporting the roof, and the almost neo-Norman shape of the windows, are sophisticated motifs for their date, with more of the 'true rust of the Barons' Wars' than anything at Strawberry Hill.

In 1808, three years after Nattes made his drawing, the building was renamed the Bourbon Tower in honour of Louis XVIII and his family, who came over to Stowe from Hartwell, where they were living in exile. It was then used by the militia, and subsequently remodelled for the 2nd Duke of Buckingham by Edward Blore. The latter's designs, dated 1842–3, survive among the Stowe papers in the Huntington Library, San Marino, California. The only other

representations of the building before this date are the very rough engravings in Bickham's and Seeley's guidebooks to Stowe, both published in 1750. Neither shows the flanking pepperpots, one possibly used as a game larder, and the other as a fodder store for the deer.

Literature: Gowing and Clarke, 1983, cat. no. 89, plate 44; Friedman, 1984, pp. 199–200.

41 View from the South Portico looking towards the Grenville Column, Stowe, Buckinghamshire, 1805

John Claude Nattes (*c*.1765–1822)

Signed and dated

Grey wash over pencil, with some ink

Watermark: J. Whatman

280 × 400mm (11 × 15$\frac{3}{4}$in)

Buckinghamshire County Museum, Aylesbury

This is one of two views drawn by Nattes within the great south portico at Stowe: one looking westwards, with a seated lady talking to a small boy; the other looking eastwards, with a view of the Grenville Column seen through the pillars, and two young ladies conversing. By chance, these figures can be identified and the exact date of the drawings established, for among the archives at Swanbourne, near Winslow, are a virtually identical sketch of the westward view (without figures) and corresponding diary entries by the lady of the house, Elizabeth (Betsey) Fremantle and her sister, Harriet Wynne.

In them, they describe their time at Stowe, coinciding with the five-day visit of the Prince of Wales in August 1805. Harriet, who had become a firm friend of the Marquess of Buckingham's daughter, Lady Mary Grenville, reports that on the 21st, 'we met at the Temple of Venus to see Mr.

40

41

Nattes draw he is very good Artist and takes views enormously well. Lady Mary took me and we were very merry, for sometime.' Then on the following day they again 'went to draw with Mr. Nattes', presumably in the south portico, for Harriet continues, 'I took a sketch passablement bien... Lady Mary and I were the whole morning with Nattes and we sang to him whilst he drew.' This impromptu entertainment may explain the high quality of Nattes's two views, one featuring Harriet and Lady Mary, and the other Betsey and her young son Tom.

The views are also interesting for the wonderfully informal arrangement of the portico, designed 35 years earlier by Earl Temple's cousin, Thomas Pitt, Lord Camelford. Flower pots massed in front of the pillars and along the inside walls soften the noble austerity of the architecture and give it a Regency flavour, as much as the ladies' high-waisted 'Grecian' gowns. The two massive statuary groups here, derived from Giambologna's famous *Hercules and Antaeus* and *Samson and the Philistine*, were sold from Stowe in 1848 and are now at St Paul's Walden Bury in Hertfordshire.

Nattes's viewpoint suggests that the portico was regarded almost as a garden building in its own right, framing different vistas – in this case to the Grenville Column on the edge of the Elysian Fields. First erected in the Grecian Valley in 1747, it was moved here a few years later and commemorates a member of the family, Captain Thomas Grenville, who died in a naval action with the French. It thus takes the form of a Doric 'rostral' column, carved with prows of ships projecting from the shaft in the antique Roman manner. The lead statue on the top, representing Heroic Poetry, was one of a large series originally adorning Lord Cobham's parterre, reused elsewhere in the gardens after that

was abandoned. She holds a scroll inscribed *Non nisi grandia canto* ('None but heroic deeds I sing') and her face is turned towards the Temple of British Worthies in the valley below.

Literature: Gowing and Clarke, 1983, p. 4, cat. nos 95, 96; Gunnis, 1951, p. 83.

42 The South Front and the King's Column, Stowe, Buckinghamshire, 1805

John Claude Nattes (*c.*1765–1822)

Signed and dated

Ink and wash over pencil

Watermark: Blackwell & Jones 1801, and crowned fleur-de-lis with monogram AB below

278 × 396mm (10$\frac{7}{8}$ × 15$\frac{5}{8}$in)

Buckinghamshire County Museum, Aylesbury

The King's Column at Stowe – wrongly identified as King William's by Nattes – is first mentioned in 1724, in a letter from Viscount Perceval (afterwards Earl of Egmont). This describes the 'noble bason of water' overlooked by Vanbrugh's Rotonda (see No. 35), 'sorounded with walks and groves, and overlook'd from a considerable heigth by a tall Column of the Composite Order, on which stands the statue of Pr. George in his Robes'. Another visitor, Thomas Knight, who came in 1727, found that a 'Statue of the Princess on 4 Columns' had also been erected at the far end of the 'bason' on axis with the Rotonda. Later in the same year the royal couple succeeded as George II and Queen Caroline, and their respective monuments were accordingly renamed. Both are likely to have been designed by Vanbrugh, with the statues carved by Rysbrack.

In 1764, as part of his 'naturalising' of the landscape, Earl Temple moved Queen Caroline's Monument to the western edge of

the gardens (where the pavilion known as Gibbs's Building had stood), but retained the King's Column, merely removing the formal planting round it. Seeley's plans of the garden in 1788 and 1797 suggest that it may then have been visible from the south portico, as a pendant to the Grenville Column on the other side of the main axis (see No. 41). The King's Column was finally removed in 1840, though the statue of George II was re-erected on a pedestal designed by Edward Blore on the site of Nelson's Seat, and finally sold in 1921; it is now at Port Lympne in Kent.

Through the trees can be seen the remodelled south front of 1771–7, designed for Lord Temple by his cousin Thomas Pitt, Lord Camelford – re-casting and refining an original scheme by Robert Adam.

Literature: Gowing and Clarke, 1983, cat. no. 55; Clarke, 1990, pp. 16, 23.

43 The Corinthian Arch, Stowe, Buckinghamshire, 1805

John Claude Nattes (*c.*1765–1822)

Pen, ink and wash, with pencil

Signed and dated

296 × 404mm (11$\frac{5}{8}$ × 15$\frac{7}{8}$in)

Buckinghamshire County Museum, Aylesbury

The great Corinthian Arch, 60 foot square in elevation, frames the visitor's first view of Stowe, approaching on the mile-long avenue from Buckingham, and also acts as a *coup d'oeil* seen from the south front of the house against the distant horizon. It was built in 1765–7, at a time when Earl Temple was extending the bounds of the gardens laid out by his uncle Lord Cobham, and his architect was once again his cousin, Thomas Pitt, Lord Camelford. The flanking columns and vases which give an

42

43

added drama and monumentality on the south side (though allowing for some exaggeration by Nattes) may well have been added by the Italian architect and painter Vincenzo Valdre, who was at Stowe for about ten years from 1778. Nattes does not show the low curving walls which link them back to the arch, so these may have been added only after 1805.

The Arch is soon to be restored by the National Trust in association with the Landmark Trust. One of the three-storey estate-workers' houses which are incorporated in the building (their windows looking east and west respectively) will then provide living quarters for staff. The other will be available for short lets to the general public, in the same way as Gibbs's Gothic Temple (see No. 39).

Literature: Gibbon, 1977, p. 43; Gowing and Clarke, 1983, cat. no. 6, plate 3.

44 View of the Temple of Friendship from the Queen's Temple, Stowe, Buckinghamshire, 1809

John Claude Nattes (*c.*1765– 1822)

Signed and dated
Sepia and grey washes over pencil
Watermark on mount: P
253 × 422mm (10 × 16⅝in)
Buckinghamshire County Museum, Aylesbury

Despite its obvious importance, the sight of one garden building from another – a picturesque view 'framed', as it were, within the confines of a door or window opening – was not often attempted by artists in the eighteenth and early nineteenth centuries. Nattes's view of the Temple of Friendship from the Queen's Temple is especially appropriate since the two were originally designed by James Gibbs to complement each other: Friendship (dated 1739) was where Lord Cobham and his supporters,

the Pitts, Grenvilles and Lyttletons – known at the time as the 'Boy Patriots' – met to drink port and discuss politics; while the Ladies' Temple (the old name, to which Nattes still adheres) was where Lady Cobham and her friends took tea, and carried out the needlework and shellwork which once adorned its walls. To emphasise these male and female characteristics, the first had a Tuscan and the second a Corinthian portico.

The interior of Friendship was gutted by fire in the early nineteenth century, but the façade was kept as a picturesque ruin, which it still remains. The exterior of the Ladies' Temple was extensively remodelled in 1773, and the interior in 1789–90, when it was renamed in honour of Queen Charlotte, who had just nursed George III back to health after his first serious bout of insanity. Nattes's view shows the Corinthian Arch (No. 46) on the hill to the right of Friendship: a vista long obscured by trees, but obviously thought important at that time. The glazed screen with its curiously narrow panes may have had a central section which lifted out, since there is no sign of a sash mechanism. However, the earliest photographs show a more conventional pair of tall French windows.

The Queen's Temple is now used as a music room by Stowe School, but is open to the public in the holidays, when concerts are also regularly held.

Literature: Gowing and Clarke, 1983, cat. no. 64, plate 24.

45 The Temple of Concord and Victory, Stowe, Buckinghamshire, 1805

John Claude Nattes (*c.*1765– 1822)

Pen, ink and wash
Signed (on loose backing sheet) 'C. Nattes del't 1805'
Inscribed: 'Stow/The Temple of Concord & Victory'
Watermarked: Double shield and crown approx 4in
280 × 375mm (11 × 14¾in)
The Governors of Stowe School

The biggest of all the garden buildings at Stowe, the 'Grecian Temple' (as it was originally known) was built in 1749, and is therefore among the earliest monuments of Neo-classicism in northern Europe. The architect is likely to have been Lord Cobham's nephew, Richard Grenville, who in this same year succeeded to Stowe, becoming Earl Temple in 1752. Despite its name, the temple owes more to Roman prototypes like the Maison Carrée at Nimes, than to Greek architecture which was still virtually unknown.

In 1763, to celebrate the end of the Seven Years War, the temple was renamed, and the interior remodelled by the Turinese architect Giovanni Battista Borra. At the same time, the pediments were crowned with six statues, brought from elsewhere in the grounds, while the one facing east was filled with reliefs by Scheemakers, originally carved for the back wall of the Palladian Bridge. Nattes shows men with ladders carrying out minor repairs or maintenance, as well as a nursemaid pulling two children in a baby-carriage and another pair of spectators. The undulating belts of trees clothing the sides of the Grecian Valley (which took its name from the temple) were mostly planted in the 1740s by Lord Cobham and his then head gardener, Capability Brown. Nattes

44

45

shows them grown to full maturity and includes conifers as well as hardwoods.

In the 1920s, sixteen of the giant Ionic columns from the peristyle were unfortunately removed to Sir Robert Lorimer's new school chapel. The National Trust intends to have replacements carved and to carry out a thorough restoration of the building at an estimated cost of over £1.5 million.

46 A view of the garden at Stourhead, Wiltshire, with the Temple of Apollo, the Palladian Bridge and the Pantheon, 1775

Coplestone Warre Bampfylde (1719–91)

Watercolour

375 × 545mm (14¾ × 21½in)

The National Trust (Hoare Collection), Stourhead, Wiltshire

Few images sum up the taste for the 'picturesque' better than this classic view of the garden at Stourhead, still hanging with its pair (No. 47) in the library of the house – next to the volumes of Virgil and Horace which were Henry Hoare's inspiration. Literature and painting, architecture and archaeology, science and religion, all meet here in one of the supreme achievements of English landscape gardening.

Coplestone Warre Bampfylde, squire of Hestercombe in Somerset, was a close friend of Henry Hoare II (1705–85), the creator of the garden at Stourhead. An amateur architect, landscape gardener and collector, he was also an accomplished painter, and several of his landscape *capriccii* are still in the Stourhead collection. His earliest drawing of the garden is dated 1753, but he also 'made an

ingenious model for the Cascade' in 1765, and some large-scale panoramic sketches of views across the lake in the early 1770s (now in the Victoria and Albert Museum).

In this view, stressing the Claudian inspiration of the layout, Bampfylde shows the Pantheon (or Temple of Hercules) built by Henry Flitcroft in 1753–4, on the far side of the lake; the bridge in the foreground erected in 1762 and based on Palladio's five-arched bridge at Vicenza; and the Temple of Apollo on the hill to the left, again designed by Flitcroft in 1765, and based on a plate from Robert Wood's *Ruins of Balbec* (1757). Visitors are seen on the serpentine path which crossed the bridge, and made a complete circuit of the lake, experiencing a series of planned viewpoints *en route*, while a coach and riders can be seen on the public road which still runs through the

garden below the Temple of
Apollo, but which is now entirely
concealed by planting.

The circuit walk has often been
represented as an allegory of the
Aeneid, with the grotto
representing Aeneas' descent into
the underworld. But this was only
one of a number of associations
which would have occurred to
Hoare and his more educated
guests. Another, more general,
view of the buildings disposed
round the lake might see Apollo on
the hillside representing the sun,
which causes trees and plants to
grow; Flora in her south-facing
temple adding the verdant lawns
and flowers; Neptune in the grotto
striking the rock to make the
waters flow; and Hercules in the
Pantheon, representing the human
labours which lay behind these
Arcadian scenes.

Both this watercolour and its
companion (No. 47) were engraved
by Francis Vivares in 1777, though
with different figures and with the
loss of much of their subtlety.
Vivares, for instance, shows the
Pantheon too large in scale, and
straight on rather than at a slight
angle.

Literature: Woodbridge, 1970,
pp. 60–1, figs. 10 a-c; Woodbridge,
1982, pp. 12–25; Rohrschach, 1983,
cat. no. 81.

47 View of the garden at Stourhead, Wiltshire, looking towards the Temple of Flora, the Bristol Cross and the Palladian Bridge, *c.*1775

Coplestone Warre Bampfylde
(1719–91)

Sepia pen and ink and watercolour
Signed: C W Bampfyld

375 × 545 mm (14¾ × 21½in)
The National Trust (Hoare Collection),
Stourhead, Wiltshire

In October 1762, Henry Hoare
wrote to his daughter Susanna
reporting that he had begun 'the
Stone Bridge of 5 arches you
always wished I would build at the
passage into the orchard and the
scheme of carrying the water up
and losing out of sight towards the
parish. This Bridge is now about. It
is simple and plain. I took it from
Palladio's bridge at Vicenza,
5 arches; and when you stand at the
Pantheon the water will be seen
thro the arches and it will look as if
the river came down through the
village and that this was the village
bridge for public use. The view of
the bridge, village and church
altogether will be a charm[in]g
Gasp[ar]d picture at that end of the
water.'

Between the bridge and church he erected the Bristol High Cross, a medieval monument which the citizens had earlier had removed as 'a ruinous and superstitious Relick', and which he was able to acquire from the Dean in 1764. The vogue for Gothick garden buildings was of course in full swing, and was also expressed at Stourhead by Alfred's Tower, the Convent, the 'druid's cell' and a Gothic greenhouse. However, Henry Hoare was in advance of his time in bringing the parish church, and indeed the village, into his garden as a picturesque incident.

On the left, Bampfylde shows the Temple of Flora (originally dedicated to Ceres) which was designed by Flitcroft in 1744 and was one of the earliest garden buildings at Stourhead. At first it stood above a rockwork cascade, with a figure of Neptune, pouring into a rectangular pond. But this was half submerged when the dam was built, raising the level of the lake, in 1754.

Literature: Woodbridge, 1982, p. 25; Rohrschach, 1983, cat. no. 80.

48 and 49 Two views of The Vyne, Hampshire, *c.*1755–9

Johann Heinrich Müntz (1727–98)

Pen, ink and wash, heightened with white, on blue paper mounted on canvas

Both 405 × 560mm (16 × 22in)

The National Trust (Chute Collection), The Vyne, Hampshire

This pair of small drawings of The Vyne shows some of the changes to the landscape made by John Chute soon after inheriting the house in 1754. According to his friend Horace Walpole, he 'enlarged the water, built the bridge, cut the walks in Morguesson [a wood to the north], and erected there the statue of the Druid [an artificial stone figure now in the garden – see No. 64]; and he too made and

planted the noble terrace that parts the road from his own grounds.' In his *Inventionary* of 1755, Walpole had also recommended making a Roman theatre with an obelisk, urns and sphinxes, but this seems not to have been attempted.

Müntz, a German-Swiss artist brought to England by Richard Bentley in 1755, was in Walpole's service until 1759, when he was dismissed partly on account of an intrigue with a serving maid at

Strawberry Hill. These drawings were presumably made before that date, and show the Tudor house built by Lord Sandys between 1500 and 1520, with his chapel at the east end more or less untouched, and John Webb's portico on the north added for Chaloner Chute, Speaker of the House of Commons, in 1654. The lake still looks very much like an earlier formal canal, whose lines have merely been softened and half-heartedly 'serpentined'. This effect

48

49

is even more noticeable in an oil painting of the house by Müntz (Harris, 1971, p. 292, cat. no. 323), which shows the north front across the lake at much less of an angle.

The line of trees on the north side of the chapel closely conceals what was then a blank wall, only later enlivened with false Gothic windows by W. L. Wiggett Chute in the mid-nineteenth century. These trees have the effect of isolating the apse, so that it looks almost like a separate Gothic garden building. The drawing presumably pre-dates the Tomb Chamber which John Chute designed soon afterwards to house the monument to his ancestor, the Speaker – and which immediately adjoins it on the south.

The bridge, with its Chinese fret balustrade in the style of Batty Langley and William Halfpenny, was probably also designed by Chute himself, since a design which

he made for a rather more elaborate bridge in the same style still exists. Beyond it, in the first drawing, can be seen two small domed garden buildings. One of these still survives and is clearly mid-seventeenth-century in date. Although an attribution to Webb has recently been doubted (Bold, 1989, p. 172), it is hard to think who else could have been responsible for such a classical and Italianate form at this date. A pair of lodges repeating the pattern of the pavilion, though a little simplified, were built on the road to the west of the house in the eighteenth century, probably again by John Chute.

Literature: McCarthy, 1975, p. 78, figs 1, 28.

50 The Hermitage at Selborne, Hampshire, with Henry White as the Hermit, 1777

Samuel Hieronymus Grimm (1734–94)

Watercolour

Signed and dated

184 × 285mm (7$\frac{1}{4}$ × 11$\frac{1}{4}$in)

The National Trust (Stamford Collection), Dunham Massey, Cheshire

The craze for hermitages which swept Britain in the eighteenth century was all part of a return to 'natural' forms after the artificiality of the Baroque garden. Among the earliest were William Kent's at Richmond (1730) and Stowe (*c.*1732), while later examples, including those at Painshill, Stourhead and Hawkstone, were equipped with a resident hermit who could surprise visitors with an ode or some philosophical reflections, supposedly based on a life in true communion with nature.

Always primitive and rustic, made of boulders, roots or bark, and with thatched or turfed roofs, hermitages were just as popular with gentry of more modest means. The Rev. Gilbert White, celebrated as the author of *The Natural History and Antiquities of Selborne* (1788), and owner of a house in the village called The Wakes, had just such a building constructed on the hill directly behind, known as the Hanger. The zig-zag path by which the Hermitage was approached was begun in 1752, so it is likely that the building followed within the next few years. It was certainly in existence by 1758, and often features in the diary of Catherine Battie who spent the summer of 1763 staying in the vicarage at Selborne. On 23 June, she records being surprised there, while drinking tea, by the appearance of Gilbert White's brother Harry (the rector of Fyfield) dressed up as a hermit, while White's own entry in his *Garden Kalendar* for 28 July records: 'Drank tea 20 of us at the Hermitage: the Miss Batties, & the Mulso family contributed much to our pleasures by their singing, & being dress'd as shepherds, shepherdesses. It was a most elegant evening; and all parties appear'd highly satisfy'd. The Hermit appear'd to great advantage.'

When it came to providing illustrations for the *Natural History*, White engaged the Swiss-born artist Samuel Hieronymus Grimm to come to Selborne in 1776, and to make a series of twelve watercolours, including this view of the building – now called the 'old hermitage' to differentiate it from a new one recently built on the lower slopes nearer the house – with his brother Harry once again performing as hermit. The conical thatched roof is crowned by an artfully crooked cross, suggesting the ancient Christian origin of the building, while the bench on the promontory behind, made of knobbly old branches, also contributes to the idea of age, and 'pleasing decay'.

The original version of the subject which Grimm painted for Gilbert White is signed and dated 1776; it was engraved as an oval vignette facing the title page of the first editions of *The Natural History of Selborne* (published as part of the *History of Antiquities* in 1789) and is now in the Houghton Library, Harvard University, Cambridge, Mass. The Dunham Massey version, dated 1777, is a repetition, with slight differences, reputedly made for Henry White. It later passed by family descent to the 10th and last Earl of Stamford through his mother, a daughter of Canon Charles Theobald, rector of Lasham in Hampshire.

Literature: Clay, 1941, pp. 72–5, fig. 80; Mabey, 1986, pp. 68–9, 88–93, 165–7, fig. 12.

51 Plan for landscaping the park at Wallington, Northumberland, c.1750

Anonymous

Pen, ink and watercolour on two sheets of vellum

Inscribed: 'References/a Part of the House/b Chinese Temple/c The Plan for the Temple/d A Ruin above the Bank/e A Large Arch for the River to Pass in a Flood/Fronted wth Large Stones like a Rock mixt wth Trees/and the Road behind it/f Cascade/g Park Wall to be taken away/i Banks Sloped in a Natural manner/k Road to the House &c/l Road to the Mill &c/n The River at the Present/o Foss'

Scale: 1in to 100ft

940 × 515mm (37 × 20¼in)

The National Trust (Trevelyan Collection), Wallington, Northumberland

Sir Walter Calverley Blackett, who inherited Wallington in 1728, had transformed both the house and estate there by the time of his death in 1777. This achievement came only after a slow start, however, for the property was much encumbered and in the hands of trustees when he inherited, and the family continued to live for most of the year at Anderson Place, their town house in Newcastle.

Daniel Garrett's remodelling of the old house at Wallington was carried out in 1738–40, but already in 1737 an estimate for extensive landscaping and planting was drawn up by a Mr Joyce: probably William Joyce, recorded as a nurseryman in Gateshead from about 1730 to 1767 (Harvey, 1972, p. 32). This estimate, amounting to over £2,000 and including making 'the terrace on the south front', may tally with an early plan rather in the style of Bridgeman, depicting straight-edged woods and ponds (including the three that still survive in the West Wood), and avenues radiating from the house.

The present plan, evidently somewhat later in date, is a proposal for the park to the south of the house, involving the diversion of the old public road from the west side of the house to the east, and the damming of the diminutive Wansbeck to make a more impressive river, spanned by a new seven-arched bridge. Though this anticipates James Paine's bridge, built in 1755 (No. 53), the provision of a 'Chinese Temple' would seem to put it before 1752, when a similar building was brought to Wallington (No. 52) and erected by Sir Walter in another part of the garden.

The plan has the same mixture of formal and informal elements found in Robert Greening's contemporary design for Wimpole (No. 20), which also features a Chinese pavilion drawn in elevation. The large turf 'rampart' west of the house may be a survivor from Mr Joyce's earlier layout, but the treatment of the lake, with serpentine paths, waterfalls and artful clumps of trees, is in the new Rococo taste.

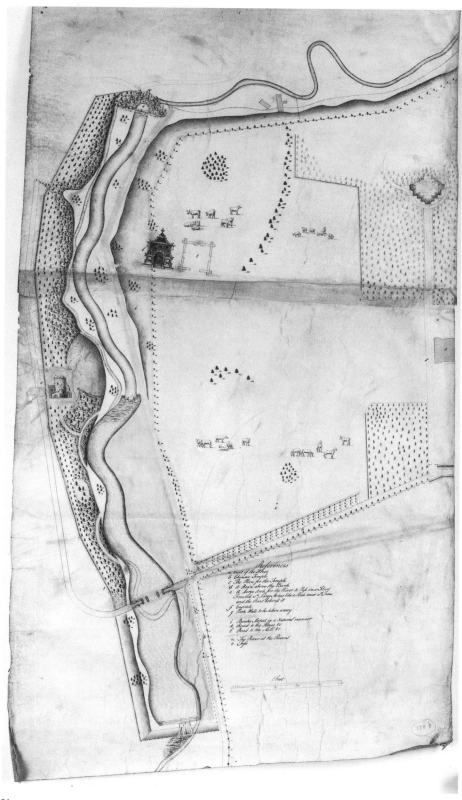

References

a. *Part of the River*
b. *Chinese Temple*
c. *The Place for the Temple*
d. *A Ruin above the Bank*
e. *A Large stone for the River to Pass in a kind
   Torrent & a Large Stone like a Rock must at Some
   and the Root behind it*
f. *Cascade*
g. *Park Walls to be taken away*

i. *Banks Slopted in a Natural manner*
k. *Road to the House &c*
l. *Road to the Mill &c*

n. *The River at the Present*
o. *Pass*

Feet

51

The great arch of rockwork framing a cascade at the head of the lake is comparable with the grotto at Forcett in North Yorkshire, another house designed by Daniel Garrett (Percy and Jackson-Stops, 1974, p. 194, fig. 8), while the artificial ruin shown on the left bank of the river recalls the much bigger ruined castle which he built for Sir Walter in Rothley Park, to the north of Wallington, in the late 1740s. If not in Garrett's own hand, the drawing may thus represent his intentions.

52 Design for a Chinese Pavilion at Wallington, Northumberland, 1752

Anonymous

Pen, ink and wash

Inscribed: on verso 'a Plan of Chinese House/come to Wallington/1752'

Watermark: HR and hunting horn in crowned shield, V under

Scale: 1in to 2ft

345 × 460mm (13⅝ × 18¼in)

The National Trust (Trevelyan Collection), Wallington, Northumberland

The early 1750s saw the height of the vogue for garden buildings in the Chinese taste. As Horace Walpole wrote, 'the country wears a new face! Everybody is improving their places... the dispersed buildings, I mean, temples, bridges etc. are generally Gothic or Chinese and give a whimsical air of novelty that is very pleasing' (Walpole, *Correspondence*, 20:166).

The inscription on the back of this drawing suggests that it may have come to Wallington ready-made from a London carver, and the design is a good deal more sophisticated than the plates in contemporary pattern-books like William Halfpenny's *Rural Architecture in the Chinese Taste* (1750–2). Perhaps influenced by Chambers's House of Confucius at Kew of 1748–9 (Harris, 1970,

52

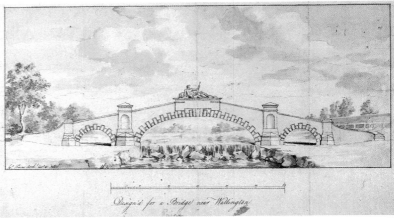

53

fig. 23), it can also be compared with the cabin of the *Mandarin*, the Duke of Cumberland's Chinese yacht, as engraved by Thomas Sandby in 1754 (Conner, 1979, fig. 41).

The pavilion was put up in the East Wood at Wallington, across the public road from the house, an area which Sir Walter Blackett began to develop after inheriting the Calverley fortune in 1749, and which is still the main garden today. A Mr Poynings, in an undated letter written from

Wallington to the Duchess of Northumberland, describes it as 'a foolish expensive Chinese Building at the end of a large fishpond' (Alnwick Castle mss.). Called the China Pond, this still survives today, though sadly nothing remains of the pavilion.

Literature: Percy and Jackson-Stops, 1974, pp. 193–4, fig. 3.

53 Design for a bridge and cascade at Wallington, Northumberland, 1755

James Paine (c.1716–89)

Pen, ink and wash

Signed: 'Jas. Paine Archt. invt. et Delint'

Inscribed: 'Design'd for a Bridge near Wallington' and on verso 'A Bridge by Mr Paine'

Scale: 1in to 10ft

240 × 380mm (9½ × 15in)

The National Trust (Trevelyan Collection), Wallington, Northumberland

The old public road from Kirkharle to Cambo ran close by the west side of the house at Wallington, and many owners would have wished to divert it way outside the perimeter of their park. However, Sir Walter Calverley Blackett was more concerned that it should make a flattering approach to his remodelled house, and act as an eye-catcher seen from it. He thus diverted it to the east, as proposed in a design of about 1750 (No. 51), damming the Wansbeck to give the illusion of a large river in the valley bottom. Part of his reason for not making this a private road may have been that other users would contribute to the cost of the bridge, eventually in the region of £300.

Daniel Garrett, Blackett's architect, died in 1753, which would explain why he approached James Paine, then working on three other Northumberland houses – Alnwick, Gosforth and Belford. This and two alternative drawings at Wallington (showing one-arch and five-arch versions respectively, the latter signed) are Paine's earliest known bridge designs, the forerunners of those at Chatsworth, Brocket Hall, Weston Park and Chillington Castle, not to mention four over the Thames, at Richmond, Chertsey, Walton and Kew. In this instance his model was evidently a design by Palladio (Ware, 1738, 3:71, plate 11), with similar 'tabernacle' niches

ornamenting the main piers. As executed, the bridge has extra piers beyond the subsidiary arches each side, and a balustrade over the arches rather than a parapet – both features taken from the five-arch design. The central figure of a river god reclining on a plinth like an enlarged label moulding – perhaps inspired by the river gods below the niches in Palladio's design – can be compared with a lead figure at Parham (once at Hagley) attributed to John Cheere, after a model by J. M. Rysbrack. This idea, too, was sadly abandoned, but the bridge still has a strength and grace that are exhilarating – more than anything due to the use of a semi-elliptical, rather than the more usual segmental, form of arch.

Literature: Leach, 1988, pp. 134, 212–13.

54 Design for Codger Crag Fort at Rothley, near Wallington, Northumberland, 1769

Thomas Wright of Durham (1711–86)

Pen and sepia ink

Inscribed: 'Plan & Elevation of a Battery for 5 Guns, with Store room, &c,/ proposed to be Erected on Codjah Crag. 29th Septr 1769/The room over the Store room is to have a fire place in the Angle or Corner/Opposite to that whereon the flagstaff is Erected, wch. will be best placed on the NW/Angle and the Stairs to be alter'd accordingly'; endorsed in sepia 'Codjah Fort' and

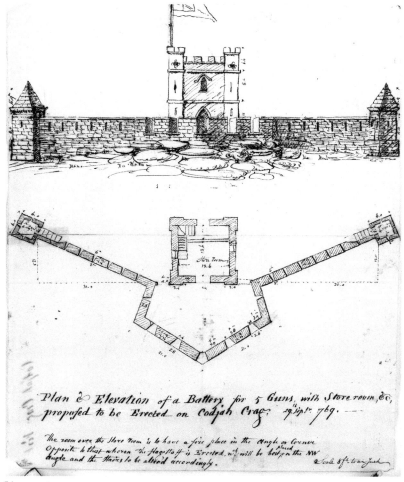

54

81

'Codjah Crag Fort' (in the same hand as recto); and in pencil '1769'

Scale: 1in to 8ft

Watermark: Crowned GR and PRO PATRIA (Britannia and lion within paling)

400 × 320mm (15¾ × 12⅝in)

The National Trust (Trevelyan Collection), Wallington, Northumberland

Rothley Park, some 5 miles north-east of Wallington on the road to Rothbury, was enclosed by Sir Walter Calverley Blackett in 1741, and as he began to exploit the agricultural potential of the estate, he also conceived the idea of a pleasure-ground which would make an agreeable day-long excursion from the house. Here the Duchess of Northumberland, writing about 1762, found 'a vast ruin'd Castle built of Black Moor Stone by Sir Walr. on a plan of Garretts on an immense craggy Rock'. Much of this building, known as Rothley Castle, still exists – and must date from before Garrett's death in 1753.

In the following decade, a chain of small ponds was turned into two substantial lakes with the advice of Capability Brown (see Nos 56 and 57), and a number of garden buildings were proposed by Brown, William Newton of Newcastle and Thomas Wright of Durham. Mathematician, astronomer, architect and garden designer, Wright moved from one country-house patron to another in the 1750s, acting as tutor and designing follies and eye-catchers, many of them published in his *Book of Arbours* (1755) and *Book of Grottoes* (1758). In 1762 he retired to his own house at Byers Green near Durham to 'Prosicute [his] Studies', but continued to design buildings for old friends and neighbours, like the Bishop of Durham at Auckland Castle. Wallington, too, was within easy reach, and as at Raby Castle, and at Horton House in

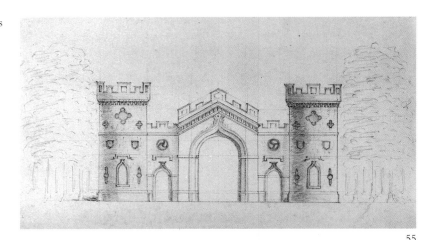

55

Northamptonshire, Wright was again following in the footsteps of Garrett.

The fort on 'Codger Crag', whose ruins still exist not far from the public road and just above the lakes at Rothley, may have been intended for the mock naval engagements which were then a popular pastime. This would explain the wide embrasures for cannon in the central bastion, and the flag, presumably the red ensign, flying so prominently from the flagstaff. Another drawing in the same hand, entitled 'Battery for 5 Guns at Codjah Crag' survives in the collection, and the boat-house designed by William Newton was also to have had two large castellated towers.

Literature: Harris, 1971, p. 614, fig. 9.

55 Design for a Gothick gatescreen at Rothley, near Wallington, Northumberland, 1769

Thomas Wright of Durham (1711–86)

Pencil

Inscribed: on verso 'By Mr. Wright/ North Gate into Rothley Park'

Watermark: Britannia in crowned circle inscribed PRO PATRIA

201 × 322mm (8 × 12⅝in)

The National Trust (Trevelyan Collection), Wallington, Northumberland

The companion drawing to this, showing the ground plan of the building, is endorsed 'By Mr. Wright 1769', presumably in Sir Walter Calverley Blackett's hand. But there is no evidence that the gate, intended as an entrance to the park at Rothley, was ever built.

The design is a rather more elaborate version of the Barbican Gate at Tollymore, County Down, which Thomas Wright built for the 2nd Earl of Clanbrassil about 1777. Designs for similar gatescreens can be found in the album of his drawings at the Avery Library, Columbia University, New York: one entitled 'An Ornamental Gate in the Saxon Stile of Gothick Architecture' was probably intended as a design for the entrance gate of Auckland Castle. The curious flat bands of applied ornament, like the Palladian label mouldings made Gothick by 'scrolling' the ends, also recall his summer-house at Nuthall in Nottinghamshire.

In general Wright's very individual form of Gothick looks back to Vanbrugh's 'castle style' in its massing of volumes and its sense of movement. Indeed, the Codger Crag Fort (No. 54) can be seen as a descendant of Vanbrugh's

Belvedere at Claremont (No. 32). Quite different from the 'cardboard' follies of Batty Langley on the one side, and the literal antiquarianism of Sanderson Miller and Horace Walpole on the other, his designs show as instinct for 'primitive' and picturesque values that is bold and original. The trees lightly sketched in on each side show his concern for garden buildings within their landscape settings, and not just as isolated incidents.

Literature: Harris, 1971, p. 614, fig. 10; McCarthy, 1987, pp. 46–8.

56 Design for a rockwork bridge at Rothley, near Wallington, Northumberland, c.1765

Lancelot ('Capability') Brown (1716–83)

Pen, ink and wash

Watermark: Crown over fleur-de-lis over VG

Scale: 1in to 12ft

340 × 530mm (13⅜ × 20⅞in)

The National Trust (Trevelyan Collection), Wallington, Northumberland

Capability Brown was born at Kirkharle, only a mile or two from Wallington, and went to school at Cambo, Sir Walter Calverley Blackett's estate village, where two of his brothers were to settle. He must therefore have seen the early improvements to the Wallington landscape made by 'Mr. Joyce' (No. 51), before moving south in 1739, and entering Lord Cobham's service at Stowe.

Much later, in the early 1760s, he returned to Northumberland to work at Alnwick, and was engaged by Sir Walter to advise on alterations to the east garden at Wallington and on the formation of the lakes at Rothley. These were created in 1765 by building a dam across the Ewesley Burn, which also served as a bridge for the road from Cambo to Rothbury. Five unsigned and undated drawings in the Wallington archives relate to this project, all in Brown's characteristic hand: two of them plans for the lakes and surrounding plantations, more or less as carried out, two for the lakeside pavilion (see No. 57), and one for the bridge-cum-dam, disguised as a five-arch grotto.

In some ways this solution seems old-fashioned, recalling Kent's grottoes at Rousham and Stowe, but the rockwork piled up above the arches and 'naturalised' with vegetation was probably intended to conceal passing carriages and farm-carts, and preserve the privacy of Sir Walter's pleasure-ground. On the other side it would also have formed a perfect frame for a cascade falling into the lower lake. In the event, this rockwork decoration seems never to have been carried out (unless removed at a later date), though the bridge is of much the same form.

Arthur Young in his *Six Months Tour through the North of England* (1771) describes the young plantations at Rothley, round the 'fine new-made lake of Sir Walter Blackett's... which is a noble water; the bends and curves of the bank are bold and natural, and when the trees get up, the whole spot will be remarkably beautiful.'

Literature: Stroud, 1975, pp. 43, 137, fig. 33b.

57 Design for a banqueting house at Rothley, near Wallington, Northumberland, c.1765

Lancelot ('Capability') Brown (1716–83)

Pen, ink and wash

Scale: 1in to 9ft

490 × 330mm (19¼ × 13in)

The National Trust (Trevelyan Collection), Wallington, Northumberland

In general, Capability Brown's emphasis on unbroken stretches of water, lawn and wood did not encourage the plethora of buildings found in earlier landscape gardens. But, where necessary, he proved himself a competent architect, especially in the Gothic style – initially inspired by James Gibbs's Gothic Temple at Stowe, which he knew well from his work there in the 1740s.

A substantial pavilion or banqueting house at Rothley was obviously considered desirable, as a place for rest and refreshment after the 5-mile journey from Wallington, and the servants would doubtless be sent on ahead to prepare dinner, usually served at about three in the afternoon. Significantly, Brown's plan of the upper lake shows a coach-house and stables concealed by trees immediately behind the building, so it is even possible that Sir Walter and his wife could have stayed there overnight.

The design is close to the Gothic bath house which Brown designed for Rosamund's Well in Blenheim Park, but which (like this) was never built. With its central bay window and castellations, it is also comparable with High Lodge at Blenheim, and the Menagerie at Melton Constable, an earlier hunting tower which Brown converted into a Gothic eye-catcher. Elegant but functional, it would have had a large west-facing porch (shown on an accompanying side elevation) where wet coats and

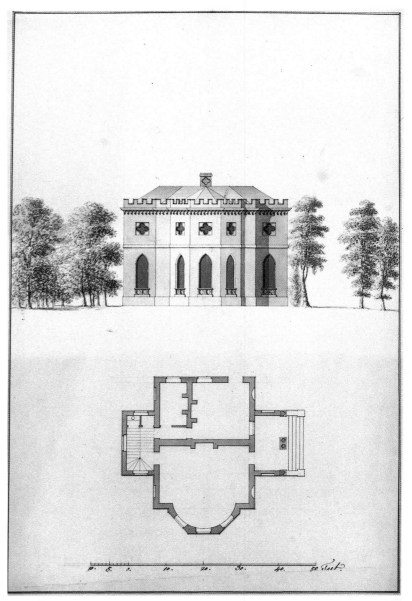

57

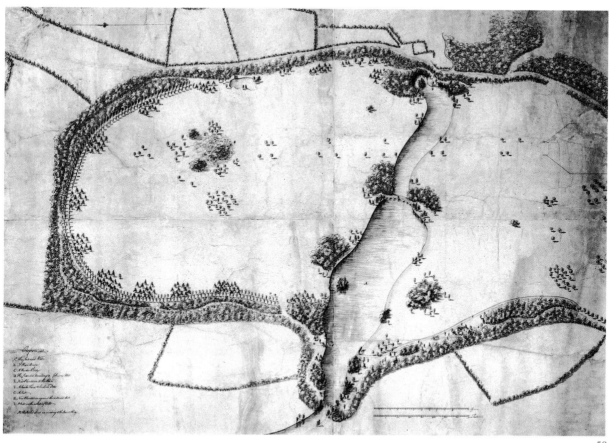

boots could be removed, or where you could sit out to admire the sunset across the lake; a water-closet under the stairs; a large symmetrical dining-room with a bow window giving a diagonal view of the grotto-bridge (No. 56); and retiring rooms on the first floor.

Without any of the 'natural' affiliations of Kent's or Wright's more imaginative garden buildings, it assumes an altogether more subservient role in the surrounding landscape – with simplicity more than symbolism as its aim.

Literature: Stroud, 1975, p. 137, fig. 32a.

58 Design for the lakes and the northern extension of the park at Wimpole, Cambridgeshire, 1767

Lancelot ('Capability') Brown (1716–83)

Pen, ink and wash

Inscribed: 'References/A. The Intended Waters/B. A Sham Bridge/C. A Wooden Bridge/D. The Intended Building on Johnson's Hill/E. New Plantation to the Water/F. A Sunke Fence to Inclose Ditto/G. A Seat/H. New Plantation against the Intended Park/I. A Ride on the outside of Ditto/ N.B. The Pricked Lines are according to the Present Plan'

Scale: 1in to 100ft

965 × 1298mm (38 × 51¼in)

The National Trust (Bambridge Collection), Wimpole Hall, Cambridgeshire

Philip Yorke, eldest son of the 1st Earl of Hardwicke, first employed Capability Brown in the 1750s at Wrest Park in Bedfordshire, part of the inheritance of his wife Jemima, Marchioness Grey. After succeeding his father in 1764, he moved to Wimpole and soon afterwards consulted Brown about extending the park far to the north of its old boundaries. In a letter written on Christmas Eve 1767, he expressed the hope that the latter would 'have the leisure in the Holy days to make out the minute for our proceedings at Wimpole' – and this plan is evidently the result, together with a scaled-down copy showing the fields vacated by Zachary Moul and other picturesquely named tenants, who were given land elsewhere on the estate.

Following this, the old straight avenue on axis with the house and leading up to Johnson's Hill (marked D on the plan) was reduced to single trees and clumps; the old hedges removed; two polygonal ponds formed into serpentine lakes, with a dam between them disguised by a sham bridge; and a tree-lined carriage drive made, some 3 miles in extent, round the outer perimeter. Lady Grey readily admitted the great man's powers of persuasion: 'Mr Brown has been leading me such a fairy circle', she wrote from Wimpole in September 1769, 'and his magic wand has conjured up such landscapes to the eye... that after having hobbled over rough ground to points I had never seen before, I returned half tired, and half foot sore.'

On the plan the tapering outline of Lord Radnor's original garden (No. 17), adapted by Robert Greening in the 1750s (No. 20), can still be seen on the far right in 'Pricked Lines'. But this was soon to be swept away, together with James Gibbs's pair of pavilions flanking the north vista, while new curving drives were made on the south. By 1770 Brown had received £2,400 under his contract with Lord Hardwicke, but a further £980 was paid later, perhaps in respect of a third lake that does not appear on this plan. Where it joins the middle lake there is still a wooden bridge (at the point marked C), with a 'Chinese fret' balustrade, dating from the late nineteenth century, but possibly reflecting the character of its predecessor.

Altogether, Brown's Wimpole plan contains all the main hallmarks of his style. His dogma that the ends of an artificial river must be concealed, whether by contours or planting, is perfectly fulfilled by the kink at the head of the upper lake here, with the wooded island in the middle of it. The gently curving ha-ha skirting the wood at the

bottom right, the perimeter drive, the clumps planted on the edge of the woodland to give it a 'natural' undulating profile – all these are archetypal 'Capability' tricks. The sole exception to the rule is the axial vista to the 'Intended Building on Johnson's Hill' – the Gothic folly that Sanderson Miller had proposed nearly twenty years before. Whether out of his friendship with Miller, or in obedience to his patron's wishes, this was something Brown must have felt he had to accept.

Literature: Stroud, 1975, pp. 140–1, fig. 40a; Stroud, 1979, pp. 758–9, fig. 3.

59 Design for the Gothic Tower at Wimpole, Cambridgeshire, c.1749–51
Sanderson Miller (1717–80)

Pen, ink and wash, with pencil

180 × 270mm (7⅛ × 10⅝in)

The National Trust (Bambridge Collection), Wimpole Hall, Cambridgeshire

In 1749 George Lyttleton, the owner of Hagley Hall in Worcestershire, wrote to Sanderson Miller that Lord Chancellor Hardwicke had desired to 'see the plan of my castle having a mind to build one at Wimpole... he wants no house, nor even room in it, but mearly the walls and semblance of an old castle to make an object from the house'. Miller soon afterwards inspected the site on Johnson's Hill (marked by a circle of trees at the end of the north avenue in No. 20), and produced this design, closely related to his earlier ruin at Hagley – which Walpole had praised as having the 'true rust of the Barons' Wars'.

In the end nothing was done to further the project until after the Lord Chancellor's death, when his son, the 2nd Earl of Hardwicke, determined to carry it out in association with Capability Brown's northward extension of the park.

Urgent messages were sent to Miller asking if he would supervise the work, but he was unable to comply (at this period he was suffering from recurring bouts of insanity), and subsequent payments to Brown show that he assumed responsibility for the construction in conjunction with the Cambridge architect and joiner James Essex. Work on it was still progressing in 1772 when Lady Grey, in a letter to her daughter, complained that 'the tower is better for being raised, but Mr. Brown has quite changed from our plan... that is, he has 'Unpicturesqued' it by making it a more continuous solid object, instead of a broken one.'

The considerable difference between Miller's design and the finished building can be seen by comparing it with the engraving which Lord Hardwicke commissioned in 1777 (No. 60). The original version is not only more scholarly, but also more believable as the ruin of a medieval castle, with proper overhanging machicolations, cracked masonry rather than smooth ashlar, an absence of string courses, and fewer windows and arrow-loops.

Literature: Jackson-Stops, 1979, p. 660, fig. 12; Stroud, 1979, p. 758.

60 The Gothic Tower, Wimpole, Cambridgeshire, 1777
Anonymous

Engraving

Entitled 'Gothic Tower at Wimple', and with a celebratory poem consisting of twelve rhyming couplets

405 × 610mm (15⅞ × 24in)

The National Trust (Bambridge Collection) Wimpole Hall, Cambridgeshire

This engraving, privately printed for the 2nd Earl of Hardwicke in 1777, bears the name neither of the artist nor the engraver. Even the author of the poem below is uncertain, though its mixture of

59

GOTHIC TOWER at WIMPLE.

When Henry stemm'd Iernes stormy Flood,
And bow'd to Britains yoke her savage brood,
When by true courage and false zeal impell'd
Richard encamp'd on Salems palmy field
On Towers like these Earl, Baron, Varvasor,
Hung high their Banners floating in the air.

Free, hardy, proud, they brav'd their feudal Lord,
And try'd their rights by ordeal of the Sword.
Now the full board with Christmas plenty crown'd
Now ravag'd and oppress'd the country round.
Yet Freedoms cause once rais'd the civil broil,
And Magna Charta clos'd the glorious toil.

Spruce modern Villas different Scenes afford;
The Patriot Baronet the courtier Lord,
Gently amus'd, now waste the Summers day,
In Book-room, Print-room, or in Terrae ernie
While Wit, Champain, and Puns and Poetry,
Virtû and Ice the genial Feast supply.

But hence the Poor are cherish'd, Artists fed,
And Vanity relieves in Bountys stead.
Oh might our Age in happy concert join
The manly Virtues of the Norman Line,
With the true Science and just Taste which rose
High in each useful Art these Modern Days.

60

87

high romanticism and playful cynicism suggest that it might be the Earl himself, whose letters and travel journals are equally entertaining. The building is shown as finally executed by Capability Brown and James Essex in 1768–72, only loosely following Sanderson Miller's original design (No. 59), made twenty years earlier. Not all of this building still survives, and the large Gothic tracery window on the return wall of the right-hand section has, for instance, long since disappeared.

It has been said that the Gothic Tower, in this final form, is 'devoid of historical associations... solely an ornamental building in the park.. to terminate the vista from the drawing room of the house' (McCarthy, 1987, p. 54). Yet archaeology was not entirely neglected. Above the north door of the middle tower (the main eye-catcher from the house) is a mitred head from a medieval statue, possibly of the fourteenth century, and a bogus Roman inscription commemorating 'Stirkeius', Abbot of Croyland and founder of Cambridge University in AD 946 – a particular hero of James Essex. Moreover the verse printed below the engraving seems to prove that its imagery was still powerful for contemporaries:

On towers like these, Earl, Baron, Vavasor,
Hung high their Banners floating in the air.
True, hardy, proud, they brav'd their feudal Lord
And try'd their rights by ordeal of the Sword.

The association of the Gothic style with ancient liberties is made by invoking Magna Carta, and then, with inspired bathos, the scene changes:

Spruce modern Villas different Scenes afford;
The Patriot Baronet, the courtier Lord
Gently amus'd, now waste the Summers day

61

The Park Building at Wimpole Hall, as remodelled by Humphry Repton, from his Red Book of 1801

In Book-room, Print-room, or in
  Ferme ornée
While Wit, Champain, and Pines and
  Poetry
Virtu and Ice the genial Feast supply.

There is of course a moral to all
this, expressed in the final couplets:

Oh might our Age in happy concert
  join
The manly Virtues of the Norman
  Line,
With the true Science and just Taste
  which raise
High in each useful Art these Modern
  Days.

Literature: Stroud, 1979, pp. 758–9,
fig. 5.

61 The Park Building at Wimpole Hall, Cambridgeshire, 1778

Daniel Lerpiniere (1745–85)
after a design by James
'Athenian' Stuart (1713–88)

Engraving
160 × 190mm (6¼ × 7½in)
Cambridgeshire County Record Office

From 1772, Capability Brown's
landscape at Wimpole was left to
mature for more than a decade,
with only one addition made on the
high western edge of the park

about 1775. Variously described as
a belvedere, prospect room or – by
Lord Hardwicke himself – as a
'modern Italian loggia', this was
(rather surprisingly) designed by
James 'Athenian' Stuart, who had
in the previous decade designed
two Yorke family tombs in the
parish church. The building
contained a tea-room with
'Etruscan figures in colours' for
which Stuart was supposed to have
been paid £700. The Earl was
delighted with the result, and had
this engraving made as a
companion to the one of the
Gothic Tower (No. 60). Sending a
copy of both to the Earl of
Dartmouth in 1778, he wrote that
'perhaps the views may strike you
as no bad contrast between ancient
and modern architecture'.

Other visitors to Wimpole were
less enthusiastic. Lord Torrington
referred to it as 'an ugly
summerhouse', and Humphry
Repton, having castigated its
inadequate foundations and 'the
absurdity of building a room on
columns' was to remodel it about
1802 – filling in the open bay on
the ground floor, and moving the
Ionic columns to form a loggia at
first-floor level, as suggested in one

of the illustrations in his 'Red
Book'. The building survived in
that form until the late nineteenth
century when it was demolished.

Literature: Stroud, 1979, p. 759,
figs 6 and 7.

62 General view of the park and monuments at Shugborough, Staffordshire, looking south, c.1780

Moses Griffith (1747–1819)

Watercolour
230 × 370mm (9 × 14½in)
The National Trust (Lichfield
Collection), Shugborough,
Staffordshire

The garden buildings which
Thomas Anson erected at
Shugborough between 1747 and his
death in 1773 were among the
pioneers first of the chinoiserie,
then of the picturesque rococo, and
finally of the Neo-classical style –
establishing the landscape there as a
landmark in the evolution of
English taste. Its appearance is also
admirably recorded in two sets of
drawings, one by Thomas Dall (see
No. 64), and another by Moses
Griffith, apparently commissioned
by Thomas Pennant as illustrations

62

for his *Journey from Chester to London* (1782). The latter were bought at the sale of Pennant's library in 1938. This particular view was not, however, engraved for use in the book.

Thomas Anson began in the 1730s by gradually acquiring the old village in front of the house, moving its occupants to Haywood, further away, and enlarging the old mill pond to form a lake. The first of his garden buildings, the Chinese House, was the result of his brother Admiral Anson's visit to Canton on his circumnavigation of 1743. Put up in about 1747 following a sketch by the Admiral's second-in-command, Sir Piercy Brett, it was, in Thomas Pennant's words 'a true pattern of the architecture of that nation, not a mongrel invention of British carpenters'.

In 1752, the Admiral's wife reported that the timber pagoda at the lower end of the mill pond was under construction 'and promises greatly'. It thus pre-dates Chambers's famous pagoda at Kew by almost ten years. Unfortunately

both it and the Palladian Bridge, seen on the far left of this drawing, seem to have been swept away in the great flood of 1795, after which the lake was drained and the River Sow re-routed. The bridge, a much modified version of a plate in Ware's *Palladio* (3:9–10), brought the main drive from Stafford over the lake, disguising the change in level with a cascade below: an idea later favoured by Capability Brown (see No. 58). It could possibly have been designed by Thomas Wright of Durham, who enlarged the house and contributed other garden buildings (No. 64) between 1748 and 1754. In the background to the right can be seen the wooden obelisk erected on Brocton Hill, which blew down later in the nineteenth century.

The two other buildings shown, still in existence, are the Triumphal Arch in the centre and the Lanthorn of Demosthenes on the far right. Both were designed by James 'Athenian' Stuart, and both were based on plates in the first volume of *The Antiquities of Athens*,

which he published with Nicholas Revett in 1762. The first was begun in November 1761 as a copy of the so-called Arch of Hadrian, but after the Admiral's death six months later cenotaphs surmounted by busts of him and his wife were installed between the upper pillars, with an *aplustre* or military trophy in the centre, carved by Scheemakers. The 'Lanthorn', started three years afterwards, was a copy of the Choragic Monument of Lysicrates in Athens, topped by a gilded tripod originally awarded as a trophy in a Dionysian festival. This final ornament was only achieved in 1771 with Matthew Boulton and Josiah Wedgwood co-operating on its manufacture: part bronze and part ceramic.

With the trees in the park now fully mature, it is difficult to see more than one of these buildings at a time. However, Griffith's watercolour shows that Thomas Anson saw no incongruity in them all appearing together: Chinese, Italian Renaissance and Greek in inspiration, yet united in the green

63

64

landscape setting of an English park.

Literature: Robinson, 1989, pp. 18–27, 74–5, 90.

Exhibited: London (Agnew), 1965, No. 41a.

63 The Tower of the Winds at Shugborough, Staffordshire, c.1780

Moses Griffith (1747–1819)

Watercolour

Signed: 'M. Griffith pinxt'

260 × 430mm (10¼ × 16⅞in)

The National Trust (Lichfield Collection), Shugborough, Staffordshire

This is another drawing from the set of fifteen views of Shugborough commissioned from the artist by Thomas Pennant and now at the house (see No. 62). It was engraved by J. Fittler as plate V in Pennant's *Journey from Chester to London* (1782), and shows 'Athenian' Stuart's Tower of the Winds, erected at the opposite end of the lake to the pagoda and completed about 1765, when the plumbers inscribed their names on the leadwork of the roof. The building is a replica of the Horologium of Andronikos

Cyrrhestes in Athens (better known as the Tower of the Winds), which dates from about 50 BC, though at the time thought to be much earlier. Stuart and Nicholas Revett had surveyed it during their time in Greece in 1751–3, even apparently demolishing an adjoining building so as to obtain a clearer view. The Shugborough version is remarkably faithful, though there are windows, while the original (a sort of public clock tower) has blank walls with sundials. Nor were the carved reliefs of the winds around the frieze executed: those shown by Moses Griffith may only have been painted in *trompe-l'oeil*.

The upstairs banqueting room, recently restored by the National Trust, has a 'domed and lozenge-coffered ceiling after the manner of Nero's Pallace' (ie the so-called 'Golden House' in Rome: a curious mixture of sources with the Greek exterior), and finely carved joinery, chimney-piece and overmantel mirror. The lower room was much simpler, but contained casts of centaurs and a statue of Mercury. It was converted into a dairy by Samuel Wyatt in 1805, the lake having by that time been drained (following the flood of 1795) and the bridges removed. The lower

windows were probably inserted at the same time, while the fanciful mermaid sundial was removed. It thereafter served as an adjunct to Wyatt's model farm, where Lady Anson could act the dairymaid, using a set of specially commissioned Wedgwood bowls and cream dishes, decorated in terracotta and black with Egyptian figures and hieroglyphs.

Literature: Robinson, 1989, pp. 24–5, 85.

Exhibited: Manchester, 1981, No. B 18.

64 View of the Conservatory and the Ruins at Shugborough, Staffordshire, c.1768–75

Nicholas Dall (fl.1756–d.1776)

460 × 1000mm (18⅛ × 39⅜in)

Staffordshire County Museum and the National Trust, Shugborough, Staffordshire

The Scandinavian artist Nicholas Thomas Dall was in England by 1756, and became a successful scene painter at Covent Garden, London. He appears to have been invited to Shugborough to paint a number of views of the house and park in oils (variously dated 1768 and 1775), and the pen-and-wash studies for these have mostly survived. At the same time he produced a design for a decorative picture on one wall of the Library (unspecified), and repaired or renewed the series of large architectural *capriccii* in the Dining Room, painted in Bologna in the 1740s.

No painting exactly equivalent to this drawing survives, but a view of the Ruins (now in the Bust Parlour) is extremely similar in treatment, with every detail of the masonry and tree planting as shown here. Moreover the drawing is of the same proportions as Dall's panoramic view of the house with the Ruins and Orangery, seen from the other side of the River Sow (Harris, 1971, p. 546, fig. 1), and the two compositions may have been intended as a pair.

Only recently acquired for the house, the drawing illustrates two phases in the creation of Thomas Anson's garden: the picturesque rococo of Thomas Wright of Durham, who created the Ruins in the centre of the view from the house about 1749; and the stricter Neo-classicism of 'Athenian' Stuart, who reconstructed the 'greenhouse' on the right in 1764. Only a small section of the Ruins now remains intact, including the triumphal arch on the right, supposedly half-buried, with an artificial stone figure of a Druid (like those at Erddig and The Vyne, see Nos 48–9) perched on a kind of neo-Norman pier behind. Eleanor Coade does not appear to have started making this model until after 1775 when she bought 'a remarkably fine figure of a Druid' with the whole of the rest of 'Mr Bridges' stone manufactory' in Knightsbridge, London. Originally, as Dall shows, the Ruins extended two or three times as far to the south, using architectural detail salvaged from the house during Thomas Wright's alterations of 1748–50 – obviously including the Venetian window

frame on the far left – as well as earlier fragments from a former palace of the Bishops of Lichfield.

Ruins of this sort, including a half-buried Arch of Constantine sprouting vegetation, had appeared in Batty Langley's *Principles of Gardening* as early as 1728. But most people found the Gothic style more suitable for ruins, suggesting the decay of superstition and despotism, and Shugborough remains among the very few classical examples. Moreover it was complemented by a classical colonnade on the far side of the river (rather confusingly viewed through the Ruins in this view), evidently based on the portico of the Temple of Saturn, near the Capitol in Rome. Whether this was also by Wright, or added at a later date by 'Athenian' Stuart, is not known, and it disappeared after the great flood of 1795. In the distance, to the left and right respectively, Dall shows the neighbouring seats of Tixall and Ingestre.

The Orangery, seen on the far right, was originally built about 1750, screening the south side of the old walled garden which lay behind. Stuart's remodelled façade, with its oval plaques and thin pilasters, is more French than Greek in feeling, though the herms in the niches at either end give a foretaste of Thomas Anson's important collection of antique sculpture shown within. At the west (or river) end was an alcove with a coffered semi-dome containing a large painting by Dall of the Temple of Minerva Polias in Rome, carried out in oils so as to be 'safe from the effluvia of the orange trees'. The building was sadly demolished about 1855, when W. A. Nesfield's new garden terraces were being laid out.

Literature: Croft-Murray, 1970, pp. 196–7; Robinson, 1989, pp. 22, 79, 81.

65 Design for the Cascade at West Wycombe, Buckinghamshire, c.1748

Attributed to Giovanni Niccolò Hieronimo Servandoni (1695–1766)

Pen, ink and wash

Inscribed: under cross-section 'Section of the Grottesco for having higher Water trough a Syphon,/than the natural Level is'; and below: 'Fol 3'

Scale: 1 in to 5 ft

450×580 mm ($17\frac{3}{4} \times 22\frac{7}{8}$ in)

Sir Francis Dashwood, Bt, West Wycombe, Buckinghamshire

Benjamin Franklin, staying at West Wycombe in 1773, wrote to his son: 'I am in this house as much at ease as if it were my own: and the gardens are a paradise.' His host, Sir Francis Dashwood, had begun to create an informal landscape garden here as early as 1739, damming the little River Wye or Wick to make a lake, and diverting the London road further south. By 1752, a survey drawing signed by Sir Francis's 'most Dutifull servant Morise Lewes Jolivet archt', shows the layout below the house much as it remains, with most of the garden buildings that still exist and a number of others that have disappeared.

A group of designs for some of these buildings, obviously French-inspired and with words like 'partie' and 'regulair' in the inscriptions, has in the past been attributed to Jolivet on the strength of his claim to be an architect. But their very high quality, and their date, now suggests an altogether more celebrated designer: the artist, scene-painter and architect Giovanni Servandoni. Trained in Rome under Pannini and G. I. Rossi, Servandoni thereafter worked chiefly in France, visiting England in 1722–4 and again in 1747–51. On this last trip he is known to have worked for Frederick, Prince of Wales, and Bubb Dodington, both intimate

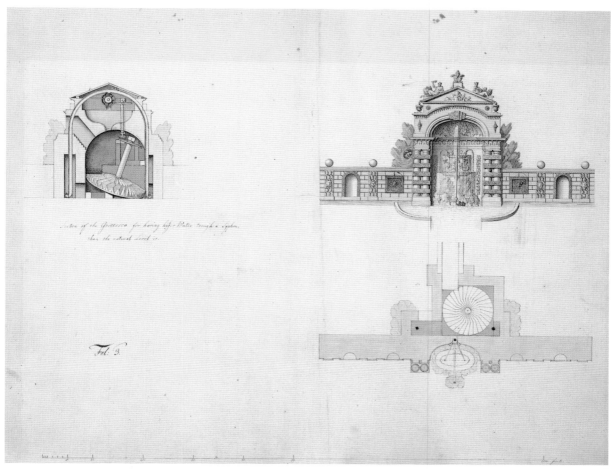

Section of the Grottesco for having high water through a syphon than the natural level is.

Fol. 3.

65

friends of Sir Francis Dashwood, while a sketch of a statue among the papers at West Wycombe is inscribed 'from a Term/ Servandoni's'.

His return to Paris in May 1751 explains a letter from Sir Francis to Colonel Gray, the secretary of the Society of Dilettanti, reporting that his 'rascally French architect has departed leaving nothing but bad debts' – a regular occurrence as far as Servandoni was concerned, explaining his constant moves from one European court to another. Maurice Jolivet is recorded as an engraver working in Dijon in the late 1750s and still active in 1772, though he was also responsible for the *decors* for a great firework display there in 1757. He must have

been related to Charles-Joseph Le Jolivet, an architect also in practice in the city at this period, and it is possible that he came to England as Servandoni's assistant (information from Mme J. Barrier of Bordeaux).

This drawing is for an elaborate 'Grottesco', where the present cascade now is, and one of the two other drawings related to the same project shows that the flint and stone walls each side were to have continued the whole length of the dam at the east end of the lake. The complicated mechanism for the fountains shown in the cross-section fits with Servandoni's reputation as an engineer, and the whole concept can be compared with the elaborate firework display which he staged in Green Park in

1749 to celebrate the Peace of Aix-la-Chapelle.

As can be seen from William Hannan's painting of *c.*1751–3 (page 16), the cascade was in fact built to a different model: a huge arch of jagged rocks with a reclining river god in the centre, probably by John Cheere to whom payments are recorded for lead figures (see No. 53). But Servandoni's alternatives, even if more architectural, also show prominent rockwork behind the central alcove – in this case with monkeys emerging from holes – so it is possible that he was proposing a building to be set against the existing arch.

Literature: Jackson-Stops, 1974, pp. 1618–20, fig. 4.

66 Design for Venus's Parlour at West Wycombe, Buckinghamshire, c.1748

Attributed to Giovanni Niccolò Hieronimo Servandoni (1695–1766)

Pen, ink and wash

Scale: 1in to 2ft

470 × 335mm (18½ × 13¼in)

Sir Francis Dashwood, Bt, West Wycombe, Buckinghamshire

Monkeys – familiar figures from Berain's *singeries* – appear in this design as in the last, reminding one that Andien de Clermont, the artist most adept at *singerie* scenes in England, collaborated with Servandoni on the setting for the Green Park firework display of 1749. This time, however, the design was certainly executed, for its oval opening to a cave between curving screen walls can still be seen under the mount in the wood to the west of the lake. Accounts for 1748–9 also refer to masons working on the 'steps att the cave' and 'plinths for figers to stand on att the cave mouth'. Sadly, these no longer exist. Facing the cave was a clearing with a circle of lead statues known as Venus's Parlour, while on the mount above it was her temple, an open rotunda similar to Vanbrugh's at Stowe (No. 34), with a copy of the Venus de Medici under it. This temple has recently been rebuilt by the present Sir Francis Dashwood, to designs by Quinlan Terry. The figure of Mercury above the cave opening can just be seen to the left of the temple and above the bridge in one of William Hannan's views (page 16).

As a founder-member both of the Society of Dilettanti and the Hell-Fire Club (otherwise known as the 'Society of St Francis of Wycombe'), Sir Francis combined scholarship with a high degree of frivolity, and a liking for practical jokes. It was said that he constructed the great golden ball on the top of the church tower at West Wycombe as an observatory, offering a view down on the gardens – part of which could then be seen to represent a naked woman. In the same way, the cave below the Temple of Venus seems to have been a very literal interpretation of the *mons veneris*, with the entrance representing a vagina, and the curving walls spread-open legs.

Literature: Jackson-Stops, 1974, p. 1619, fig. 5.

66

67 Design for a bridge at West Wycombe, Buckinghamshire, c.1748

Attributed to Giovanni Niccolò Hieronimo Servandoni (1695–1766)

Pen, ink and wash

Inscribed: below parapet wall on left: 'but contind if wonted'

Scale: 1in to 6ft

330 × 540mm (13 × 21¼in)

Sir Francis Dashwood, Bt, West Wycombe, Buckinghamshire

One of William Hannan's view
paintings of West Wycombe dated
between 1751 and 1753 (page 16)
shows a timber bridge over the
little river at the point where it
enters the north-west corner of the
lake, not far from the Temple of
Venus. This was a reduced-scale
version of the famous timber
bridge over the Thames at Walton,
constructed by the master-carpenter
William Etheridge in 1748–50, and
soon afterwards painted by
Canaletto. This design, in the same
practised hand as the previous two
drawings, shows the West
Wycombe version slightly extended
and with matching pavilions at
either end, surmounted by open
loggias. These would doubtless
have come into their own during
the *fêtes-champêtres* which Sir
Francis was so fond of giving, or as
viewing points for the mock naval
battles regularly held on the lake.

Two other related drawings are
still at West Wycombe: a plan
showing the structural timbers at
ground- and first-floor levels, and a
cross-section of one of the
pavilions showing a large staircase
ascending to the upper viewing
platform.

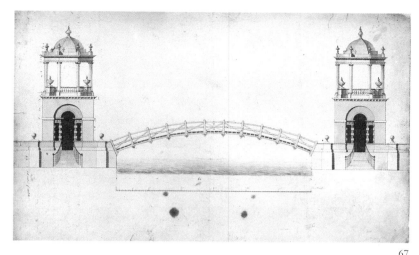

67

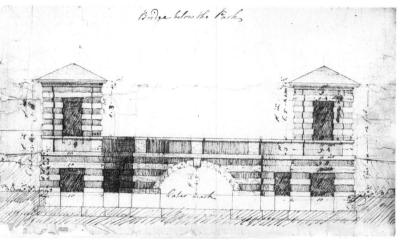

68

68 Design for a bridge at West Wycombe, Buckinghamshire, c.1778–80

Nicholas Revett (1720–1804)

Pen and ink
Inscribed: 'Bridge below the Park'
195 × 320mm (7¾ × 12⅝in)
Sir Francis Dashwood, Bt, West
Wycombe, Buckinghamshire

Between 1770 and 1781, the rococo
layout at West Wycombe was
transformed into a more natural
landscape by Thomas Cook,
described by a contemporary as 'an
eminent land-surveyor & pupil of
the celebrated *Capability* Browne'.
At the same time, Sir Francis
Dashwood (now Lord le
Despencer) commissioned a series
of chaster, less artificial, garden

buildings from Nicholas Revett,
co-author with James 'Athenian'
Stuart of *The Antiquities of Athens*.
Revett's west portico of the house,
based on the Temple of Bacchus at
Teos, was completed in 1771, and
itself treated as a separate garden
building. But he also received
payments for work in 1778–80,
almost certainly in connection with
the Music Temple on an island in
the middle of the lake – now the
focal centre of the landscape seen
from the house – and the so-called
Pepperbox Bridge, at the far end of
the new eastward extension of the
park, next to St Crispin's, a
shoemaker's cottage disguised as a
church.

By contrast with its humorous
neighbour, Revett's bridge has all
the *gravitas* associated with the
Neo-classical revival. Yet in detail,
its heavy rusticated bands of
flintwork (a local speciality),
alternating with red brick, seem
more Italianate, even Mannerist, in
inspiration – almost as if looking
back to Vanbrugh and
Hawksmoor. A carefully measured
drawing of a simpler rusticated
bridge in the collection at West
Wycombe suggests that Revett may
simply have been remodelling an
existing structure.

Literature: Jackson-Stops, 1974,
pp. 1684–5, figs 8 & 9.

95

69 Inscription from the Temple of Cloacina at West Wycombe, Buckinghamshire, c.1750–60

Anonymous

Engraving
Watermark: GR under crown
200 × 160mm (7⅞ × 6¼in)
Sir Francis Dashwood, Bt, West Wycombe, Buckinghamshire

The Cloaca Maxima was the great sewer of ancient Rome, parts of which were excavated in the seventeenth and eighteenth centuries, becoming something of a tourist attraction for the young English *milordi* in Italy. Possibly the origin of the word 'cloak-room' it was also the inspiration for a certain number of 'Temples of Cloacina': a punning name for privies or water-closets disguised as garden follies. Bishop Pococke describes one example at Wentworth Woodhouse in Yorkshire in 1750 as 'a beautiful temple to Cloacina with a portico round it supported by columns made of the natural trunks of trees' (Pococke, 1888–9); and the Earl-Bishop of Bristol mentions 'my Casino at Derry – that temple of *Cloacina*...', writing to his daughter in 1796 (Fothergill, 1974, pp.175–6).

The whereabouts of Sir Francis Dashwood's Temple of Cloacina at West Wycombe remains a mystery, but this printed version of the inscription within it is a good example of his somewhat bawdy humour. The 'nine' invoked in the penultimate line must refer to the Nine Muses.

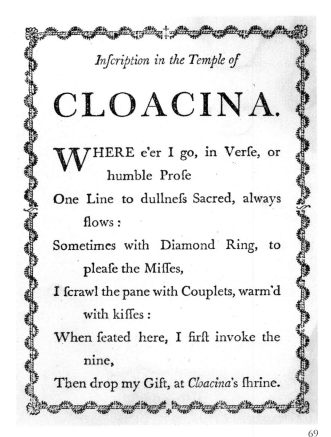

Inscription in the Temple of

CLOACINA.

WHERE e'er I go, in Verse, or humble Prose

One Line to dullness Sacred, always flows :

Sometimes with Diamond Ring, to please the Misses,

I scrawl the pane with Couplets, warm'd with kisses :

When seated here, I first invoke the nine,

Then drop my Gift, at *Cloacina*'s shrine.

69

70 Sketch plan for landscaping the Pleasure Ground at Kedleston, Derbyshire, 1759

Robert Adam (1728–92)

Pen and sepia ink and wash
Inscribed: 'Sketch for the Pleasure Garden/A. Pastures. for Red Deer/B. Scotch Cattle & Indian Sheep'
467 × 412mm (18⅜ × 16¼in)
The National Trust (Scarsdale Collection), Kedleston Hall, Derbyshire

Thought to be the only known plan for a garden in Robert Adam's hand, this is a page torn from the sketchbook which he made on his first visit to Kedleston Hall in the spring of 1759: a sketchbook that also contained watercolour designs (much influenced by his drawing-master, Clerisseau) for the North Lodge, the Bridge and Cascade between the two lakes, an ambitious stable block between the upper lake and Hare Hill, and a panoramic view of the Pleasure Ground looking north-west from the house (Harris, 1987, cat. nos 61–6). The last of these (page 14) coincides most closely with the plan, showing a rectangular pavilion on the hill to the left, a domed rotunda in the middle distance, and another alcove seat to the right below Harepit Hill.

While in Italy between 1755 and 1757, Adam had kept his hand in at landscape gardening, perhaps for fear that architectural commissions might not come so easily on his return to Britain. In a letter to his brother James, he boasted that he had 'a great ease in drawing and disposing of trees and buildings and ruins picturesquely, which Kent was not quite master of, as all his trees are perpendicular and stiff and his ruins good for nothing'. It may well have been such

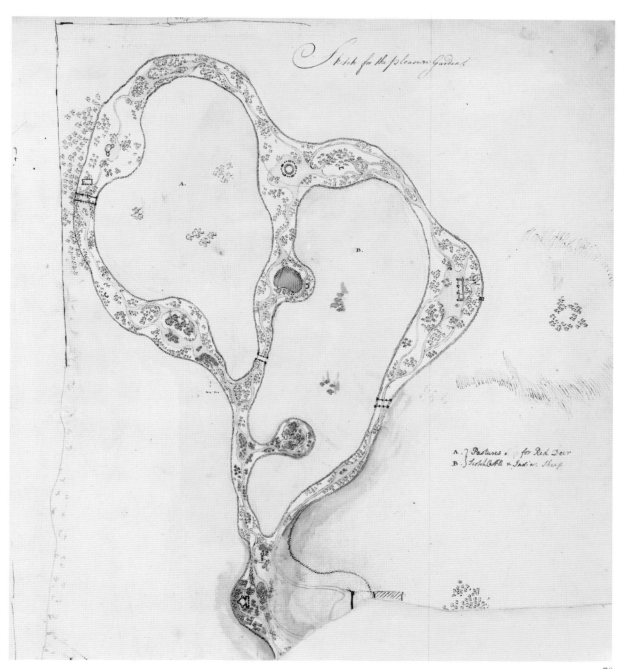

Sketch for the pleasure Garden

A. } Pastures . . for Red Deer
B. } Scotch Cattle & Indian Sheep

70

97

drawings that captivated the young Nathaniel Curzon (later 1st Lord Scarsdale), for only a few days after their first meeting in December 1758, Adam wrote to James that he had 'got the intire managdement of his Grounds put into my hands with full powers as to Temples Bridges Seats & Cascades'.

A survey of the estate made in 1764 shows the long walk very much as in Adam's plan, though without the dividing belt of trees between the two pastures – one reserved for 'Red Deer' and the other for 'Scotch Cattle & Indian Sheep'. Buildings are also indicated in most of the same places, though the alcove seat was abandoned in favour of a more rustic 'Hermitage', constructed in 1761–2, and now the only structure to survive – albeit in a ruinous state.

The Long Walk itself, with a 'fosse' or ha-ha on each side, was already being laid out as far as the Hermitage in the spring of 1760, and the surviving lists of plants used include laburnums, syringas, lilacs, honeysuckles, jasmine, broom and many other species of flowering and fragrant trees and shrubs. The remaining sections, amounting to 3 miles in total, were only completed in the 1770s.

Exactly how much credit Adam should take for the landscape at Kedleston is still open to question – for by April 1760 he had secured the dismissal of James Paine and his own appointment as architect of the house. On the other hand William Emes's departure in the same month, and the absence of any other landscape designer's name in the accounts, suggests that Lord Scarsdale followed his advice throughout the following decade.

Literature: Harris and Jackson-Stops, 1987, pp. 98–101, fig. 6.

71 Design for a View Tower at Kedleston, Derbyshire, c.1760

Robert Adam (1728–92)

Pen, ink and wash

Signed and dated

Inscribed in office copperplate: 'Diagonal Elevation of a View Tower Designed for the Right Honble The Lord Scarsdale/for Kedlestone in Derbyshire'

Scale: 1in to 4ft 6in

646 × 393mm (25⅞ × 15½in)

The National Trust (Scarsdale Collection), Kedleston Hall, Derbyshire

Adam records beginning the design of this tower in his first letter to Nathaniel Curzon in July 1759, and a model of it was sent a year later; sadly, it has not survived. Although this, and six other drawings for the building, are all dated 1760, they were evidently made after 1761 (when Curzon was created Lord Scarsdale), proving that the drawings from the Adam brothers' office were usually inscribed with the date of the original conception, rather than the year they were actually produced.

One of the keys to the development of Kedleston was the spirit of competition between the Tory Curzons and the Whig Cavendishes. Adam's single-arch bridge design was enlarged to three arches, immediately after the construction of James Paine's at Chatsworth; the sash bars of the windows on the north front were gilded in direct emulation of the Devonshires'; and there is good reason to think that this 'view tower' was conceived as a bigger and better version of Robert Smythson's Elizabethan hunting tower on the hill above Chatsworth. The projected site for this curious building is not known, but it could have been on the summit of Harepit Hill, dominating the upper lake and clearly visible from the house.

The cross-section (Harris, 1987, cat. no. 77) shows that it was to have had four substantial rooms, all with elaborate chimney-pieces, and the one on the ground floor with pilasters and a shallow coffered dome. One of the turrets was to house the staircase, and the overall height was to have been just under 85 feet. With mammoth building operations in progress on the house, it is hardly surprising that the project remained on the drawing board. Many years later, however, in 1777, Adam was to build a Gothick version: the 78-foot high Brizlee Tower at Alnwick, designed for the Duke of Northumberland.

Literature: Harris, 1987, cat. nos 76–7 (related drawings).

72 & 73 Designs for a gateway at Nostell Priory, Yorkshire, 1776

Robert Adam (1728–92)

Pen, ink and wash

Signed and dated 1776

Elevation and ground plan inscribed, in office copperplate: 'Design of a Gateway for the Park at Nostel/One of the Seats of Sir Rowland Winn Bart./to be situated at the approach to the House/from the York & Pontefract roads'; side elevation, cross sections and roof plan inscribed: 'End front of the Gateway/Section through the Gateway from A to B on the Plan/Section across the Gateway from C to D'

Scale: 1in to 5ft

(a) 617 × 452mm (24¼ × 17⅞in)
(b) 480 × 620mm (18⅞ × 24⅜in)

The Lord St Oswald, Nostell Priory, Yorkshire

Sir Rowland Winn, 5th Bt, who succeeded to Nostell Priory in 1765, lost no time in replacing his father's architect, James Paine, with the young and energetic Robert Adam. Over the next ten years, most of the interiors of the house were remodelled, and in 1779–80 Adam also built the family wing, originally intended to be one of four, replacing Paine's more modest pavilions.

Diagonal Elevation of a View Tower Designed For the Right Hon.ble The Lord Scarsdale for Kedlestone in Derbyshire.

Rob.t Adam Architect 1760

71

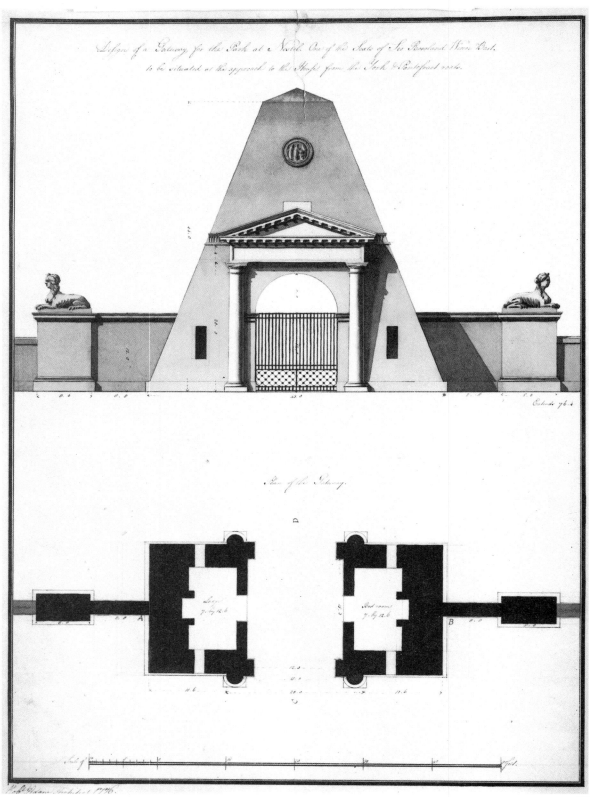

Design of a Gateway, for the Park at Nostel, One of the Seats of Sir Rowland Winn Bart. to be situated at the approach to the House from the York & Pontefract roads.

Plan of the Gateway.

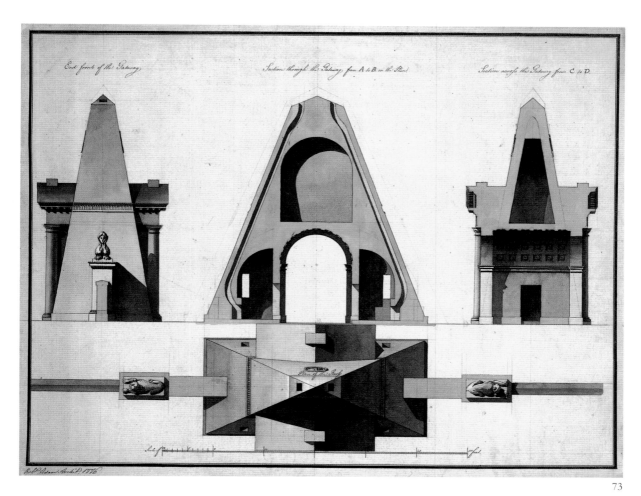

End front of the Gateway;

Section through the Gateway, from A to B on the Plan;

Section across the Gateway from C to D.

Plan of the Roof

Rob.t Adam Arch.t 1776

73

(Right) The 'Needle's Eye'
gate at Nostell Priory,
Yorkshire

In between these operations, Adam also contributed to the park and gardens, designing a large orangery or greenhouse backing on to the stables about 1770; extending the Menagerie, a Gothick garden house on the far side of the lake in 1776; and designing the lodge and gates at Foulby in the following year. However, much the most interesting of his buildings at Nostell is the gateway on Featherstone Moor, originally on the approach to the house from Pontefract but now a largely disused drive.

Sir Rowland probably intended this gate as a direct answer to the 'Needle's Eye', a much earlier folly at nearby Wentworth Woodhouse, built (again on a drive to Pontefract) in 1722–3, and featuring an obelisk pierced by an arch (Binney, 1991, p. 61, fig. 2). It is significant that the nickname (derived from the famous biblical quotation about the rich man entering the kingdom of heaven) was also applied to the Nostell gate from an early date. The drawings for the building are dated 1776, and bills from the mason, Cosmo Wallace, show that it was completed in the same year. Adam's inspiration may well have been the Arch of Titus in Rome, whose left-hand supporting wall was built at an angle of 45 degrees (as illustrated in Desgodetz's *Edifices Antiques de Rome*, 1682, plate 179). At the same time those who had been on the Grand Tour would also have recalled the famous Pyramid of Cestius on the Aventine – next to the Protestant cemetery.

The cross-section shows the ingenuity with which Adam concealed the chimney flues within the pyramid itself, though it is hard to imagine a lodge-keeper actually living in the two diminutive rooms flanking the arch. The loft above is, curiously, a void, with no apparent means of access. The two sphinxes are similar to a pair once on the Foulby gate-piers, but have disappeared if they were ever executed. Nor is there any record of the bas-relief in the central medallion, now an empty recess.

The happy relations between patron and client are illustrated by a letter which Adam wrote to Sir Rowland in this same year, 1776, reporting that 'we had a glorious lunch of your excellent venison yesterday when we remembered with much pleasure the founders of the feast'.

Literature: Jackson-Stops, 1982, pp. 25–6, 31, 34.

74 Design for a bridge at Osterley Park, Middlesex, 1768

Robert Adam (1728–92)

Pen, ink and wash

Signed and dated

Inscribed with heights, and in office copperplate: 'Designs of a Bridge for Osterley Park in Middlesex. The Seat of Robert Child Esquire'

Scale: 1in to 5ft 4in

395 × 1205mm ($15\frac{1}{2}$ × $47\frac{1}{2}$in)

Victoria and Albert Museum (on loan to the National Trust, Osterley Park, Middlesex)

This is the grandest of two alternative designs, each accompanied by a plan, almost certainly proposing a bridge which would take the drive from the Wyke Green lodges (the main approach from London) across the dam between the two lakes, at the same time acting as an eye-catcher from the entrance front of the house. Like the similarly positioned bridge at Kedleston, it may well have had a cascade below it, falling into the lower lake on the other side. Whereas the other design has three equal arches, more conventional statues in niches on the piers, and garlanded urns above, this drawing shows a flatter and more graceful central span, and larger urns in bold pedimented aedicules, with putti riding sea-monsters and pairs of sphinxes on the balustrade. Both designs have his favourite Neo-classical medallions carved in bas-relief in the spandrels. Sphinxes occur in a similar position on Adam's rather simpler bridge at Compton Verney, also dating from the late 1760s.

Altogether, Adam's proposal would have been utterly different in character from Chambers's rusticated 'Roman' bridge built in the 1750s over the lower lake at Osterley, leading to the aviary, and reminiscent of his Ruined Arch at Kew (Bolton, 1922, 1:300, wrongly attributing the drawing to Adam). Elegant, sophisticated, even feminine in character, it may have been an intentional riposte to the latter's rugged Piranesian grandeur.

Literature: Rowan, 1988, cat. no. 107, plate 33.

75 Design for a ruined castle at Osterley Park, Middlesex, 1774

Robert Adam (1728–92)

Pencil, pen and ink and wash with watercolour

Signed and dated

Inscribed: 'Remains of the Old Castle of Osterley in Middlesex, one of the Seats of Robert Child Esqr.'

Scale: 1in to 8ft

440 × 592mm ($17\frac{1}{4}$ × $23\frac{1}{4}$in)

Victoria and Albert Museum (on loan to the National Trust, Osterley Park, Middlesex)

This remarkable drawing, in Adam's own hand, is a key document in the development of his late 'castle style'. Needless to say, there never was an old castle on the Osterley estate, the first house having been built there by Sir Thomas Gresham in the 1570s. But ever since Vanbrugh's impassioned plea to the Marlboroughs to save the remains of old Woodstock Manor in the park at Blenheim, the idea of picturesque ruins suggesting the antique origins of a place had become increasingly fashionable. No one could have needed to stress

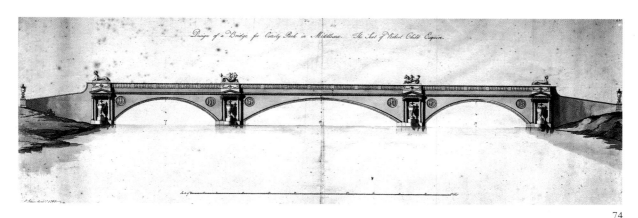

Design of a Bridge for Osterly Park in Middlesex. The Seat of Robert Child Esquire.

74

Remains of the Old Castle of Osterly in Middlesex, one of the Seats of Robert Child Esq.

75

antique origins more than the Childs, nouveau riche bankers whose extravagant remodelling of the Elizabethan house, begun by Chambers and continued by Adam, was the talk of London society.

As Alastair Rowan has pointed out, the idea of a quasi view picture was 'a mode of display which Adam particularly favoured for his castle projects, where the novelty of composition and style might otherwise confuse a client'. Nevertheless, 'pencil lines behind the towers to the right suggest that, despite its haphazard appearance, the elevation has been constructed from a plan.' No other drawings for the project survive, and it is hard to know where the building would have been sited, though the far end of the lower lake is a possibility, given the distant view of water on the left.

Rowan also identifies themes in the drawing to which the architect returned in later commissions: the round tower with its heavy machicolations derived from Theodoric's mausoleum at Ravenna, resurfaces in Adam's mausoleum to David Hume in the Carlton Hill Cemetery, Edinburgh, in 1777, and a year later as a tea-house at Auchencruise in Ayrshire. It is also used as a central feature in later castle-style houses like Dalquharran, Culzean and Pitfour. The battlemented archway is a pre-cursor of the gateway at Culzean.

In style, the drawing owes much to Clerisseau, with whom Adam visited Ravenna in 1755, and the Italianate figures drawn in picturesque attitudes are an important ingredient of the whole composition. The implication for a client like Robert Child was that he could have his own 'Old Master' or ruin *capriccio* brought to life in three dimensions, and erected in the park with almost as much ease as buying a picture to hang.

Literature: Rowan, 1988, cat. no. 108, plate 54.

76 Design for the park at Dudmaston, Shropshire, 1777
William Emes (1729–1803)

Ink on vellum

Inscribed on left: 'A PLAN/of the Intended Sheep Pasture &c at/ DUDMASTON/the seat of Wm Whitmore Esqr/by Wm Emes/1777'; and on right 'REFERENCE/No. 1. House and Offices/2. Stables/3. Farm Yard/4. Approach Roads/5. Garden'

Scale: 1in to 2 chains

280 × 400mm (11 × 15¾in)

The National Trust (Labouchere Collection), Dudmaston, Shropshire

In 1775 a young sailor from Southampton named William Whitmore inherited, by a circuitous route, the Wolryche family house at Dudmaston, built between 1695 and 1701, and probably designed by Francis Smith of Warwick. This main part of the house was joined on to the buildings of Tudor origin which had succeeded the original fortified manor of the twelfth century. By the time William inherited, the house and estate were both in a poor condition. The park cannot have been very large, for an anonymous account of life at Dudmaston in the 1750s records that 'dinner was ready every day at one o'clock for twenty persons, and when the Bell rang any neighbouring Farmers out working in their fields were welcome to come and any friends of the family who chose to partake of the plain hospitable dinner provided'.

Having repaired the house and begun to organise the woods, Whitmore commissioned the landscape designer William Emes to draw up a plan for the park along the picturesque lines made popular by Capability Brown and others. Emes had already built up a considerable practice in the West Midlands and the Welsh borders, producing schemes for Erddig and Chirk among other houses. His Dudmaston layout is characteristic of his style, with its clumps of trees in open parkland, woods with

purposely ragged edges, and serpentine drives approaching the house always at an angle. Only the straight edges of the ends of the lakes would have offended Brown, betraying their origin as earlier eighteenth-century fishponds. One curious feature of Emes's drawing is that the compass point at the top is entirely wrong: north as indicated actually representing south-west. This aberration might suggest that it was produced some time after his visit, and from inadequate notes.

Some of Emes's ideas may have been acted on, but William Whitmore's wife, Frances Lister, and their gardener Walter Wood, seem to have gone their own way, making a particular feature of the 'Dingle' – the valley south of the house, the steep escarpment of which can be seen on Emes's plan. The Whitmores' daughter, another Frances, later recalled that 'the Dingle was a pet of our dear mother's. She laid out the walks therein, placed seats and formed cascades in conjunction with Walter Wood, whom we called Planter, and who was many years gardener at Dudmaston and died there. This man had imbibed his notions of taste at Shenstone's Leasowes – & the Badger and Dudmaston Dingle were long picturesque rivals. My mother and Aunt Dora were good Botanists – I believe Botany became at that period a favourite pursuit of ladies owing to Dr. Darwin's then famed poem of the loves of Plants.'

This connection with the poet William Shenstone's famous *ferme ornée* at The Leasowes, near Halesowen in Warwickshire (now largely taken over by a golf course and municipal park), makes the Dingle an important survival today. The National Trust has recently restored it, uncovering ancient paths, cascades, abutments, niches and stone revetments – all very much in the spirit of Shenstone's *Unconnected Thoughts on*

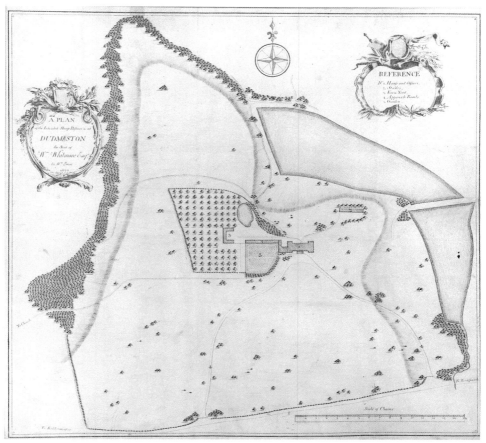

76

77

Gardening (1764), a copy of which is in the library at Dudmaston. Like Shenstone, the Whitmores could not afford to build lavish follies in their garden, but would anyway have considered them too artificial in a landscape that (in Gray's words) 'trusts to nature and simple sentiment'.

Literature: Cornforth, 1979, p. 818, fig. 2.

77 View of the house and park at Dudmaston, Shropshire, 1793

Moses Griffith (1747–1819)

Watercolour

Inscribed: 'Dudmaston/The Seat of William Whitmore Esq./May 16 1793'

219 × 300mm (8⅝ × 11¾in) (outside ruled margin)

The National Trust (Labouchere Collection), Dudmaston, Shropshire

This watercolour of Dudmaston from the south-west shows the house as built by Francis Smith in the 1690s, but with an extra roof constructed over the valley of the original hipped roof, presumably constructed by William Whitmore in the 1760s. The lake in the foreground, merged with its neighbour in the 1850s and since known as the Big Pool, still appears very much as in Emes's plan of 1777 (No. 76), with the Dingle lying out of sight to the right. The informal planting of trees and shrubs to form a picturesque setting for the house could be considered an archetypal statement of English landscape gardening in the late eighteenth century.

The screening of the servants' wing on the right; the carefully controlled scale of different trees so as to accentuate the 'depth' of the whole composition, and emphasise its serpentine lines; the removal of the lower branches by grazing livestock allowing vistas through the trunks – all these are classic examples of a style that was to sweep away the formal gardens of

an earlier era, and become fashionable all over Europe.

Soon after 1816, when he inherited, William Wolryche Whitmore constructed a series of terraces between the house and lake, with stone steps, urns and elaborate gravel paths, parts of which still survive.

Literature: Cornforth, 1979, p. 714, fig. 1.

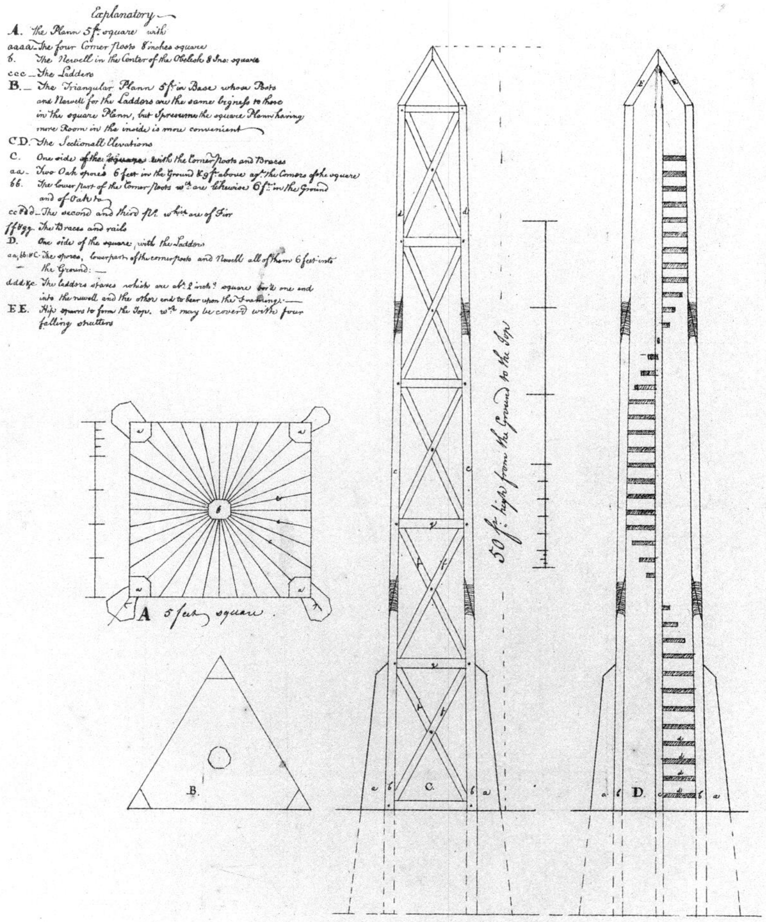

78

78 Plans, elevation and cross-section for a timber obelisk at Blickling Hall, Norfolk, c.1765–70

Attributed to William Ivory (1746–1801)

Pen and sepia ink, with pencil

Inscribed: 'Explanatory/A The Plann 5ft square with/aaaa The four corner posts 8 inches square/b The Newell in the Center of the Obelisk 8 Ins square/ ccc – The ladders/B. – The Triangular Plann 5ft in Base whose Posts and Newell for the Ladders are the same bigness to those/in the square Plann, but I presume the square Plann having more Room in the inside is more convenient./CD The Sectionall

Elevations/C One side of the square with the Corner posts and Braces/aa Two Oak sparrs 6 feet in the Ground and 9ft above/agt the Corners of the square/bb The Lower part of the Corner Posts Wch are likewise 6ft in the Ground/and of oak/to./cc & dd The second and third flos. which are Firr/ff & gg The Braces and rails/ D One side of the square with the Ladder/aa,bb,&c The Sparrs, lower part of the Corner posts and Newell all of them 6 feet into the Ground/ddd & c The ladder stares which are abt 2 inchs square bor'd one end into the newell and the other end to bear upon the Framing:–/Hip sparrs to form the Top. wch may be covered with four falling shutters'; and to right of C: '5oft high from the Ground to the Top'

Watermark: IV

Scale: approx. 1in to 4½ft

380 × 290mm (15 × 11⅜in)

The National Trust (Lothian Collection), Blickling Hall, Norfolk

This design for an obelisk viewing tower, with alternative square and triangular ground plans, shows a great deal of technical knowledge about carpentry – and is almost certainly from the office of the Norwich architects, builders and timber merchants Thomas and William Ivory, who worked at Blickling for the 2nd Earl of Buckinghamshire from 1765 until his death in 1779. Although still very young, William seems to have usually acted as the draughtsman, though a group of cruder, unsigned drawings for the house are likely to be by his father, Thomas.

Many garden buildings of the eighteenth century were constructed solely of timber, and have disappeared through later lack of maintenance. There is no firm evidence that this obelisk was ever erected, unlike the Gothic Tower on the western edge of the park, built in 1773 and used as a grandstand for the adjoining racecourse, the Lady's Cottage depicted by Repton (No. 79), or the pyramid mausoleum designed by Joseph Bonomi in 1793. On the other hand, the number '5' on the corner ties up with a table of contents from an eighteenth-century album of drawings at Blickling, now dismembered. It is described here as 'A plann, Elevation, Section of the building in the Park', perhaps suggesting that the design had been executed. One of its limitations must have been that only one person at a time could climb to the top and raise the four shutters to admire the view. Nor would its height have been a match for the great stone obelisk at Holkham, built as early as 1729 and 80 feet high.

79

79 View of the Lady's Cottage at Blickling Hall, Norfolk, c.1780

Humphry Repton (1752–1818)

Pen, ink and watercolour, with some body colour

Signed: *H. Repton delin*

295 × 355mm (11⅝ × 14in)

The National Trust (Lothian Collection), Blickling Hall, Norfolk

In 1778, on the death of his parents, the young Humphry Repton decided to abandon his career as a merchant in Norwich, and to buy a modest manor house at Sustead near Aylsham. Here he lived the life of a country gentleman, occupying himself with topographical drawing and some political activity on behalf of his neighbour William Windham of Felbrigg. It was only in 1786 that reduced circumstances caused him to move to Hare Street in Essex, and two years later to embark on a new career as landscape gardener.

This drawing, somewhat hesitant and naive in style, is among Repton's earliest known watercolours, and depicts the Ladies' Cottage in the Great Wood at Blickling, built for Mary Anne Drury soon after her marriage to the 2nd Earl of Buckinghamshire in 1761. The picturesque composition foreshadows the watercolours in Repton's later 'Red Books', and the combination of conifers and crumbling statuary contribute to the atmosphere of pleasing melancholy.

In an inventory of 1793, the Ladies' Cottage was furnished with a dining-table and chairs as well as an impressive array of cutlery, crockery and cooking equipment. In the late nineteenth century it was abandoned, however, and only the foundations and some overgrown box now mark its site.

To the right can be seen an early seventeenth-century fountain which the 1st Earl bought at the sale of Oxnead, the neighbouring seat of the Paston family in 1732. This was moved to the centre of Sir Matthew Digby Wyatt's new east parterre in 1873. The urn on a pedestal behind is also similar to those now on the parterre, and in the adjacent wilderness.

Another signed version of this view, executed in monochrome and rectangular rather than oval in format, also survives in the collection at Blickling. Though identical in most respects, it shows a headless statue on the plinth in the foreground, apparently the Diana from Oxnead (attributed to Nicholas Stone), now housed in the east wing of the house.

Literature: Carter, Goode and Laurie, 1982, pp. 6–8, 99, cat. no. 87(i), plate 96; Maddison, 1987, p. 68.

80 Elevation and ground plan for a greenhouse at Gunton Park, Norfolk, 1816

Humphry Repton (1752–1818) and John Adey Repton (1775–1860)

Pen, ink and watercolour (with a pencil sketch of a plant stand on the verso of the elevation)

Signed and dated

Inscribed: (on elevation) 'A design for a Greenhouse at Gunton in Norfolk as proposed by H & J A Repton 1816'; (on ground plan) 'For the Right Honble Lord Suffield &c &c/at Gunton/Ground Plan of the Greenhouse proposed by H & J A Repton/This is supposed to be about 40 feet long &c may be extended if required/to 50 feet with five windows – or 60 feet with Seven'

Scale: 1in to 10ft for the ground plan; 1in to 5ft for the windows
Both 185 × 255mm (7¼ × 10in)
The National Trust (Lothian Collection), Blickling Hall, Norfolk

The 2nd Earl of Buckinghamshire's heir was his daughter Caroline, who had married William Assheton Harbord, later Lord Suffield, owner of the neighbouring estate at Gunton. After inheriting Blickling in 1793, Lady Suffield made a number of improvements to the gardens of both houses, often consulting Humphry Repton while he was staying with his sister Dorothy Adey at nearby Aylsham. This advice was not always given on a formal basis, for in one of his letters to Dorothy, about 1800, suggesting an enlargement of the flower garden at Blickling, he writes: 'You may perhaps like to explain [this] to Lady Suffield as your own idea, for I know by experience that the opinion of a professional man is only valuable in proportion as it is paid for...'

From 1800 Repton severed his previous connection with the architect John Nash and took his eldest son, John Adey Repton, into partnership, collaborating with him on many important commissions which entailed building work. Born almost stone-deaf, John Adey had shown promise as a pupil of the Norwich architect William Wilkins the elder, and later worked as Nash's assistant. This design for a greenhouse at Gunton, signed by father and son together, shows a chaste Neo-classical building rather in the French manner, set off by a little formal parterre.

The ground plan shows heating pipes beneath the floor, and a flue for hot air also concealed in the back wall. The plan shows no planting beds and it is very likely all the plants were kept in pots which was typical of the period. Small black dots on the plans suggest cast-iron columns and the dotted lines possibly the lines of the

roof structure. Two sheds for gardeners are provided at the rear, and the central niche is intended for a 'Seat or Aviary'. The detail of the windows shows how they are swung open on central vertical pivots to air the plants on hot days.

The building is modest in size and forms a backdrop for Repton's flower garden, encircled by a low lattice fence, almost as if it were a painted screen at the back of a theatrical stage. The typically Reptonian formality of the flower beds makes an interesting comparison with the looser 'gardenesque' style of planting in front of the Tatton conservatory (No. 89), following J. C. Loudon's precepts.

Literature: Goode, Carter and Laurie, 1982, p. 129, cat. no. 58; Maddison, 1987, p. 58.

A Design for a Greenhouse at Gunton in Norfolk as proposed by H & J A Repton 1816.

80a

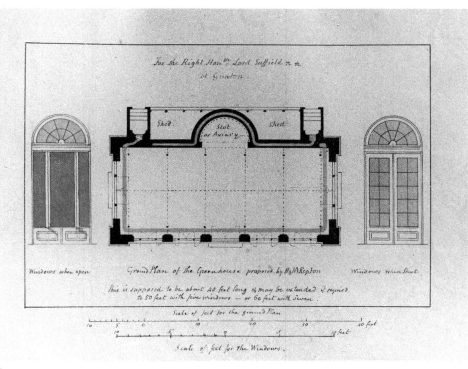

For the Right Hon.ble Lord Suffield &c &c at Gunton.

Shed.　　　Seat for Aviary.　　　Shed.

Windows when open.　　Ground Plan of the Greenhouse proposed by H.J.A.Repton.　　Windows when shut.

This is supposed to be about 40 feet long & may be extended if required
to 50 feet with five windows — or 60 feet with seven.

Scale of feet for the ground Plan

Scale of feet for the Windows.

80b

81 Design for a flower basket on a tall stand, probably for Gunton Park, Norfolk, *c.*1816

John Adey Repton (1775–1860)

Pen and ink

Inscribed: 'Plan of the Iron basket/Plan of the Post (if executed in Oak?)/ A 1½ × 1/B 1 by ⅝ to halve into each other/A.A. horizontal Bars 1¼ inch by ¾ thick/B.B. Cross.d Bars/¾ of an inch by ⅖'

Watermark: fleur-de-lis

Scale: 1in to 6in

410 × 250mm (16¼ × 9⅞in)

The National Trust (Lothian Collection), Blickling Hall, Norfolk

This design almost certainly relates to the four flower baskets on tall triangular stands shown in Humphry and John Adey Repton's design for the greenhouse at Gunton (No. 80). Like Nash, with whom he collaborated for many years, the elder Repton was interested in the development of cast iron for decorative purposes – suggesting its use for whole buildings, like the projected conservatory at Plas Newydd (page 19) – and his son, John Adey, was often called upon to produce working drawings for such items after 1800, when they began to work in partnership.

Repton's re-establishment of the flower garden as a self-contained element in the landscape, rather like an outdoor room, demanded 'furniture' in the shape of pergolas, urns, vases, trellis screens and fountains. In this case the four stands seem actually derived from the torchères or tripod candlestands fashionable in the Neo-classical interior, and almost invariably placed (as here) in the four corners. The analogy may be taken still further, for these torchères often supported perfume-burners as well as candelabra, and the wafts of scent from honeysuckles, jasmines and other plants climbing the stands, or tumbling down from the baskets, would similarly have been at nose level.

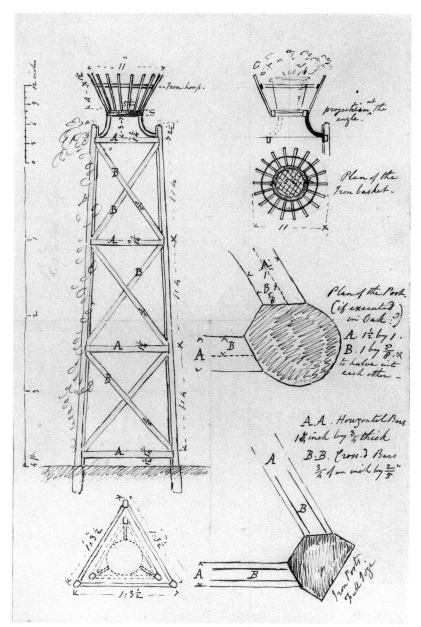

81

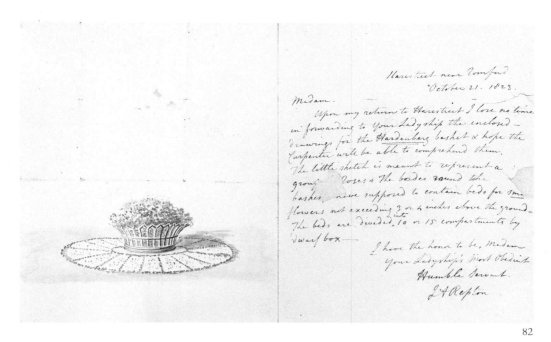

Literature: Carter, Goode and Laurie, 1982, p. 57.

82 Design for a 'Hardenberg Basket' at Blickling Hall, Norfolk, with an accompanying letter to the Dowager Lady Suffield, 1823

John Adey Repton (1775–1860)

Pen, ink and wash

Signed and dated

Inscribed: recto 'Harestreet near Romford/October 21. 1823/Madam/ Upon my return to Harestreet I lose no time in forwarding to Your Ladyship the enclosed – drawings for the *Hardenberg* basket & hope the Carpenter will be able to comprehend them. The little sketch is meant to represent a group... Roses. The border round the basket... have supposed to contain beds for *small* flowers not exceeding 3 or 4 inches above the ground. The beds are divided into 10 or 15 compartments by dwarf box/ I have the honour to be, Madam/ Your Ladyship's Most Obedient/ humble Servant/ J. A. Repton'; verso 'Cross Post/To the/Dowager Lady Suffield/Blickling Hall, Aylsham/ Norfolk/[Postmark] Romford/12' and with a half-plan and elevation detail of basket'

Watermark: W. Thomas 1822
Scale: 1 in to 1 ft
230 × 380mm (9 × 15 in)
The National Trust (Lothian Collection), Blickling Hall, Norfolk

The idea of the *corbeille*, or flower bed resembling a wicker basket full of blooms, is found in one of Humphry Repton's earliest 'Red Books', made for Courteenhall in Northamptonshire in 1791. Derived from William Mason's flower-edged beds at Nuneham Park, Oxfordshire (dating from the 1770s), it recurs in many of his later plans, most spectacularly in his proposals for the Royal Pavilion at Brighton (1808), where baskets are scattered in great profusion over the lawn overlooked by the Regent's private apartment.

John Adey Repton's design for a 'Hardenberg basket' was a refinement of this idea, and derived its name from Prince Hardenberg, one of the patrons for whom he worked (at Neu Hardenberg near Frankfurt-am-Oder, and at Glienicke near Potsdam) on his Continental tour of 1821–2. The size of the drawing is misleading, for the wooden basket, filled with roses, was to be over 8 feet wide and at the centre of a miniature circular parterre. In the past it has been assumed that this feature was intended for Gunton, but Lady Suffield was widowed in 1821 and spent most of the rest of her life at Blickling, to which this letter was addressed.

Literature: Carter, Goode and Laurie, 1982, cat. no. 74.

83 Design for a circular trellis enclosure at Blickling Hall, Norfolk, c.1823

John Adey Repton (1775–1860)

Pen, ink and watercolour

Inscribed: 'Trellis $1\frac{1}{4}$ by $\frac{1}{2}$ inch thick'; and 'The lower rail B to be the same as A. but to be reversed'

Watermark: fleur-de-lis
Scale: 1 in to 1 ft and 1 in to 5 ft
394 × 210mm ($15\frac{1}{2} × 8\frac{1}{4}$ in)
The National Trust (Lothian Collection), Blickling Hall, Norfolk

In his *Fragments on the Theory and Practice of Landscape Gardening* (1816), Humphry Repton claimed, rather dubiously, to have reintroduced the fashion for trellis

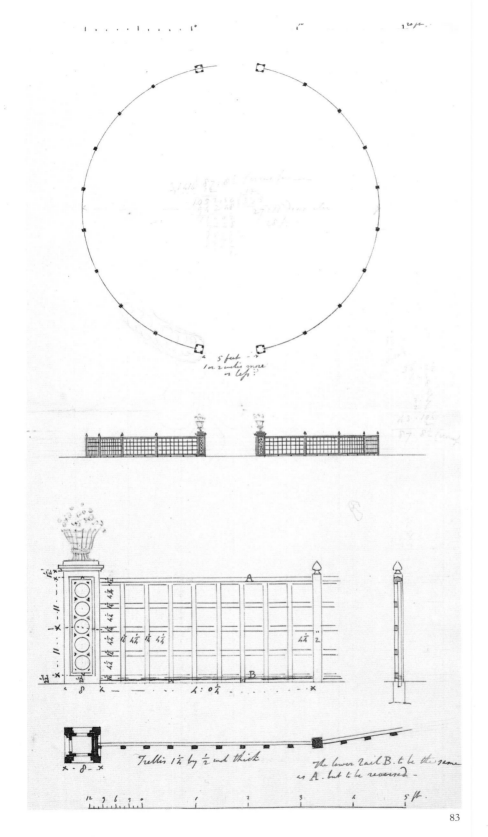

5 feet
1 or 2 inches more
or less

A

B

4½ 1½ 4½

4¼ 2

Trellis 1¼ by ½ inch thick

The lower rail B. to be the same
as A. but to be reversed.

112

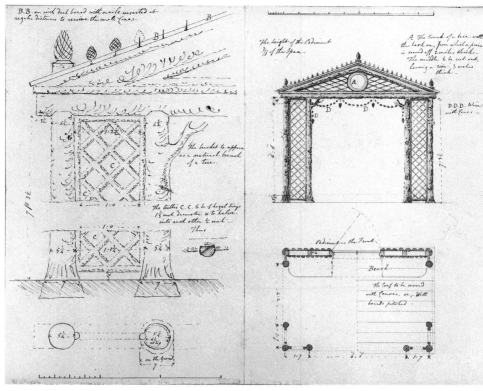

in England, and some of the illustrations to the book deliberately suggest a return to trellised hedges and arbours of seventeenth-century design. The device was certainly a useful one for demarcating the boundaries of formal parterres and flower gardens, without resorting to the expense or artificiality of brick and stone walls. At the same time, he was fond of condemning the flimsy 'cottage-porch' type of English trelliswork, and advocating the more substantial French variety.

This design by John Adey Repton is true to his father's principles, showing a large circular enclosure bounded by a trellis fence, probably intended to contain a flower garden in the centre of what is now the east parterre at Blickling.

84 Design for a trellis arbour at Blickling Hall, Norfolk, c.1825

John Adey Repton (1775–1860)

Pen, ink and wash, with pencil
Inscribed: 'A The trunk of a tree with the back on, from which a piece is sawed off 2 inches thick, the middle to be cut out leaving a rim 3 inches thick/ B.B. an inch deal board with nails inserted at regular distances to receive the small Cones/The trellis CC to be of hazel twigs $1\frac{1}{3}$ inch diameter and to halve into each other $\frac{1}{2}$ inch – thus/ D.D.D. Wire with Cones/The bracket to appear as a natural branch of a tree/ The Roof to be covered with canvas or, – with braids pitched'; on verso, design for another trellis arbour to be made out of planed timber
Watermark: J. Whatman Turkey Mill 1824
Scale: 1in to 2ft on elevation; 1in to 6in on detail
330 × 405mm (13 × $15\frac{7}{8}$in)
The National Trust (Lothian Collection), Blickling Hall, Norfolk

As an architect, John Adey Repton is best known as an antiquarian, reviving Gothic and Elizabethan forms. At Blickling itself he reconstructed the central clock-tower about 1828, and designed the linking arcades between the house and wings in a remarkably scholarly Jacobean manner. However, this charming design for a trellis arbour, with its tree-trunk columns and pediment, its pine-cone acroteria, and garlands of cones strung above the entrance, shows that he was equally adept at the Neo-classical style, and familiar with current theories about its primitive origins. His father, Humphry, had earlier explored such theories in the introduction to his *Designs for the Pavillon at Brighton* (1808), with vignettes derived from a knowledge of Laugier's *Essai sur l'Architecture*, and perhaps also a familiarity with Soane's garden buildings in the primitive manner (Du Prey, 1979, fig. 3, plate I).

The arbour has much in common with the Menagerie at Woburn Abbey, as illustrated in the 'Red Book' of 1804, and in Repton's *Fragments*; it is also similar in detail to the rather simpler trellis seat which still stands in the Secret Garden at Blickling today.

Literature: Carter, Goode and Laurie, 1982, plate 110, cat. no. 76; Maddison, 1987, pp. 58, 64.

85 Design for a garden pavilion at Dyrham Park, Gloucestershire, *c.*1803

Humphry Repton (1752–1818) and John Adey Repton (1775–1860)

Pen, ink and watercolour

Inscribed on Elevation and Ground Plan: 'Design for the pavilion at the end of the Terrace at Dyrham Park, Somersets:/to be build of Bath Stone/ Ground Plan of the same whether built with Stone or Wood/The same plan may suit this building of wood Covered with Bark of trees'

270 × 145mm (10⅝ × 5¾in)

National Trust (Blathwayt Collection), Dyrham Park, Gloucestershire

Humphry Repton visited Dyrham in September 1800 with his son John Adey, whom he had taken into partnership as architect only a few months before. Repton was paid £66 3s in 1801 and £24 3s in 1803, writing to William Blathwayt to acknowledge the last payment, 'being the balance of my Acct', but apologising that 'you did not receive the designs for the Stairs & Pavillon – which were sent a few days after the plan for the terraces'. Unfortunately no 'Red Book' survives and this drawing for a pavilion (at the west end of the long terrace seen on the left in Nos 5 and 6) is all that remains of his proposals. The building does not survive, if indeed it ever existed.

The style of draughtsmanship suggests that John Adey was chiefly responsible, with his father adding the trees and the strolling couple (for scale) in the perspective sketch. The alternative suggestion of bark to face the building instead of Bath stone looks back to earlier follies like Thomas Wright's 'Root House' at Badminton – besides representing a cheaper option.

Literature: Mitchell, 1977–8, p. 91, fig. 12.

86 View from the north front looking towards the Gothic Tower from the Wimpole 'Red Book', 1801

Humphry Repton (1752–1818)

Watercolour and pencil (with two flaps)

161 × 490mm (6⅜ × 19¼in) (inside drawn frame)

The National Trust (Bambridge Collection), Wimpole Hall, Cambridgeshire

In his manuscript *Memoir*, now in the British Library, Repton recalled how he came to make his reports for clients in the form of books, 'accompanied with maps and such sketches as at once shewed the present, and the proposed, portraits of the various scenes capable of improvement'. This idea came from 'my old friend Squire Marsham' (his Norfolk neighbour, Robert Marsham of Stratton Strawless), but 'the effect produced by my invention of the Slides made the Sketches interesting'. Not only were these charming watercolours to become his trademark, demanded by clients even when the extent of his 'improvements' scarcely justified it, but they were also to prove archetypal statements of the Picturesque style, setting out its principles with clarity and humour.

In all, Repton claimed to have produced over 400 of these 'Red Books' (called after the red morocco in which they were often bound), but only about 70 are known to have survived. The Wimpole book is one of the few to have been disbound, and its cover is now missing. Repton's preface, addressed to the 3rd Earl of Hardwicke, who was then serving as Lord Lieutenant in Ireland, shows that it was the result of two visits, in June and September 1801, and that the plans were finished in the following October.

As usual the text is somewhat verbose, but there are some key passages which cast light on his philosophy. Talking of the view from the north front of the house illustrated here, for instance, he comments: 'there is no part of Mr. Brown's system which I have had more difficulty in correcting than the absurd fashion of bringing cattle to the windows of a house. It is called natural, but to me it has ever appeared unnatural that a palace should rise immediately out of a sheep pasture...' Instead Repton recommended 'an iron rail that does not affect to be concealed' stretching between the ends of the two flanking wings, and enclosing a flower garden as 'a rich and appropriate foreground to the View'.

The Gothic Tower, built by Capability Brown after an earlier design by Sanderson Miller (see Nos 59 and 60), was praised as 'one of the best buildings of its kind extant' but the narrow view of it, framed by two heavy clumps of trees (shown on the overlay) was again to be improved – 'a glimpse of the distant hill and fine shape of ground on which it stands suggests the propriety of removing one of these clumps and loosening the other'. Besides this, Repton suggested adding 'two distant objects': a 'covered seat or shed' on the hillside seen on the far right, 'near where the Drive now finishes', and a sailing boat on the lake below. 'Although the water itself can never be seen from the house, yet the sail or mast of a vessel might, and it would... give a hint that water existed there.'

Design for the pavillon at the end of the Terrace at Dyrham Park. Somerset: to be built of Bath Stone

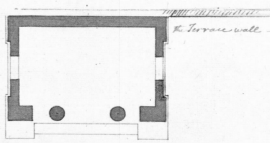

the Terrace wall

Ground Plan of the same whether built with Stone or Wood.

The same plan may suit this building of wood covered with Bark of trees.

85

Whether Lord Hardwicke succumbed to these verbal and visual blandishments is unlikely: the 'covered seat' was never built, and old trees from the left-hand clump still survive. However, iron railings set rather further away from the house, and with much larger urns on pedestals, were erected in the 1840s as part of H. E. Kendall's work for the 4th Earl (see Nos 96–100).

Literature: Stroud, 1979, figs. 9, 10.

Exhibited: Norwich and London, 1982–3, no. 33.

87 View of the lake, with an urn, from the Wimpole 'Red Book', 1801

Humphry Repton (1752–1818)

Pen, ink and watercolour

145 × 188mm (5¾ × 7⅜in) (inside drawn frame)

The National Trust (Bambridge Collection), Wimpole Hall, Cambridgeshire

Not all of the illustrations in Repton's 'Red Books' were equipped with slides or overlays. Some of his most poetic effects were achieved in monochrome or very simple colour washes, and show the value of the topographical views made early in his career when he was living in

Norfolk (see No. 79). This little sketch from the Wimpole Red Book shows part of Capability Brown's lake, with an urn on a pedestal placed on the far bank. This is probably one of the pair shown flanking the two clumps of trees on the overlay of No. 86, and identifiable with a pair shown in the same position in Greening's 1750s plan (No. 20).

After criticising 'Vases in the park, some of which have kept their ancient stations, altho' the trees which formerly accompanied them have been removed', Repton goes on to admit that 'there are certain situations in which some object is absolutely necessary to break the monotony of green; and

87

88

it is nowhere more desirable than in these dark recesses of water where it may be doubled by reflection. With this view I have supposed a vase placed in one of the bays... where a Painter's eye will instantly be aware of the great importance which may be derived from an Urn so placed or even a garden chair upon the margin of the water.' The view was engraved by John Peltro for William Peacock's almanac, *The Polite Repository*, representing the month of March 1803.

Exhibited: as No. 86.

88 Survey map of the park and farm showing proposed alterations, from the Wimpole 'Red Book', 1801
Humphry Repton (1752–1818)

Pen, ink and wash
Inscribed: 'Wimpole/Park and Farm/ belonging to the/Earl of Hardwicke/ Copied from the Original Plan in his Lordships possession/I have made use of this Map to explain/my opinion, altho the situation of/the trees is very inaccurately laid down/& many changes seem to have been made/since the survey was taken/H. Repton'
Scale: 1in to 12 chains
357 × 334mm (14¼ × 13¼in)
The National Trust (Bambridge Collection), Wimpole Hall, Cambridgeshire

The map from the Wimpole 'Red Book' is chiefly of interest in showing the trees Repton proposed to remove hatched out, and the different carriage drives – both for the approaches to the house, and for excursions round the park – indicated in different colours. The main drive from Cambridge via the old eastern avenue was indeed re-routed along these lines, looping northwards from Orwell Field to the edge of Cobb's Wood ('this wood being one of the principal game covers ought not perhaps to be disturbed'), and then southwards so as to approach the main entrance front at a satisfactory

angle. If Repton had had his way, the whole vast red-brick building would also have been coated in a limewash 'of the colour of Sussex or Suffolk bricks' to accord better with its landscape setting.

The number of different drives available through the park, a development from Capability Brown's single belt walk, encouraged the opening up of new vistas, like the one which 'would unite the lawns of No. 19 and 18', and open up a view of the 'row of cottages near the old kennel'. 'With the help of a wash over the bricks' (as shown in another of Repton's sketches), this would become 'as pleasing an object of its kind as the far more sumptuous and costly buildings at the Tower and upon the hill' (see Nos 60 and 61). The Tower itself, with its curtain walls clearly visible here, on Johnson's Hill, was to be 'made more useful, by adding floors in the Tower and outbuildings in the yards behind to form a keeper's lodge', while the ground floor of 'Athenian' Stuart's Park Building (No. 61; due west of the house on this plan) was also to be made into a labourer's cottage, with a 'prospect room' above, changing the central bay into an open loggia. Both these changes appear to have been made, and a great deal of overgrown timber removed (though not as much as Repton intended), so the Wimpole Red Book was not as ineffective as has sometimes been thought.

Literature: Stroud, 1979, fig. 12.
Exhibited: as No. 86.

89 Elevation and ground plan for the conservatory at Tatton Park, Cheshire, c.1812
Lewis Wyatt (1777–1853)

Pen, ink and watercolour
Inscribed: 'Plan of a Conservatory for Mrs. Egerton. Tatton Park/NB The roofs will be form'd with a glass lantern/the Sizes and forms of the beds – and lead flats over the Walks/ The blue lines represent iron columns and arch'd/ribs to support the roofs – and form'd for Climbing plants'
Scale: 1in to 10ft
510 × 330mm (20⅛ × 13in)
The National Trust (Egerton Collection), Tatton Park, Cheshire

The rebuilding of Tatton Park was begun by Samuel Wyatt in the 1770s but only completed by his nephew Lewis between 1808 and 1816, working for Wilbraham Egerton and his wife Elizabeth Sykes. A design for the conservatory is recorded as being exhibited at the Royal Academy in 1812, though it appears not to have been built until 1818. The dedication to Mrs Egerton is interesting and suggests that the building may have been inspired by the large conservatory at her old family home, Sledmere in Yorkshire – where Samuel Wyatt was again involved.

Probably influenced by his cousin Jeffry Wyatville's conservatory at Belton (No. 91), exhibited at the Academy only the year before, Lewis Wyatt's design for Tatton is wonderfully assured, achieving more by proportion than decoration – here confined to the Doric pilasters and the small square panels in the parapet above.

The drawing shows the original form of the roof, with a glazed lantern directly over the long central bed, and lead flats over the surrounding walks. The resulting effect of light and shade was lost when a new, entirely glazed, roof was substituted first by Joseph Paxton or his son-in-law G. H. Stokes, who were responsible

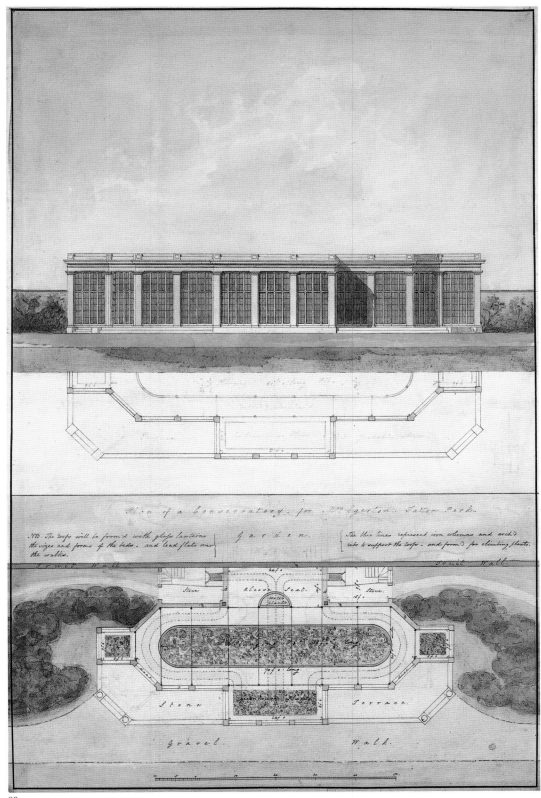

Plan of a Conservatory, for Mᵗ Egerton. Tatton Park.

N.B. The roofs will be form'd with glass lanterns the shape and forms of the beds, and lead flats over the walks.

Garden.

The thin lines represent iron columns and arch'd ribs to support the roofs, and form'd for climbing plants.

Fruit Wall   Fruit Wall

Stove   Alcove Seat.   Stove

Stone   Terrace.

Gravel.   Walk.

89

90

for the neighbouring Fernery, about 1859, and again at the end of the century. The original roof was carried on cast-iron columns, some of which still survive, and which also functioned as rainwater down-pipes. The two central lower lights of each bay were intended to open with direct access on to the terrace and steps, but these were also replaced by larger plate-glass panes about 1900. Similar plate-glass panes were also inserted in the lower lights.

Very few architects' plans of this date show planting schemes in such detail, but Lewis Wyatt's interest in horticulture is demonstrated by another drawing in the collection at Tatton, dated 1814, showing a kidney-shaped garden with an alcove seat in trelliswork: possibly one that still survives, rechristened Lady Charlotte's Arbour. The hot air flues are also clearly shown below the stone paving, fed by two

stoves in sunken areas at the back, approached by short staircases. These flues pass under a small pond in the central alcove intended for tropical 'water plants'.

90 View of the conservatory at Tatton Park, Cheshire, 1820

John Buckler (1770–1851)

Watercolour

Signed: 'J. Buckler', and dated

250 × 375 mm (9⅞ × 14¾ in)

The National Trust (Egerton Collection), Tatton Park, Cheshire

About 1820, Wilbraham and Elizabeth Egerton celebrated the completion of the rebuilding of Tatton by commissioning four watercolours from the leading topographical artist of the day, John Buckler. These consisted of a view of the south front, the interior of the library, Lewis Wyatt's Knutsford Lodge built in the form

of a triumphal arch, and finally – a measure of the importance they attached to it – his new conservatory in the garden to the west of the house.

Buckler's view is of particular interest in showing the planting round the conservatory, with irregular-shaped flower beds on the lawn in the foreground; greenhouse pots brought out and arranged on the steps to the left; and a rockery and shelter belt of trees and shrubs concealing the low service wing of the house. Wyatt's work on the garden was carried out in conjunction with John Webb, who is credited with 'improvements' at Tatton in Neale's *Views of Seats*, published in 1818, and who also worked at several other Cheshire houses: Oulton Park, Somerford, Rode Hall, Bradwell Manor and Eaton Hall. At Oulton he was described as a pupil of 'the celebrated landscape gardener,

120

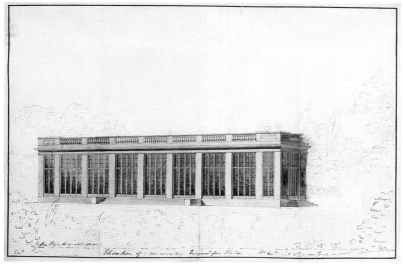

91

The orangery and rose garden at Belton House, Lincolnshire

William Eames [Emes]' (see No. 76).

The trellis arches to the left led into the alcoves shown on Wyatt's ground plan (No. 89), giving access to the stoves, and this trelliswork was continued right round the back wall of the interior of the conservatory. Some of Repton's designs show similar devices, helping to dissolve the boundaries between internal and external architecture. Buckler also demonstrates that the plants – mostly camellias and magnolias rather than climbers – were only grown up to the top of the trellis, or in other words, the level of the main transoms of the windows. The lusher effects of later palm houses, imitating tropical rainforests, were a Victorian development yet to come, aided by more sophisticated heating.

91 Perspective design for the conservatory at Belton House, Lincolnshire, 1810

Sir Jeffry Wyatville (1766–1840)

Pen and ink, pencil & watercolour
Inscribed: 'Jeffry Wyatt Archt 1810/ Elevation of a Conservatory designed for Belton – Rt. Honble Lord Brownlow'; verso 'Perspective Drawing of the Conservatory for Belton [etc.]'

$337 \times 500mm$ ($13\frac{1}{4} \times 19\frac{5}{8}$in)
The National Trust (Brownlow Collection), Belton House, Lincolnshire

The major Georgian changes to the seventeenth-century house at Belton were made by James Wyatt in 1776–8. But from 1809 onwards the 1st Earl Brownlow employed Wyatt's nephew Jeffry (afterwards Wyatville) to make alterations to the interior, including the creation of a new library. Soon afterwards the architect submitted plans for the whole area previously occupied by the kitchen gardens, and now known as the Italian Garden. His main proposal was for a large conservatory to be built near the site of the original manor house, and next to the medieval parish church, which still survives. This was to look south, over a circular 'bason' with a fountain, towards a dairy in the form of a small classical temple. However, the latter was never built and its place was finally taken by the Lion Fountain and exedra (see below, No. 92).

This sketch is probably a study for a finished watercolour, exhibited at the Royal Academy in 1811. But a number of more detailed drawings for the conservatory are dated 1819–20, and the long delay in building may have been partly caused by the death of the Earl's first wife, Sophia Hume. The design incorporates two quite modern features for its time: a wrought-iron supporting structure carrying a timber-framed roof and sliding sashes; and a balustrade of artificial stone round the parapet. The account books of the Coade Manufactory of Lambeth for 1819–20 record the delivery of 183 'small balusters [to] Earl Brownlow, Mr. Jeffry Wyatt, Architect'. The latter also provided a drawing for the internal layout showing the position of the beds, two aviaries, and the central pond with its statue of Flora. The six statues crowning the parapet are not shown in a sketch of the Italian Garden attributed to Elizabeth Cust, c.1821, and were added later, probably again in the 1850s.

Pared down to the bare essentials, with plain piers where others might have used a classical order (see No. 89), Wyatville's design is functional yet supremely elegant: a masterpiece of the genre, which he did much to develop during the second and third decades of the century. By comparison with his similar conservatories at Longleat (c.1814), Bretton Hall, Yorkshire (1815), Woburn Abbey, Chatsworth and the Aroid House at Kew (1836), Belton is chaste and understated,

92

achieving more by proportion than decoration. The interior survives intact, with the exception of the roof, which was replaced in 1857 with a totally glazed version. As at Tatton (No. 89) this change introduced more light at a time when tropical plants were becoming increasingly fashionable. Several very old camellias survive inside the conservatory.

92 Design for the Lion Fountain at Belton House, Lincolnshire, c.1817

Attributed to Sir Jeffry Wyatville (1766–1840)

Pen, ink and watercolour
Watermark: Turkey Mills J. Whatman 1817
Scale: 1in to 2ft
330 × 217mm (13 × 8½in)
The National Trust (Brownlow Collection), Belton House, Lincolnshire

The Lion Fountain at Belton forms the central section of an exedra, that favourite form of Roman garden building, revived in the Italian Renaissance, and again by William Kent at Chiswick and Stowe in the early eighteenth century (see No. 37). However, in this case, the ten niches in the surviving wing walls contain ledges for flowerpots rather than seats for disputing scholars and orators. The lion's mask itself is thought to be by Richard Westmacott, who was much employed at Belton in these years.

As originally designed by Wyatville for the 1st Earl Brownlow, the exedra was the main feature of the Dell, a damp and shady area planted mostly with evergreens, immediately to the west of the Italian Garden. Pedestals were being built there in 1816, according to the accounts – implying further urns or statues – and a trellis for climbing plants was erected in the following year. It was only in 1921 that the fountain and exedra were moved to their present position on the southern edge of the Italian Garden, on axis with the centre of the conservatory.

93 Designs for a flower stand and a basket container for flowers at Belton House, Lincolnshire, 1818

Elizabeth Cust (1776–1858)

Pen, ink, pencil and watercolour on laid paper

Watermark: 1815

Inscribed: 'Design for La *Citadelle de Flore*/being a hors d'oeuvre on each side of the north/Steps at Belton by/E. C. P. O. T./January 12 1818'

(a) 187 × 230mm (7⅜ × 9in)
(b) 105 × 185mm (4¼ × 7¼in)

The National Trust (Brownlow Collection), Belton House, Lincolnshire

These two charming amateur drawings for flower baskets and boxes are by Elizabeth Cust, eldest daughter of the 1st Baron

Brownlow, then living at Belton with her brother, who had recently been raised to an earldom. In a note of 'Works designed and executed by members of the family' drawn up by the 3rd Earl in 1896, the 'Hon. Miss Cust and the Hon. Miss Lucy Cust' are credited with the 'pictures in each end of the alcove in the library' – roundels in James Wyatt's plasterwork which still survive, and which have wrongly been attributed to Biagio Rebecca – a 'lunette (unfinished) in the ante-library', a portrait of their brother

Richard Cust 'in his "Montem [ie Eton College] dress"', and lithograph views of Belton church and village. In addition the Earl records that 'the garden seats were designed, and executed by them – the little room at the back of the Conservatory was their workshop'.

It is significant that the drawing for the large flower boxes on the north front steps is dated 1818, for it was in that year that Wyatville replaced the balustrade round the roof of the house (removed by his uncle, James Wyatt, in the 1770s),

93a

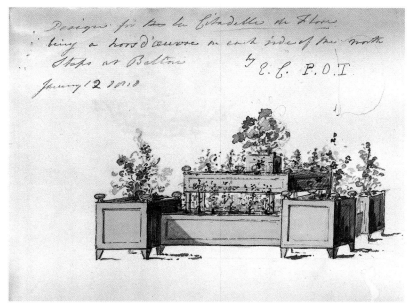

93b

and made other major changes indoors and out. The sketches also illustrate the accomplishments of ladies in the Regency period, not only confined to needlework, shellwork, silhouette-cutting and other genteel occupations.

94 Design for a parterre at Cliveden, Buckinghamshire, c.1835

Comte Alfred d'Orsay (1801–52)

Watercolour with faint pencil drawing on left

Inscribed: 'D'orsay fecit', and, bottom right: 'Je Conseille a Sir G. Warrender s'il adopte le Plan, de placer des Statues en marbre aussi que des Vases, car cela correspondroit avec le Style du Jardin et l'Architecture de la Maison.'

475 × 670mm (18¾ × 26⅜in)

The Viscount Astor

Painter, sculptor, collector and dandy, the Comte d'Orsay is best known for his long affair with his mother-in-law, the Countess of Blessington, who was also among

Byron's closest friends. The couple lived in London (though very respectably, in neighbouring houses) from 1831 until 1849, when his debts obliged him to return to Paris, taking her with him.

Sir George Warrender, who had bought the burnt-out shell of Cliveden in 1824 and rebuilt it to designs by William Burn, moved in the fashionable London circles to which d'Orsay and Lady Blessington belonged – and where he was nicknamed Sir Gorgious Provender.

This design appears to be for the main parterre on the east of the house overlooked by William Winde's terrace, and with sensational views down on to the Thames below (see No. 10). However, it may exclude the raised circular platform at the far end, created by Lord Orkney to give some relief to the plainness of what he called his 'quaker parterre'. D'Orsay's scheme, including formal flower beds with orange trees in Versailles tubs at the

corners, a large central fountain, a row of vases and the possibility of additional statues (as suggested in the inscription), looks forward to Charles Barry's parterre designs of the 1850s, made for a new owner, the Duke of Sutherland – and the somewhat simplified planting that remains today.

Literature: Jackson-Stops, 1976–7, p. 111, fig. 18.

95 Design for the garden at The Argory, Co. Armagh, 1821

Arthur (fl. 1820s) and John Williamson (d. 1831?)

Pen, ink and watercolour, with pencilled additions

Signed and dated

Inscribed: 'A Map/for laying out the site/of the Garden and sundry/Building &c &c at/Derrycaw County/Armagh/Belonging to/Walter McGeough Esqr/A. & J. Williamson Archts/November 23d 1821'

Scale: 1ft to 30ft

94

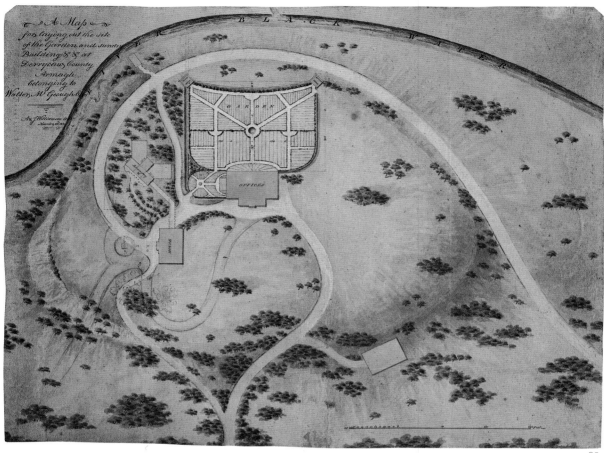

460 × 606mm (18⅛ × 23⅞in)

The National Trust (MacGeough Bond
Collection), The Argory, Co. Armagh,
Northern Ireland

The Argory is a Greek Revival
villa on the banks of the River
Blackwater, the dividing line
between County Armagh and
County Tyrone, west of
Portadown. The house was built
for Walter McGeough in 1819–24
by the architect brothers Arthur
and John Williamson of Dublin,
pupils of the more celebrated
Francis Johnston, and this drawing
shows that they also designed the
surviving walled garden behind the
stable yard, with a gently curving
rampart wall at the far end
overlooking the river, and
terminating in a 'pump house' and

'garden house' at either end. In a
letter of April 1823, the builder
Thomas Duff of Newry warns
Walter McGeough that 'the Rock
work of the Rampart wall &c I
think is enormously dear', and the
carpenter's accounts for the
following year include the
'ornamental Dwarf sashes for. . .
the Garden houses'. So these
charming little pavilions, with their
shallow-pitched roofs and central
chimneys, must then have been
nearing completion.

Apart from some formally
trained yew arbours in the centre,
little of the original planting
survives, and what was probably a
combined flower and vegetable
garden has now become a more
conventional Victorian pleasure-
ground with specimen trees and

shrubs. However, the small circular
garden to the west of the offices
still survives, with old roses in box-
edged beds, and a central sundial
by Lynch and Sons of Dublin,
dated 1820.

In the early 1830s, the house was
enlarged by the addition of a wing
to the north, and at that point a
new forecourt was made on the
east, while the previous main drive
passing below the rampart and the
two pavilions became merely a
garden path.

Literature: Jackson-Stops, 1983,
p. 24, fig. 12.

96–100 Five designs for the conservatory at Wimpole Hall, Cambridgeshire, c.1842

Henry Edward Kendall (1776–1875)

Watercolour

North, south and west elevations: 510 × 830mm (20⅛ × 32¾in); ground plan: 310 × 540mm (21¼ × 12¼in); interior perspective: 850 × 560mm (33½ × 22in)

The National Trust (Bambridge Collection), Wimpole Hall, Cambridgeshire

The original orangery at Wimpole, built by the 2nd Earl of Radnor between 1693 and 1707, was a large detached block to the left of the south, or entrance, front – balancing the service wing to the right (see No. 17). Gibbs's addition of a library and ante-room on this side of the house had the effect of joining the orangery to the main block, as seen in Robert Greening's plan (No. 20). About 1806, the 3rd Earl of Hardwicke commissioned Soane to remodel the ante-room as a second library, with large french windows leading down a short flight of steps into the orangery; and three years later the latter was converted into an up-to-date conservatory by Humphry Repton, and his son John Adey.

The 4th Earl, a naval captain (known in the family as 'Blowhard'), succeeded in 1834, became Lord-in-Waiting to Queen Victoria in 1841, and entertained her and the Prince Consort at Wimpole in 1843. Perhaps because he felt it should be fit to receive crowned heads – particularly after visits to Berlin and St Petersburg, as guest of the King of Prussia and the Tsar – the Earl embarked on a series of grandiose additions to the house, designed by Henry Kendall, a pupil of Thomas Leverton and John Nash, and apparently costing over £100,000. These included the complete rebuilding of the service wing on the east, and the addition of a porch, heavy balustrade and massive central chimneystack to the

main block, visible in the drawing of the west elevation (No. 98). With a letter to Lord Hardwicke dated 7 February 1840, Kendall also sent 'a proposal for altering the west wing to approximate in a great measure with the proposed new East wing without taking down the same, except the extremity which would be rendered necessary for the construction of a similar Tower to that Eastward. I should also propose putting on a glazed Roof and having carried out the same features in Decoration of Ballustrade etc. as characterize the new Building.'

The idea of a conservatory leading out of a library, as illustrated in Repton's *Fragments* of 1816, was adopted by many country-house architects in the Regency period, and remained a popular idea throughout the Victorian period – perhaps most notably at Capesthorne in Cheshire, where the conservatory was designed by Paxton about 1837, and Flintham Hall in Nottinghamshire, of 1851–4, where both rooms rise through two storeys. If there was a new development here, it was the far bolder architectural treatment of the conservatory from the late 1830s onwards, urged by writers in the *Builder* and other magazines, and reacting against the plainer, more utilitarian, glass-houses which J. C. Loudon and his followers had advocated in the previous decade. At the same time, the conservatory also began to take on the role of sculpture gallery, with nymphs crouching among succulent ferns, and vases and sarcophagi used as tubs for plants.

Kendall's designs for the Wimpole conservatory perfectly illustrate these trends, and at the same time show him to have been one of the great architectural draughtsmen of his day. The bold red-brick walls with contrasting stone ornaments are in an Italianate Baroque style probably intended as

a tribute to Gibbs – like the cupola of Kendall's neighbouring stable block. As such, they are also an interesting precursor of the 'Queen Anne' style later popularised by Norman Shaw. The urns along the balustrade match those on the south parapet of the main block, which were made of terracotta by M. H. Blanchard. The fountain shown on the north side of the conservatory, on axis with the tower, could also have come from Blanchard's manufactory in Lambeth, along with other decorative elements inside and out.

The ground plan shows the formal garden setting which Kendall proposed for the conservatory in more detail. Vast numbers of urns on pedestals, and axial paths and sets of gate-piers, create an opulent Mediterranean feel, appropriate to the tender plants housed within. The large potting ground, backing on to the blank back wall of Gibbs's library, is a reminder of the huge amounts of plants constantly being brought in and out of the house and conservatory, and in need of repotting: a small lobby off Soane's Book Room (here called the 'Anti-Library') was also provided, so that the indoor servants could collect them from the gardeners and vice versa.

Both the ground plan and the interior perspective show the floor covered in brightly coloured encaustic tiles, very like some of the Minton tiles (incorporating the Hardwicke motto and monogram) which Kendall laid in the entrance hall. The interior itself could hardly be more eclectic: the hammerbeam roof looks back to Elizabethan great halls like that at Burghley; the great shell doorcase to the Book Room is Italian Renaissance in style; the arabesque pattern of the tiles is more Spanish; while the statues and vases look back still further to the worlds of ancient Greece and Rome.

The colza-oil chandeliers help to

96

97

98

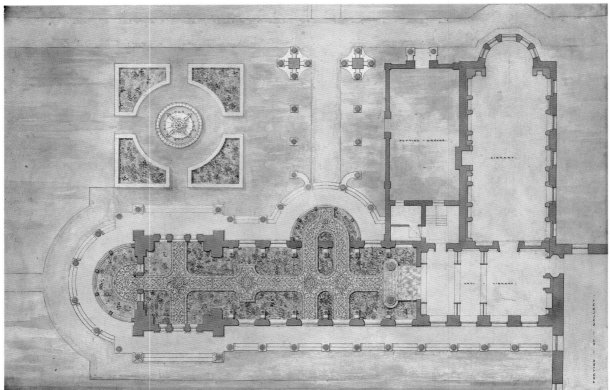

99

100

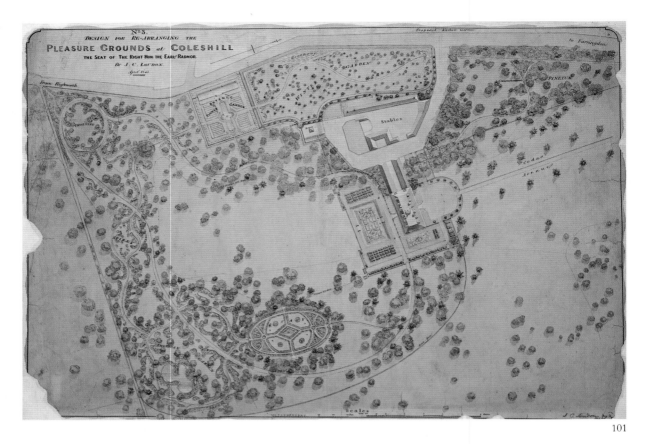

give the effect of a lived-in room rather than a mere greenhouse, and would have enabled the conservatory to be used after dark, especially as a retiring room during the great balls which the 4th Earl had in mind.

The effect must have been like that of the great winter garden at Somerleyton in Suffolk, erected about 1866 but demolished in 1912. Sadly, the Wimpole conservatory was to share its fate. After the depredations of the Second World War, when the house was occupied by the army, its owner Mrs Bambridge (Rudyard Kipling's daughter) employed the architect Trenwith Wills to demolish both the east and west wings with their towers. Only a few relics, such as the bronze lamps on the staircase leading up to the front door, now remain to tell of this extravagant and eccentric edifice.

101 Design for the garden at Coleshill, Berkshire, 1843

John Claudius Loudon
(1783–1843)

Watercolour with ink and pencil
Signed and dated
Inscribed: 'No 3/Design for Re-Arranging the Pleasure/Grounds at Coleshill/The Seat of the Right Hon: The Earl of Radnor/By J.C. Loudon/April 1843'
Scale: 1in to approx. 50ft
580 × 840mm (22¾ × 33in)
National Trust (on loan to Berkshire County Record Office)

John Claudius Loudon, the son of a Scottish farmer, became, in the words of his American contemporary A.J. Downing 'the most distinguished gardening author of the age'. His designs for individual commissions, often reproduced in his books, were also very influential, although as his

career progressed he was more concerned with public parks and botanical gardens (including squares in London and other cities) than in the private gardens of great country houses. This was in keeping with his firm liberal convictions, which earned him the friendship of Jeremy Bentham.

Curiously, it was these advanced political views which must have led to one of Loudon's most important private commissions, carried out in the last year of his life and among the finest of all his landscape designs. William Pleydell-Bouverie, 3rd Earl of Radnor, was for nearly half a century considered 'the most radical and reform-minded aristocrat in England', and was also a close associate of Bentham. His estate at Coleshill in Berkshire was run on the most progressive lines, and he first employed Loudon as early as 1814 to design a ducted hot-air system for the house. After 1828, when he succeeded his father, he moved to the main family seat, Longford Castle, near Salisbury, but continued to spend several months every summer at Coleshill.

Loudon's three alternative plans for the grounds were drawn up in the spring of 1843, each more elaborate than the last, and culminating in the drawing shown here. These plans were clearly meant to speak for themselves, and his accompanying *Report* gives little more than a breakdown of the expenses: in this case requiring an outlay of about £10,200 and a staff of one gardener, one groundsman and three labourers.

Early on in his career, Loudon's gardens were entirely irregular in plan, influenced by the picturesque principles of Uvedale Price. By this time, however, the French theorist Quatremère de Quincy had inspired a return to regular layouts in the 'ancient style', combined with a type of planting known as the 'gardenesque', which required each variety to be displayed to its best advantage – usually marshalled together to form what he saw as a perfect combination of art and science.

These principles are clearly demonstrated in the Coleshill design, covering some 50 acres. The original formal gardens surrounding Roger Pratt's famous seventeenth-century house (usually attributed to Inigo Jones in the nineteenth century) had been swept away in the late eighteenth century during the vogue for 'natural landscape'. Loudon proposed to restore some formality to the immediate surroundings, with a cedar avenue on the main approach, and flower gardens and fountains on the south and west. The main parterre (on the west) fills a sunken terrace so that its geometrical forms could be clearly read from the windows of the house, while at the same time it would be barely visible from the

102

open meadow beyond – only enough to increase the apparent height of the building. A gravelled walk round the perimeter of this meadow would then introduce visitors to a succession of specialised gardens with contrasting characters and shapes: the rosary, the American garden, the spiraea garden, the thornery, the botanic flower garden, the winter garden (including a heathery) and finally the pinetum. A curving ha-ha separated this garden area from the park to the south, while the meadow in the centre would have a 'strained wire fence' to enclose grazing sheep or cattle.

Some of Loudon's recommendations for tree planting may have been carried out after his death, but very few features shown on the plan are now discernible, and it is unlikely that Lord Radnor actually carried out much of the scheme. Coleshill House was tragically gutted by fire in 1952 and subsequently demolished, though the parkland (with some of Pratt's outstanding stone gate-piers) still belongs to the National Trust.

Literature: Simo, 1988, pp. 185–7, fig. 81.

102 View of Sudbury Hall, Derbyshire, with a Gothick gazebo c.1770

Samuel Botham

Pen, ink and wash

Signed: Saml. Botham delint

115 × 240mm (4½ × 9¾in)

The National Trust (Vernon Collection), Sudbury Hall, Derbyshire

Sudbury is largely the creation of one man, George Vernon, who succeeded in 1660 and almost immediately began to rebuild the old manor house, probably to his own designs. The elaborate formal gardens which he laid out to the south are shown in a bird's-eye view by Jan Griffier. However, his parterre with its walls and gate-piers, statues and fountains, was swept away by his grandson, the 1st Lord Vernon, who 'naturalised' the landscape in the manner of Capability Brown.

A serpentine lake was made out of the straight-sided canal shown in the foreground of Griffier's picture, the old avenues were reduced to clumps of trees, and an extensive deer-park laid out to the north. At the centre of this park Lord Vernon built a large Gothick deercote, which still exists, and

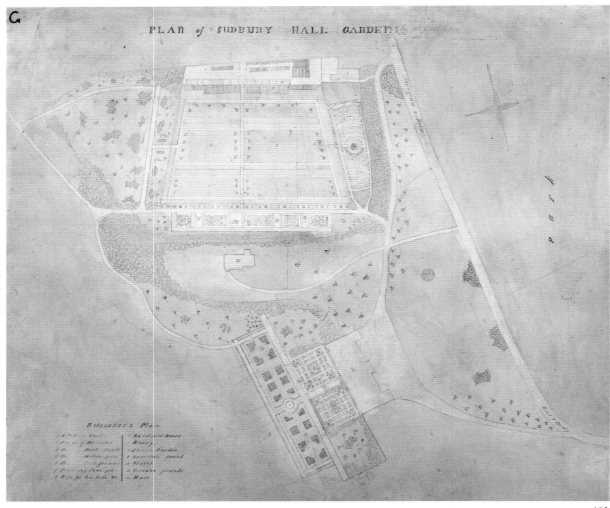

which may have been designed by the same architect as the long-vanished Gothick summer-house shown on the right in Botham's view.

Bishop Pococke, who visited Sudbury some time between 1751 and 1765, noted that 'a serpentine river runs through the lawn behind the house, and in the park is a square arcade, with a turret at each corner [ie the deercote], and trees being planted about it, through which it is seen, has a very fine effect...' (Pococke, 1888–9, p. 219).

Nothing is known of Samuel Botham, who may have been an amateur artist in the locality.

103 Design for the garden at Sudbury Hall, Derbyshire, c.1830–5

William Sawrey Gilpin (1762–1843)

Pen, ink and wash
Inscribed with the letter 'G' at top left; and the title 'Plan of Sudbury Hall Gardens' with the pencil addition 'by Mr. Gilpin'. The key at bottom left, entitled 'References to Plan' lists '1 Kitchen Garden/2 Range of Hot houses/3 Do. ... Back-sheds/4 Do. ... Mellon pits/5 Do. ... Cold frames/ 6 Fruteing Pine-pit/7 Beds for Sea-kale &c./8 Gardeners House/9 Rosery/ 10 Flower Garden/11 American ground/12 Church/13 Terrace grounds/ 14 Hall.'

520 × 635 mm (20½ × 25 in)
The National Trust (Vernon Collection), Sudbury Hall, Derbyshire

The 4th Lord Vernon, who succeeded to Sudbury in 1829, married the daughter and heiress of a Cheshire landowner, Sir John Borlase Warren, and it was evidently her fortune which encouraged ambitious plans for the remodelling of the house and garden in the following decade. It is not entirely clear when W. S. Gilpin first arrived on the scene, but it was evidently before Lord Vernon's death in 1835, for the formal parterre beds on this plan correspond with another drawing in the collection, which is annotated in the 5th Baron's hand: 'Copied by my Father from the plan of the Garden at Dereys Cross – near London (Lord Ravensworth's) with these exceptions that the walls there of fine yellowish gravel with white brick borders rounded at the top. This was not adopted at Sudbury 1st on accont of expense & 2ndly from doubt as to whether being close to gravel walk the effect would be counteracted – Grass Walks have disadvantages 1st damp 2ndly that the walks get uneven & 3rdly labour of mowing and rolling.'

In a fascinating letter, dated 20 August 1837, and written to his cousin Vice-Admiral Octavius Vernon-Harcourt, Lord Vernon writes: '. . . Mr Paxton from Chatsworth has promised to come here on Tuesday afternoon so as to meet Gilpin on Wednesday . . . Mr. Paxton quite agrees with you about the Lower Terrace. Gilpin is an old man and Heaven knows when one may see him here again . . . so much was done last year that I do not wish to do anything this year but planting or cutting down trees and altering a little the form of the groups on the lower Terrace.' He then goes on to acknowledge the Admiral's own 'advice and assistance', admitting that 'not being a draughtsman I cannot originate things so well myself'. The fountain, seen in the centre of the lower terrace on Gilpin's drawing, 'looks pretty, but . . . I do not think the Basin large enough and . . . instead of a good broad jet from the boy's conch it is a weak piddling concern . . .'.

The meeting of the 75-year-old Gilpin with the 34-year-old Joseph Paxton – later to achieve fame as the architect of the Crystal Palace – aptly symbolises the moment of transition from the old-fashioned Picturesque style to the grandiose formality of Victorian bedding-out.

W. S. Gilpin was the nephew and pupil of one of the great pioneers of the Picturesque, the author and watercolourist William Gilpin. His own book, *Practical Hints upon Landscape Gardening*, published in 1832, was one of the last to advocate Uvedale Price's extreme form of landscape aesthetics. Yet in his later commissions, like Scotney Castle in Kent and Balcaskie in Scotland, he uses formal terraces to overlook painterly, naturalistic scenes. Sir Walter Scott described the garden at Balcaskie as 'in the good old style with its terraces and yew hedges. The beastly fashion of bringing a bare ill sheared park up to your very door seems going down' (Tait, 1980, p. 228).

The same ideas can be found in this design for Sudbury, with two broad formal terraces below the house on the south, overlooking the lake; a formal flower garden with intricately shaped beds beyond the church, next to the walled kitchen garden; and a contrasting American Garden, with trees and shrubs in asymmetrical beds of curious zig-zag outline, closely corresponding with plates in his *Practical Hints* (Tait, 1980, plate 147). Much of this scheme was certainly implemented, including the two terraces – but excluding the intricate beds on the upper level, already referred to.

Gilpin may also have introduced the architect Anthony Salvin to the 5th Lord Vernon, for the two were working as partners at Scotney in 1837, and in the very same year Salvin produced designs for turning Sudbury into another Harlaxton, bristling with gables, towers, cupolas and strapwork balustrades. Fortunately, Lord Vernon rejected this plan, and two years later shut up the house and went to live in Italy, where he remained for much of the rest of his life.

The initial 'G' on the top of this plan is almost certainly a mistake for 'C': a key at the front of the

folder of architectural drawings at Sudbury attributes those in the latter category to 'Mr. Gilpin' and those in the former to 'Mr. Nesfield' (see No. 104). Other drawings by Gilpin, correctly marked 'C', include an alternative sketch for the planting of the lower terrace, and a design for two large benches with panelled back and sides, to stand at either end of the long cross-walk between the two terraces.

104 Design for the garden at Sudbury Hall, Derbyshire, 1852

William Andrews Nesfield (1793–1881)

Pen, ink and wash

Signed and dated: 'W. A. Nesfield/ 5 York Terrace/Regents Park/Sep^{r}'

Inscribed at top left with the letter 'G'; at top right 'No. 1 Detailed Plan of proposed architectural treatment of Approach Parterres &c.'; along right hand edge 'The red lines shew the present surface of Terraces &c.'; and on left 'NB. An incorrect distance from the landing place to the Island is purposely given to avoid an otherwise elongation of this Plan'

Scale: 1in to 40ft (plan); 1in to 20ft (sections)

810 × 565mm ($31\frac{7}{8}$ × $22\frac{1}{4}$in)

The National Trust (Vernon Collection), Sudbury Hall, Derbyshire

If Salvin's introduction to the 5th Lord Vernon came through W. S. Gilpin, he in turn recommended his own brother-in-law, W. A. Nesfield, to succeed Gilpin as landscape designer at Sudbury. In a letter of 7 October 1851, he gave his patron Nesfield's address and added 'I believe he charges 5 gns per day & travelling expenses'. Despite Lord Vernon's prolonged absences in Italy, where he became a leading authority on Dante, many alterations had continued to be made to the house by Salvin, and the idea of a grander formal garden descending all the way to the lake may have suggested itself after visits to the Italian lakes, with their villa gardens dating back to the Renaissance.

Nesfield, a painter by training, had first achieved fame in the 1840s for his work on the Royal Botanic Gardens, Kew. His 'General Observations & Remedial Propositions' submitted to Lord Vernon with this plan, in September 1852, amounts to a devastating attack on Gilpin's earlier work. In place of the 'diagonal Approaches' to the house ('common-place, modern & quite out of harmony with its style'), he proposed an axial drive and paved stone courtyard lined with junipers and Portugal laurels. On the other side of the house 'the great flaw in the whole scene' was the way in which 'the general lines run parallel with the House' instead of away from it, preventing any kind of 'agreeable perspective'. In general, 'neither the design nor the quality of the details are after the manner of "the olden time", but modern and nondescript.'

Nesfield's answer was to propose 'a total reconstruction of the present artificial surface', with a central vista towards the island in the lake, and terraces of very much larger scale giving longitudinal rather than transverse vistas. As at Worsley Hall in Lancashire, his parterre beds (aligned on the two bay windows of the south front) are based on a design from Dezallier d'Argenville's *Theory and Practice of Gardening*, translated into English by John James in 1712: a scholarly approach to 'olden-time' gardening that was quite new at this date. A very full key to the plan (amounting to five pages of foolscap) also survives at Sudbury, and reveals many details that were to become hallmarks of his later work. These include the avenue of standard roses flanking the central walk between the two *broderie* parterres (marked 5); the use of crushed red tiles and cream-coloured Derbyshire spar to

contrast with the cut box and beds of low flowers in the *broderie* itself (marked N); the many statues and vases; the large blocks of rhododendrons edged with azaleas on the lower terrace (marked 18); and the planting of Halmias (16), *Yucca gloriosa* (17) and Irish yew (21).

The central path in this lower section was to have a 'chain of broad beds for tall flowers, such as Dahlias or Holyhocks (on the circles) edged with Box upon gravel' (Q), while at each end of the Lake Terrace there was to be a 'Pavilion and Bastion' (X), flanked by 'Beds edged with Box for dwarf Roses'. Nesfield found the existing island in the lake too central to be satisfactory as an irregular feature, and thus proposed 'to treat this geometrically so as to form an Apex to the entire arrangement'. The intention was to construct 'a Pavilion seat as a commanding Architectural feature', here backed by a mass of Portugal laurel which would also serve as 'a breeding place for Aquatic birds'.

Lord Vernon was not in the end persuaded by these arguments, and the 'large Plans & Sections to a working scale', which Nesfield offered to draw up as a next stage, seem never to have been executed. However, the plan remains one of his most interesting, on a par with his classical Italianate gardens that survive at Castle Howard and Broughton Hall in Yorkshire, Holkham Hall in Norfolk, and Witley Court in Worcestershire.

105 Design for the garden at Kingston Lacy, Dorset, *c.*1835
Sir Charles Barry (1795–1860)

Watercolour and pencil
Inscribed: 'No. [blank] Kingston Lacy/ Design for Terrace flower garden &c'; on blue areas under terrace 'Violet Beds', with 'Grass border' below; on green areas at end of parterre 'Evergreen border'
Scale: 1in to 20ft
440 × 570mm (17¼ × 22½in)
The National Trust (Bankes Collection), Kingston Lacy, Dorset

This drawing, combining elevations of the south and east fronts of Kingston Lacy with a plan of the parterre and terraces immediately adjoining the house, shows the care Charles Barry took to integrate his buildings with their surroundings. Perhaps more than any other great Victorian architect, he was interested in the details of garden planning, and his masterpieces in this field – Trentham, Cliveden and Shrublands – were achieved with the close collaboration of three outstanding horticulturists: respectively George and John Fleming, and Donald Benton.

At Kingston Lacy, he found a client, William John Bankes, who was perfectly in tune with his Italianate tastes, and turning to Rubens's *Palazzi di Genova* for inspiration, they completely remodelled the 1660s house designed by Sir Roger Pratt, but already greatly altered by R. F. Brettingham in the 1780s. The work began in 1835 and was largely completed by 1841, when Bankes was prosecuted for a sexual indiscretion and went to live in exile in Italy. This drawing is likely to be early in date, for it shows several architectural features not found in the executed building: notably the triangular pediment over the south front door (which was to become segmental), and two small extra dormers on the east front (which were to be omitted).

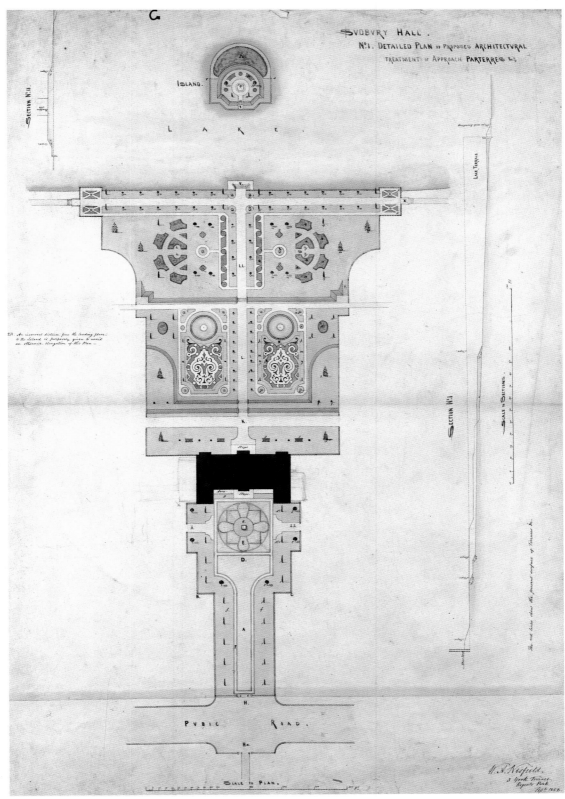

From Brettingham's time, the main entrance to the house had been on the east, by way of a sunken forecourt. Barry reverted to Sir Roger Pratt's original intention and made the entrance on the north, though at the lower (basement) level, under a new *porte-cochère*. The old forecourt then became a formal parterre, overlooked by the great arched windows of the loggia, which not only formed a broad half-landing on Barry's new marble staircase, but also acted as a garden entrance with a double flight of steps outside, descending to the parterre. The marble staircase was almost complete by December 1837, when Bankes wrote to his brother: 'there is no staircase in England equal to it, not even Wardour, and not

many that surpass it in Italy. I delight in the rich Eastern external Loggia which is finished...'

Whether the parterre with its central pond and fountain was ever laid out to Barry's design is difficult to discover, for in 1899 the area was completely remodelled as a 'Dutch Garden', designed by the Salisbury diocesan architect C. E. Ponting, and with advice on planting from William Goldring of Kew. The long double staircase along the south side of the parterre seems never to have been built, and the balustrade here was replaced by a lower retaining wall, set with urns. The two large rectangular buildings shown in outline at the far end of the parterre are also somewhat mysterious. The one shown in elevation cannot have

been a conservatory since it is screened by an 'evergreen border' on the south side, and it is more likely that these were earlier stable and office buildings, demolished at a later date when a new stable block was built on the other side of the house.

In the nineteenth century, it was held that Inigo Jones had designed the original Kingston Lacy, and many of Barry's internal features were borrowed from other buildings attributed to him. The idea of the terrace on the south front with its long stone balustrade is likewise derived from Jones's *perron* at the Queen's House, Greenwich, though with a single instead of a horseshoe staircase in the centre. Once again there are differences between the drawing

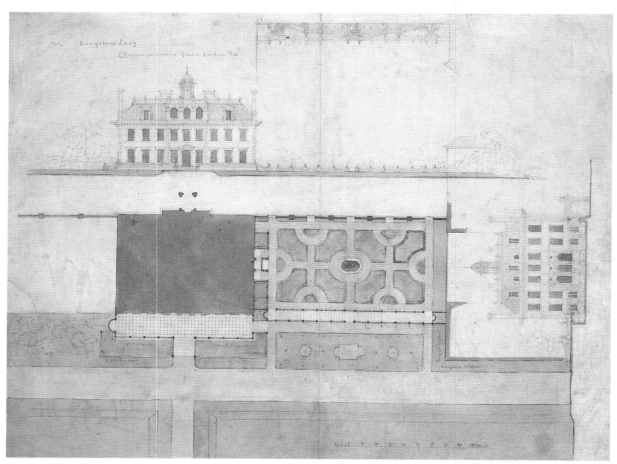

105

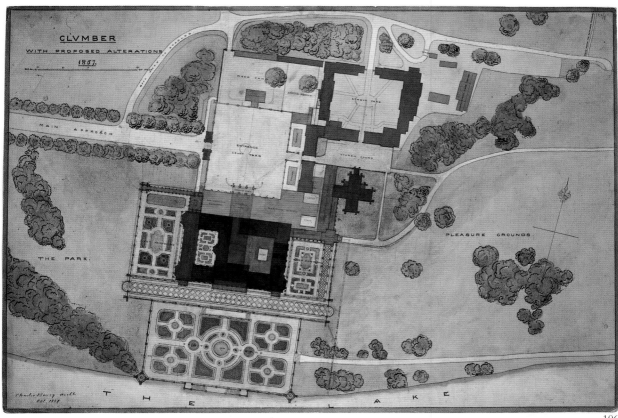

and what was executed: there are semicircular stone benches at both ends; the outer piers are doubled up; and the staircase sweeps outwards at the bottom. But the proportions are much the same, and so are the wide gravel paths – that on the main axis leading to the great Egyptian obelisk from the island of Philae, which William Bankes had brought to England in 1821.

106 Design for the garden at Clumber Park, Nottinghamshire, 1857

Sir Charles Barry (1795–1860)

Pen, ink, watercolour and pencil

Signed and dated: Oct. 1857

656 × 960mm (25¾ × 37¾in)

Drawings Collection, Royal Institute of British Architects, London

The original house at Clumber was designed by the Palladian architect Stephen Wright, a pupil of William Kent, in 1768–78. In 1857, the 5th Duke of Newcastle approached Charles Barry to enlarge the building and the latter proposed a vast Italianate mansion crowned by a dome. As usual, the architect took equal trouble with the setting of the house, suggesting a long terrace walk along the south front, a main terrace with fountains and formal beds extending as far as the lake, and subsidiary parterres on the east and west fronts.

Although his plans for the house were never fully implemented, old photographs of the garden show a balustraded main terrace and fountain, with steps down to the water very much in Barry's manner, and covering much the same area. So it is possible that his plans for the garden were at least

partly achieved. However, W. A. Nesfield was also employed on the garden in 1862, and he rather than Barry may have been responsible for the final form of the parterre. In 1879 the central part of the house was entirely destroyed by fire, and was subsequently rebuilt by Charles Barry the younger. The house was finally demolished in 1938, but the remains of the garden and landscape park, the stable yard, and the spectacular chapel built by G. F. Bodley for the 7th Duke in 1886–9, were acquired by the National Trust in 1946.

Barry's parterre designs, strictly architectural in treatment, often recall antique mosaic or marble floors, of the type which he had sketched on his extensive Mediterranean tour of 1817–20. Yet he also took a keen interest in how the beds were planted, as his correspondence and annotated drawings bear out. This proposal also shows what importance he attached to the overall landscape setting, controlling the views to and from the house by irregular belts of trees.

Literature: Brown, 1990, p. 92, No. 60.

107 Preliminary design for the south front and garden at Knightshayes Court, Devon, c.1868
William Burges (1827–81)

Watercolour

195 × 300mm (7¾ × 11¾in)

The National Trust (Heathcoat-Amory Collection), Knightshayes Court, Devon

Though undoubtedly emanating from William Burges's office, this preliminary sketch for the south front of Knightshayes may well have been commissioned by the architect from a professional perspectivist like E. S. Cole or Axel Haig – the author of the lithograph view of Knightshayes which appeared in *The Architect* for 2 July 1870. Another watercolour in the same hand (though circular in format) shows the proposed entrance front, again dominated by the huge staircase tower, which Burges had abandoned by the time the lithograph appeared.

Haig's view for *The Architect* shows the house set on somewhat intimidating ramparts with two terraces and corner bastions, increasing the vertical emphasis of the façade. The effect is softened only by a small cascade falling into a bason, between the two long flights of steps leading up to the house. In this earlier drawing, by contrast, the flower beds are full of vivid colour to complement the polychrome finish of the building, and to give the idea of a medieval 'pleasaunce', while the stone benches in the centre, forming a circle round a plashing fountain, strike a Moorish note: a synthesis

so often found in William Burges's designs.

A strong interest in horticulture can be traced throughout Burges's career, from the neo-Jacobean parterre at Gayhurst in Buckinghamshire of the late 1850s, to the roof and moat gardens of Cardiff Castle in the late 1860s, and the elaborate Pre-Raphaelite setting of his own Tower House in Melbury Road, Kensington, London, in the late 1870s. Here, within a very similar double *exedra* made of Jura marble, recalling the paintings of Alma-Tadema, Burges would (according to a later writer in the *Art Journal*) 'give tea to a few friends, who lounged on the marble seats or sat on Persian rugs and embroidered cushions round the pearl-inlaid table, brilliant with a tea service composed of things precious, rare and quaint' (Crook, 1981, pp. 308–9).

As it happened, the three steeply descending terraces on the south front proudly overlooking the Heathcoat-Amorys' textile mill in the valley below, were probably Burges's only contribution to the garden at Knightshayes. In 1874 he and his patron, Sir John Amory, fell out over the expense of his projected interiors, and the cheaper and more conventional decorator, John Diblee Crace, was hired in his place. At the same time the gardens were entrusted to Edward Kemp, who had been Paxton's chief assistant at Chatsworth and had gone on to design municipal parks like that at Birkenhead, influencing Olmsted's Central Park in New York, among others. He also wrote several standard books, including *How to Lay Out a Garden* (published in several editions beginning in 1850).

Some of Kemp's planting on the terraces, his tall yew hedges enclosing the bowling green, and his tradition of planting 'luxuriant' creepers on the house, have still been retained. But the fame of the woodland garden today is mostly

due to the work of the late Sir John Amory and his wife, the champion golfer, Joyce Wethered. Knightshayes has been maintained by the National Trust since Sir John's death in 1973.

108 Design for a Parterre at Wallington, Northumberland, 1882
Edward Milner (1819–84)

Pen, ink and watercolour

Signed and dated: 1882

Inscribed: 'Wallington/Plan of Flower Garden'; later inscription in pencil, bottom right, 'On west Lawn, now all turned back to Grass 1908'

Scale: 1in to 10ft

500 × 530mm (19¾ × 20⅞in)

The National Trust (Trevelyan Collection), Wallington, Northumberland

Like Edward Kemp, Edward Milner began his career at Chatsworth as one of Joseph Paxton's apprentices. Having spent four years in Paris, studying at the Jardin des Plantes, he superintended the laying out of Prince's Park, Liverpool, in 1844, and the grounds of the Crystal Palace at Sydenham in 1852–6, both to Paxton's designs. As well as public parks, he later took on many private commissions – mostly from industrialists, but also from a few Liberal landowners like the 2nd Earl of Durham at Fenton in Northumberland (c.1874).

Lord Durham could in turn have recommended Milner to his neighbour, Sir Charles Trevelyan of Wallington, who had inherited the property from his cousin in 1879. At that time, the only flower garden at Wallington lay across the public road, within the old eighteenth-century walled enclosures. Sir Charles and his second wife, Eleanora Campbell, evidently wanted something nearer the house, and Milner thus designed a formal parterre, rather in the French manner, to be seen

107

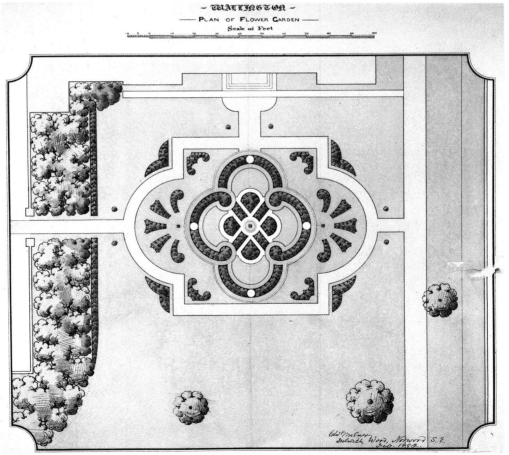

~ WALLINGTON ~

PLAN OF FLOWER GARDEN

Scale of Feet

Edw.d Milner
Dulwich Wood, Norwood S.E.
Feb. 1882.

108

immediately below the windows of the west front, where they had their private rooms.

Two other designs by Milner exist in the collection, both on tracing paper: one showing the irregular belts of trees beyond the parterre, enclosing the west lawn; and the other with a key to the planting of the beds. The suggestions include white, pink, scarlet and bronze geraniums, pink petunias, blue lobelias, calceolaria, ageratum, scarlet and yellow tropaeolum, phlox and asters: a brave display of colour to offset grey Northumbrian skies. As the pencilled note on the drawing indicates, this garden was to have a short life, but during a drought, the outlines of the beds can still be discerned in the grass.

Literature: Hodges, 1977, pp. 68–76.

109 A view of Bateman's, East Sussex, from the south-west, 1913

Sir Edward Poynter PRA (1836–1919)

Watercolour
Signed and dated: EJP 1913
368 × 536mm (14½ × 21⅛in)
The National Trust (Kipling Collection), Bateman's, East Sussex

Bateman's is an early seventeenth-century stone manor house, south of the village of Burwash in Sussex, which Rudyard Kipling and his American wife Caroline Balestier discovered 'down an enlarged rabbit-hole of a lane', and which they bought in 1902. Probably built by a prosperous ironmaster involved in the Wealden iron industry, it bears the date 1634 carved over the porch. The age and romance – and essential Englishness – of the house appealed to a writer who had spent so much of his life abroad, in India and America, and at Bateman's he

was to produce some of his best-known work: books like *Traffics and Discoveries* (1904), *Puck of Pook's Hill* (1906) – the hill that can be seen from the garden looking south-west – and *Rewards and Fairies* (1910). Much of his poetry also dates from this time, including *If* and *The Glory of the Garden*, while his last work, the autobiographical *Something of Myself* is in part a memorial to Bateman's.

The avenue of pleached limes seen on the right of this view had been planted in 1898, before the Kiplings bought the house, but they were responsible for laying out the paths and yew hedges that enclose this formal garden, and for making the large square pond, fed by the water turbine which was installed in 1903 in the mill on the River Dudwell. The curved garden seat within an alcove of yew at one end of the pond is of a form often used by Lutyens and possibly invented by Walter Godfrey (see page 5).

Sir Edward Poynter, son of the

painter and architect Ambrose Poynter, and Kipling's uncle, is the only man ever to have served concurrently as President of the Royal Academy and Director of the National Gallery. His son – also called Ambrose – became an architect like his grandfather, and helped the Kiplings to alter Bateman's, in particular giving one of the two oast houses its present mansard roof.

Literature: Ottewill, 1989, p. 115, fig. 168.

110 Sketch for the Planting of the Rose Garden at Bateman's, East Sussex, 1906

Rudyard Kipling (1865–1936)

Pen, ink and watercolour

Signed: 'R.K. del:/p.n.s./Aug 1906/ Bateman's'

Inscribed: 'All inside dotted/lines to be made/beds with seat/next year/as pr. sketch/opposite' [accompanied by sheet of watermarked paper (GR under crown), torn through middle, inscribed twice in ink 'Rudyard']

212 × 135 mm (8⅜ × 5¼in)

The National Trust (Kipling Collection), Bateman's, East Sussex

'Our England is a garden, and such gardens are not made/By singing:– "Oh, how beautiful" and sitting in the shade,/While better men than we go out and start their working lives/At grubbing weeds from gravel paths with broken dinner-knives.'

Kipling's attitude, expressed in *The Glory of the Garden*, was fully borne out by the hard work which he put into his own garden at Bateman's, designing most of it himself. The rectangular pond in this drawing is the one shown in Poynter's view (No. 109). This was made with a flat concrete bottom so that it would be used for boating and bathing by the Kipling children and their young friends. Sometimes an entry in the visitor's book is followed by the initials F.I.P., which stand for 'Fell In Pond'; the mysterious initials 'p.n.s.' which

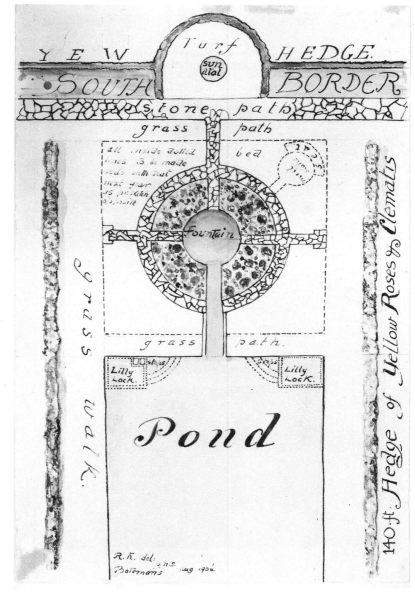

110

appear after Kipling's initials on this drawing may also have a punning explanation.

The rose garden with its central fountain, connected by a channel to the pond, remains just as it is shown here, with the sundial in a yew alcove beyond – answering the alcove seat seen in Poynter's view at the other end of the pond. On the sundial, the poet engraved the words 'It is later than you think',

and behind it is the original stone which marked Kipling's grave in Westminster Abbey. The wide-flagged southern terrace, which he always called the Quarter Deck (useful for pacing up and down in thought), extends westward to the boundary of the garden, where the planting becomes less formal, with trees and flowering shrubs planted in rough grass, carpeted with wild flowers in the spring.

111 Design for the garden at Polesden Lacey, Surrey, 1907

Frank Stuart Murray
(fl.1880–1910)

Pen and ink

Signed and dated: 1907

Endorsed: 'General View of Garden as planned 1907'

410 × 1190mm (16⅛ × 46⅞in)

The National Trust (Greville Collection), Polesden Lacey, Surrey

Once the home of the playwright Sheridan, Polesden Lacey was rebuilt as a Regency villa in 1821–3 to the designs of Thomas Cubitt.

Introduced to the Arts and Crafts Movement by his aunt, Georgina Burne-Jones, and influenced by the writings of Gertrude Jekyll, Avray Tipping and other contributors to *Country Life* in its early days, Kipling managed to make – in the magazine's own words – 'precisely the retreat which the English-speaking world would desire one of its wisest thinkers and most brilliant writers to have created for himself... a typical old English home, of which every part, within and without, both what is original and what has recently been added, is in ordered harmony, while the whole is redolent of the British soil and an epitome of generations of its men.'

In 1902 it was enlarged by Ambrose Poynter for Sir Clinton Dawkins, but on his death in 1906, it was bought by Captain the Hon. Ronald Greville and his young wife, Margaret McEwan, heiress to a Scottish brewing fortune.

Mrs Greville, who was to become one of the great society figures of her day, regularly entertaining Edward VII and other members of the Marlborough House set, had the interior of Polesden remodelled by Mewes and Davis, architects of the Ritz Hotel, and also commissioned a series of designs for the garden from the landscape architects Durand, Murray and Seddon. These drawings, all signed by one of the partners, Frank Stuart Murray, and dated 1907, show a grandiose Edwardian garden, dwarfing the house itself. Many influences can be traced – French parterre beds, Italian cypresses and junipers, Moorish pergolas – rather in the manner of Philip Tilden's later gardens at Port Lympne.

Durand, Murray and Seddon appears to have been a short-lived partnership between the ecclesiastical architect John Pollard Seddon (1827–1906), who worked principally in the Gothic style, Frank Murray – primarily a painter and decorative artist, who had collaborated with Seddon on the W. H. Smith memorial window in St Margaret's, Westminster, in 1893 – and Arthur Durand, who later established his own practice, exhibiting designs for the Park Lane Hotel at the Royal Academy in 1920. In 1905, the firm also showed at the Academy designs for painted decoration at Christ Church, Bristol, giving its address as 85 Newman Street, London W1. Seddon's obituary in the *Builder* the following year records that 'in conjunction with Mr. Murray, he prepared [this] scheme for the decoration, after the Italian Renaissance manner'. Murray himself had been a regular contributor to the Society of British Artists and other exhibitions from 1880 onwards, and held a one-man show of watercolours at 23 Hanover Square, London in 1908.

Seddon's name was presumably kept by the firm after his death, which would explain why it still appears on this group of Polesden Lacey drawings in 1907. It was probably Captain Greville's sudden death in 1908 which brought these ambitious schemes to an end, and the garden which was subsequently laid out with the help of J. Cheal & Sons was rather more conventional, with a series of hedged and walled enclosures filled with roses, peonies, iris and lavender, and giving views through 'windows' over the valley below.

112 Design for a pond in the garden at Polesden Lacey, Surrey, 1907

Frank Stuart Murray

Pen, ink and wash
Signed and dated: 1907
Inscribed: 'The Terrace Pond'
280 × 490mm (11 × 19¼in)
The National Trust (Greville Collection), Polesden Lacey, Surrey

The fountain and balustrade proposed in this drawing for Mrs Ronnie Greville could almost be called Elizabethan Art-Deco in style. The stylised dolphins grouped round a trident, and placed on a tall pedestal of faceted blocks, would feel almost as much at home in the public park of an early garden suburb as in the private domain of an Edwardian hostess.

Other watercolours in the series include one for the 'Gate to the Ladies Garden', rather in the manner of Voysey (who had indeed been a pupil of J. P. Seddon), and one for the 'Long Walk' (a grass terrace originally laid out in 1671, and extended by Sheridan) with stone vases on pedestals set against the backdrop of trees on one side, and a low hedge on the other with large semicircular bays providing viewpoints.

113 Design for a country cottage and its garden, 1907

Charles Paget Wade
(1883–1956)

Pen, ink and watercolour and shell gold, with inset mother-of-pearl
Signed and dated
Scale: 1in to 16ft
Inscribed: with numerous identifications of trees, plants, etc. and on the scroll below a poem by Christina Rossetti
615 × 475mm (24¼ × 18¾in)
The National Trust (Wade Collection), Snowshill Manor, Gloucestershire

A variant of this drawing, without the scroll at the top and signed with the pseudonym 'Peaceful Hours', won the young Charles Wade second prize in a competition for the design of a 'small garden', offered by *The Studio* magazine in 1907. But it anticipates many features of the garden at Snowshill Manor, Gloucestershire, which he bought in 1919, and which was laid out with the help of his friend and mentor, M. H. Baillie Scott (see No. 116).

When he won the prize, Wade had only qualified as an architect a few months before, and had just joined the drawing office of Raymond Unwin, architect to the Hampstead Garden Suburb Trust, under the overall supervision of Edwin Lutyens. Baillie Scott, one of the leading figures in the Arts and Crafts Movement, was also involved with the Hampstead project as an independent designer, and Wade had already come under his spell. Not only does the drawing betray many of Scott's favourite ideas, and the same style of draughtsmanship, but the explanatory notebook that accompanies it is full of quotations and paraphrases taken from his *Houses and Gardens*, published the year before.

One of the key ideas here was that the garden, with its 'apartments and leafy corridors', should be 'an outdoor extension of the house plan, so that the house

112

and garden are each part of a whole comprehensive scheme'. But another vital principle was the importance of vistas, 'necessarily more interesting than the mere disposition of winding walks, which never fulfil the promise they seem to convey of some vision beyond'. On the other hand, Wade continues, 'the defect of the formal treatment often lies in a certain barrenness, a lack of mystery, and those surprises and dramatic effects of light and shade which are such essential attributes of the garden. Open flower gardens are best approached through dim and shady alleys. Broad and open sunlit spaces should be contrasted with the shade of pergolas and embowered paths.'

To Baillie Scott's strictly practical philosophy, Wade also added an elaborate veneer of Pre-Raphaelite whimsy. His architectural plans, often dressed up with inlays of silk, ribbon and mother-of-pearl, are also notable for their calligraphy, with all the empty spaces filled with poetry and quotations. Even the planting could have an artistic source, as with the borders at either end of 'My Lady's Garden' in this drawing – marked 'Carnation, Lily, Lily, Rose', after Sargent's famous painting in the Tate Gallery painted in 1885–6.

Literature: Venison, 1980, pp. 1178–80, fig. 4; Ottewill, 1989, p. 138, fig. 208.

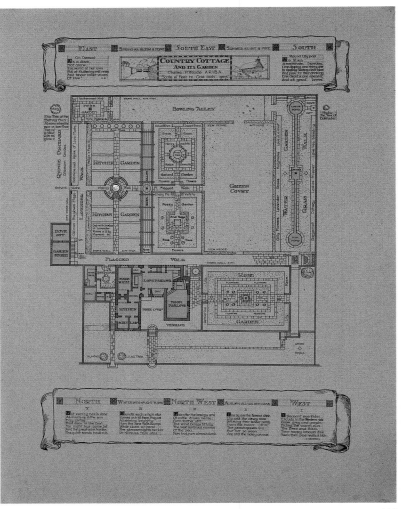

113

114 Design for part of the Dutch Garden at 'Caldicott Court', 1912

Charles Paget Wade (1883–1956)

Watercolour on cardboard

Inscribed: in pencil on verso 'Caldecote Court/Part of the Dutch Garden/March 1912 pinxit et inv./at Mansion/S. Kitts'

102 × 166mm (4 × 6½in)

The National Trust (Wade Collection), Snowshill Manor, Gloucestershire

During his time in Raymond Unwin's office, Charles Wade developed his unique talent as an illustrator, producing what Unwin called the 'charming and imaginative Pictures' for his book *Town Planning in Practice*. But his artistic temperament, and the restrictions put upon his designs by clients, finally decided him against a career as a professional architect, and in 1911 he left Unwin's office and spent the next few years (up to the outbreak of the First World War) illustrating books, including *Bruges* by Margaret Stratton, and *The Spirit of the House* by his Hampstead neighbour Kate Murray.

This watercolour and its companion (No. 115) were made for *The Spirit of the House* – 'Being an account of Caldicott Court an imaginary House – and of some who dwelt there', as explained on the title page. As its name implies, Caldicott was an idealised Cotswold manor house, obviously not far from Broadway and Sapperton,

those twin founts of the Arts and Crafts Movement, and foreshadowing in an almost uncanny way the house Wade was to buy for himself at Snowshill, after his return from the war in 1919. He must already have made a number of visits to this part of the world, and in his garden at Hampstead he even constructed a model Cotswold village, complete with station and clockwork train, for the amusement of Kate Murray's daughter, Elizabeth.

This view of part of the 'Dutch Garden' at Caldicott shows a combination of formality and simplicity characteristic of Wade's interest in the vernacular, and very different from the grandiose Italianate gardens being laid out by many of his contemporaries. Flowers were never as important to him as the architecture of a garden – here expressed by the yew 'walls', the stone-flagged paths and well-head, and the lawn carpeted with daisies. Only the cherry trees, purposely breaking this symmetry,

introduce a picturesque note. As he was later to write in his Snowshill notebook (No. 116), 'a delightful garden can be made in which flowers play a very small part, using effects of light and shade, vistas, steps to changing levels, terraces, walls, fountains, running water . . . few indeed are the botanists that can make a garden, they have instead a "Nurseryman's Catalogue" come to life.'

115 Design for the Herb Garden at 'Caldicott Court', 1913

Charles Paget Wade (1883–1956)

Watercolour on cardboard

Inscribed: on verso 'Caldecote Court/ The Herb Garden./inv. Ap.1913 – S. Kitts'

168 × 128mm (6⅝ × 5 in)

The National Trust (Wade Collection), Snowshill Manor, Gloucestershire

Once again made as an illustration for Kate Murray's *The Spirit of the*

115

116 Frontispiece and garden plan from a notebook describing Snowshill Manor, Gloucestershire, c.1951

Charles Paget Wade
(1883–1956)

Pen and ink, illustrated with watercolours, plans and sketches

Key to plan, written on opposite page, headed 'NOTE. The Garden slopes steeply down to the West from the MANOR HOUSE/1. Willow Grove/ 2. Gate House/3. Fore Court/4. Inner Court/5. Bird Cherry Tree/6. Gate Piers and old Sundial/7. Yew Hedge/ 8. Hornbeam Trees/9. Grass Terrace/ 10. Arbour/11. S George/ 12. Northumberland Shield & trappings[?]/13. Courtyard/ 14. Gate House to Cloisters/15. Tower/ 16. Grass Terrace/17. Sundial Court/ 18. Yew Trees/19. Bronze water spout/ 20. Horoscope/21. Pond/22. "Jolly Roger"/23. Grass Terrace/LOWER GARDEN/24. Lily Pool/25. Water Springs/26. Well Head/27. Garden House Hall of Heraldry/28. Garden House/29. Elder Glade/30. Dovecote/ 31. Clock, seat in arch recess below/ 32. Kitchen Garden Gate/Position of Garden Seats shown in Green, S.'

Frontispiece: 190 × 120mm (7½ × 4¾in)

Notebook, closed: 202 × 162mm (7⅞ × 6⅜in)

The National Trust (Wade Collection), Snowshill Manor, Gloucestershire

House (published by Hodder and Stoughton in 1915), this imaginary view of the Herb Garden at 'Caldicott Court' is another essay in Wade's Cotswold vernacular style. The feeling of enclosure, like the room of a house entered through 'doors' in the high yew hedges, and the controlled colours, seem to anticipate V. Sackville-West's famous White Garden at Sissinghurst, while the combination of box-edged beds, stone-paving, terracotta pots and sundial, are in the same spirit as the simple, hand-carved furniture of an Arts and Crafts interior.

Despite its quintessentially English character, both this watercolour and its companion (No. 114) were produced by Wade at St Kitts in the West Indies, on an estate which he had recently inherited (after the deaths of his father and uncle), and whose revenues enabled him to leave Raymond Unwin's office, and ultimately to buy Snowshill.

Snowshill is a typical Cotswold manor house, not far from Broadway, dating back to about 1500, but with seventeenth- and early eighteenth-century additions giving its south-facing entrance front a charming lop-sided look. When Charles Wade bought it in 1919, the house 'stood sad and desolate in the midst of a wilderness of chaos, the result of long years of neglect... nettles covered the slope from the very walls... right down to the kitchen garden, strewn with old iron, bones, broken crocks and debris.' The rest of his life was largely devoted to the restoration and embellishment of the house and garden, and the formation of its extraordinary collections –

116a

everything hand-crafted, from furniture, ceramics and glass to musical instruments, clocks, dolls, ships' models, bicycles and Japanese armour.

In 1951 he handed over the property to the National Trust, and this manuscript notebook, entitled 'SNOWSHILL.MANOR./THE. GARDEN./"FAR ESTRANGED FROM MAD/-DENING RIOT AND THE/ HAUNTS OF MEN"'', was probably made in that year, as a draft guidebook for early visitors. Instructions to a printer regarding spacing can be seen pencilled in some of the margins.

The watercolour pasted in as a frontispiece (and now temporarily removed), may be earlier in date. It illustrates one of the 'four most attractive pictures in my Garden', which he describes in the text as '(iii) From the Dovecote looking up flight of steps to the House partly screened by Alley of Yews, the chimney towering above against the sky. Particularly lovely at Sunset time when entrancing shadows play on the walls.' The bright blue-green colour of the sash window may come as a surprise, but bears out one of Wade's *dicta* in the notebook: 'Never paint a "nature" green, turquoise is the most satisfactory colour, a foil to the grass and foliage' – a tradition still kept up in the painting of the front door and entrance gates.

The layout of the garden at Snowshill used always to be attributed to Wade himself, but plans by M. H. Baillie Scott, dated 1920, were discovered fairly recently among the papers in the house, together with correspondence proving that he was undoubtedly responsible for the initial conception. Naturally Wade was to make important alterations and additions as work progressed – in the Sundial Court (17), for instance, Scott's two cross-paths were omitted; the four segments round the sundial, which he marked 'flowers', were laid as

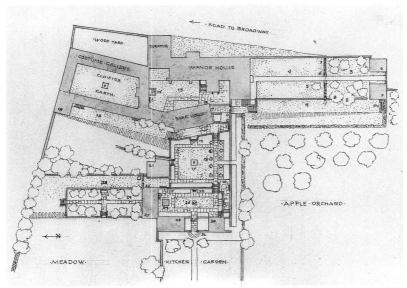

116b

Beatrix Potter (1866–1943)

Pen and ink, sepia ink and watercolour
Both 107 × 87mm (4¼ × 3⅜in)
The National Trust, Beatrix Potter
Gallery, Hawkshead, Cumbria
© Frederick Warne PLC

The vogue for the cottage garden, crammed with 'old-fashioned' flowers, goes back to the poetry of Tennyson, and William Morris's philosophy of the homespun. An important influence on garden designers like Gertrude Jekyll, it was also disseminated at another level by book illustrations like those of Kate Greenaway, Helen Allingham and Beatrix Potter. The garden at Hill Top, the Lake District farm which Beatrix Potter bought in 1905, partly with the proceeds of her first book, *The Tale of Peter Rabbit*, was to be the setting for many of her books, starting with *Tom Kitten*, published in 1907.

Though she was already experienced at botanical drawing, with an advanced knowledge of plant forms, it was the picturesque qualities of the garden that appealed above all. Gwaynynog in Denbighshire, the home of her uncle Fred Burton (and home also of the *Flopsy Bunnies*), provided her with a model – 'very productive but not tidy, the prettiest kind of garden, where bright old fashioned flowers grow amongst the currant bushes'. The borders at Hill Top, like the other Sawrey cottages depicted in *The Pie and the Patty-Pan*, were to be a jostling mass of snapdragons, pinks and pansies, old roses, lavender and lilies. Like Gertrude Jekyll, she subscribed to the notion that bare earth should be visible only in a vegetable patch.

In one of these scenes, Mrs Tabitha Twitchit, the farm cat at Hill Top (and Tom's mother), has pulled the kittens off the wall and is giving them a good smack for

lawn; and the low central pedestal was replaced by a tall column with an armillary sphere – so it would perhaps be more accurate to call the garden a work of friendly collaboration.

As with the *Studio* competition entry of 1907 (No. 113), and as with Baillie Scott's *Houses and Gardens* plans, the Snowshill garden consists of a series of courts linked by long and cross-vistas not only with each other, but also with the various barns and outbuildings which cling to the side of the steep hill. Most of these are adequately identified on the key, printed above, but it should perhaps be mentioned that the 'Horoscope' (20) is an astrological dial set into paving representing the stars at the moment of Wade's own birth, while 'Jolly Roger' (22) is 'a little summer cabin originally placed in connection with the ½″ scale model of a [Cornish] sea-port for which the pond formed the sea'.

The Bake House, otherwise known as the 'Priest's House', just below the manor to the west, was Charles Wade's own cottage until his death in 1956. The two ancient bread ovens below provided the only means of heating for his

bedroom above, for there was no electricity anywhere on the property. The 'Costume Gallery', 'Cloister Garth' and tower (15) were designed just before the Second World War, but never built. Their appearance on this plan suggests that the idea was still in Wade's mind in his last years. Age had by no means dimmed his romantic spirit, as the poems in the notebook prove, and one of them, entitled simply 'Snowshill Manor', wonderfully evokes the magic of the place in its opening stanzas: 'An old house in the Cotswolds/ Stands dreaming in the dusk,/ Fragrance sweet of Lavender/ And perfume of the musk...'

Literature: Venison, 1980, pp. 1178–80, fig. 7.

117a

117b

having lost their party clothes to the Puddle-Ducks. In the other (used as the frontispiece to the book) she is hurrying them indoors, where they are sent up to bed, unfit to be seen by the guests at her tea-party. The mixture of vegetables, espaliered fruit trees and flowers, the riot of climbing plants on the house itself, and the sense of enclosure given by the grey slate walls and simple timber gates, reflects something of the author's own complex character: that combination of the idyllic and the severely practical which makes her work so quintessentially English.

Literature: Taylor, etc., 1987, p. 130, fig. 281.

118 Perspective view of Castle Drogo, Devon, from the south-east, 1923

Cyril Farey (1888–1954) after Sir Edwin Lutyens (1869–1944)

Watercolour

Signed and dated: 'Cyril A. Farey/ Del.1923' and also bottom right 'Edwin L. Lutyens 1923'

630 × 540mm (24¾ × 21¼in)

The National Trust, Castle Drogo, Devon

Soon after the First World War, with the curtailment of his original plans for the great castle commissioned by Julius Drewe, Lutyens and his patron also decided to abandon the idea of a large garden on the east, which would have necessitated massive earthworks and terracing, and instead chose a new site on the hillside to the north. The wild landscape of heather, bracken and pines on the hillside below was thus preserved, and in his biographer's words, Lutyens agreed that 'the dark firs against the metallic granite walls and the whispering of the wind in their branches contributed to the whole effect' (Hussey, 1953, p. 220).

Probably the leading

architectural draughtsman of his day, Cyril Farey was often employed by Lutyens to produce coloured perspectives of his buildings for presentation to a client, or for exhibition. He also occasionally worked as an architect in his own right. This drawing, with its pair, was acquired by the National Trust in 1982, with generous support from the National Art-Collections Fund.

Exhibited: Hayward Gallery, London, 1981, No. 159(9).

119 Design for the garden and carriage approach at Castle Drogo, Devon, 1915

Sir Edwin Lutyens (1869–1944)

Pen, ink and wax crayon on tracing paper

Signed and dated: E. L. Lutyens A. R. A./17 Queen Anne's Gate/ London S.W. Nov 1915

Inscribed: 'Castle Drogo, Devon/ Layout of Garden Carriage Approach Etc/Drawing no 183'

Scale: 1in to 16ft

687 × 758mm (27 × 29¾in)

The National Trust (Drewe Collection), Castle Drogo, Devon

Begun in 1910, Lutyens's Castle Drogo was not originally intended to be the intriguing essay in asymmetry it now appears. On the contrary, the great hall range – part of whose undercroft is now occupied by the chapel – would have been approached across an enclosed courtyard, with the gatehouse range framed by balancing splayed wings on the east and west (the latter never begun). This makes it easier to understand the idea of a great formal garden, which Lutyens originally intended on the east side of the building, as seen in this plan, overlooked by the windows of the drawing-room, library and billiard-room, and the private family rooms in the wing. Massive terraces and bastions would have been needed here, jutting out above the ravine that

118

bounds the site, but the effect would certainly have been spectacular.

Ever since his early association with Gertrude Jekyll (or 'Bumps' as he affectionately called her), Lutyens had developed an abiding interest in the settings of his buildings – giving the architectural bones of their garden layouts, which she then fleshed out with her planting schemes. From 1894 (when they worked together on her own house at Munstead Wood) up to 1912, they created some 70 gardens in partnership, and he always remained acutely conscious of the importance of her role. Giving a vote of thanks to T. H. Mawson after one of his lectures in 1908, he stressed that 'the true adornment of a garden lies

surely in its flowers and plants. No artist has so wide a pallette as the garden designer, and no artist greater need of discretion and reserve. When a design begins to appear as merely a collection of features, then I think it is time to look in which direction our india-rubber has bounced' (Hussey, 1953, p. 174).

In this design for Castle Drogo, Lutyens's skill in relating the garden to the building is immediately apparent. The upper terrace walk is aligned on the bow window of the library, continuing the axis right through from the front door, while the suggestion of a tree circle turning into an avenue brilliantly solves the awkward change of axis at the point where the house itself is 'hinged'. Despite

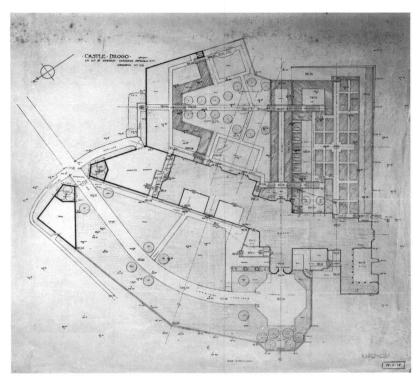

119

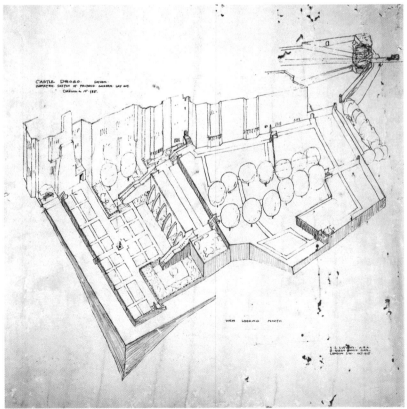

120

this formal architectural treatment, much freedom has been left to the garden designer – evidently Miss Jekyll, who had already been called to advise on the planting along the drive – to fill in the various borders and compartments, and to supply the detail.

120 Sketch of proposed garden layout at Castle Drogo, Devon, 1915

Sir Edwin Lutyens (1869–1944)

Pen, ink and pencil

Signed and dated: E. L. Lutyens A.R.A./17 Queen Anne's Gate/London S.W. Oct 1915

Inscribed: 'Castle Drogo, Devon/ Isometric Sketch of Proposed Garden Lay Out/Drawing No 185'; and at bottom 'View looking North'

511 × 522mm (20⅛ × 20½in)

The National Trust (Drewe Collection), Castle Drogo, Devon

The technique of the isometric sketch, often favoured by Lutyens for his more complex buildings, was also crucial for the design of a garden on so many levels and with so many elements as this Castle Drogo project. The gridiron of small (presumably grass) plots round a central fountain on the lower parterre looks back to sixteenth- and seventeenth-century precedents, while also exaggerating the bulk of the great granite walls of the castle looming above. The buttresses supporting the upper terrace walk have flower beds between them, as if interrupting one long herbaceous border, while the 'hanging' gardens either side recall Italian Renaissance gardens like the Villa Lante, visited by Lutyens in 1912 while helping with the rebuilding of the British School in Rome.

It is interesting to note that the idea of a gatehouse on the main drive, mocked-up at full scale in timber and canvas in 1913, still appears a possibility. In the end, this too was abandoned, and the

121

triangular enclosures shown behind were carried out as solid blocks of clipped yews.

121 Design for the path and shrub borders between the rose garden and croquet lawn at Castle Drogo, Devon, c.1924

Sir Edwin Lutyens (1869–1944)

Pencil on tracing paper

Inscribed: 'Castle Drogo'

782 × 516mm (30¾ × 20¼in)

The National Trust (Drewe Collection), Castle Drogo, Devon

In 1922, the idea of a garden on the east side of the castle was finally abandoned, having already been very much simplified in the

preceding year. Perhaps because Gertrude Jekyll's eyesight was fading, and perhaps also because Lutyens's patron, Julius Drewe, had his own ideas about planting, the landscape gardening firm of R. Wallace and Co. from Tunbridge Wells was employed to make a large new rose garden north-west of the castle, entirely surrounded by yew hedges, with three terraces at the upper end. From here, a central path led up to a huge circular croquet lawn at the top – once again enclosed by clipped yew.

One of the partners in the firm, George Dillistone, had earlier advised Julius Drewe on the garden at Wadhurst (just outside Tunbridge Wells) and his name appears on the detailed planting

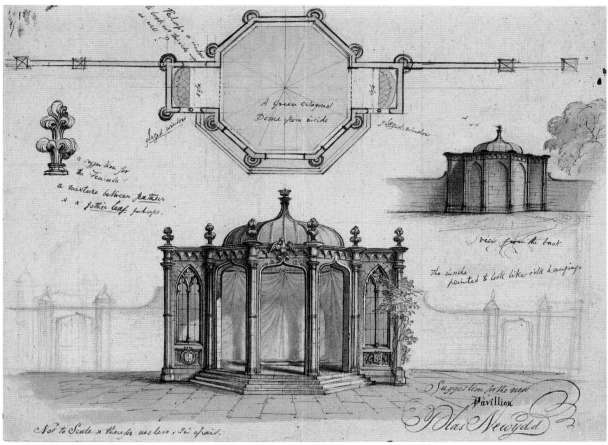

Handwritten annotations on the drawing include: "Perhaps a roof glazed as real?", "Glazed window", "A green octagonal Dome from inside", "Glazed window", "a proper Vase for the Finials — a mixture between feathers & a gothic leaf perhaps.", "view from the back", "The inside painted to look like silk hangings", "Suggestion for the new / Pavillion / Plas Newydd", "Not to Scale & therefore useless, & so forth."

schemes still in the collection. However, the general outlines were almost certainly given by Lutyens. The twisting border paths in particular owe their origin to a pattern he had seen in India, and which he was to re-employ in the gardens of Viceroy's House, New Delhi.

Lutyens also submitted two alternative designs for the pathway ascending from the rose garden to the croquet lawn: this one with its yew 'buttresses', contrasting with the natural foliage between; and a less severely architectural solution with pairs of unclipped Irish yews separated by paler shrubs. Playing with an idea already seen in the larger garden design for Castle Drogo years before, the 'buttress' scheme has the same monumental simplicity found in the corridors of the house itself: a response to the past that is entirely individual, never descending to the mere pastiche.

122 Design for a Gothick pavilion at Plas Newydd, Isle of Anglesey, 1936

Rex Whistler (1905–44)

Watercolour, ink and pencil with shell gold; pencil sketches on verso
Inscribed: bottom right: 'Suggestion for the new/Pavillion/Plas Newydd'; and bottom left: 'Not to scale so therefore useless'
Watermark: TL
230 × 300mm (9 × 11⅞in)
The Marquess of Anglesey

While Rex Whistler was working on the great dining-room mural at Plas Newydd between 1936 and 1938, he made various sketches and proposals for architectural features at the house. It was, for instance, he who modified H. S. Goodhart-Rendel's design for a screen wall on the west front (dividing the new car-park from the garden) by including the present rusticated archways either end, with grilles over heavy panelled doors. Another perspective view shows a more ambitious scheme, with a parallel wall forming a paved courtyard, a central fountain, and a Baroque doorcase added to the house.

This, one of the most elaborate of his architectural drawings, is a suggestion for a Gothick summer-house to be built in the centre of Goodhart-Rendel's wall between the two arches – which are lightly sketched in, rather too small in scale. In an accompanying letter, Whistler explained that the interior was to be decorated with 'painted hangings [which] we could do in one afternoon & the gold stars on top next day'. Despite this optimistic assessment, the 6th Marquess of Anglesey did not pursue the idea. Having just stripped the house of much of Joseph Potter's playful early seventeenth-century Gothick ornament, it is indeed hard to imagine him taking the proposal seriously. Like Repton's earlier Gothick greenhouse (page 19), Whistler's pavilion joined the ranks of the 'might-have-beens'.

Literature: Jackson-Stops, 1977, p. 287, fig. 5.

123 Design for the Nymphaeum at West Green House, Hampshire, 1977

Quinlan Terry (b.1937)

Pen and ink

Signed and dated

Inscribed: 'True Elevation (not Perspective)' and with various instructions to the builder

Scale: 1in to 1ft

615 × 615mm (24 × 24in)

Quinlan Terry, Esq.

West Green House, near Hartley Wintney, is an early eighteenth-century house that once belonged to General Hawley, a vindictive pursuer of Jacobites after the 1745 Rebellion. The garden was laid out by Evelyn, Duchess of Wellington, from 1904. In 1957 West Green was acquired by the National Trust, and from 1973 to 1990 let to Lord McAlpine, who proceeded to develop what has recently been called 'the best post-war garden in Britain'.

Quinlan Terry, a pupil (and later partner) of the classical architect Raymond Erith, was commissioned

(Right) The Nymphaeum at West Green House, Hampshire, seen on the vista from the walled garden

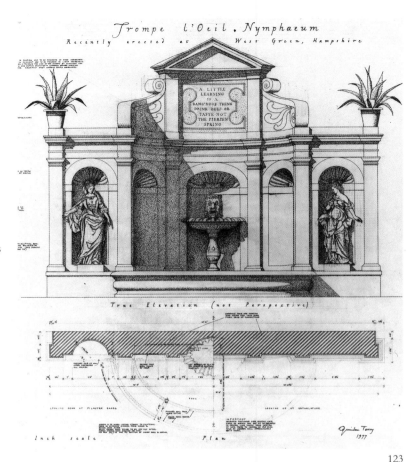

123

to design a large number of eye-catchers and follies in the garden, including a Chinese bridge, a 'primitive' hut with tree-trunk columns, a grotto, aviaries and a tin 'tent'. One of the most elaborate is the Nymphaeum or *Prospettiva*, which terminates a long vista from the old walled garden south-west of the house, and which also conceals a cow-shed accessible from the park behind.

The building is an essay in false perspective, as can be seen from the plan, with the 'shadows' in darker-coloured rendering than the rest. Only the tablet carved with the inscription from Pope, and the fountain basin below, are of carved stone. Like the house itself, the Nymphaeum is in the Palladian style, and reminiscent of the central fountain in the *cortile* behind the Villa Maser: quite a common feature in country houses of the Italian Renaissance. The terracotta flowerpots contain imitation yuccas, perhaps inspired by Charles Barry's copper-leaved 'plants' in urns placed along some of the parapets at Cliveden.

Literature: Brown, 1990, p. 206, fig. 28.

124 Design for the Column at West Green House, Hampshire, 1976

Quinlan Terry (b.1937)

Pen and ink

Signed and dated

Inscribed: 'The New Column at West Green', and with a translation of the Latin inscription on the pedestal: 'This Monument was built with a large sum of money, which would have otherwise fallen, sooner or later, into the hands of the officials of the Inland Revenue'

Scale: 1in to 1ft

920 × 227mm (36¼ × 8⅞in)

The Lord McAlpine

The Column at West Green has become something of a local landmark, placed just inside the entrance gates, and at the end of a long, narrow *allée* of lime trees leading to the centre of General Hawley's battlemented north front. The only major difference in execution is that the rusticated bands of stone on the pillar are carved to resemble blocks of irregular length.

The inscription on the pedestal, a criticism of high taxation under a Labour government, has proved particularly appropriate given Lord McAlpine's subsequent role as treasurer of the Conservative Party for much of Mrs Thatcher's time in office. This openly political statement also revives an eighteenth-century practice, best seen in the Elysian Fields at Stowe (see No. 37). Among other unfulfilled projects at West Green was the creation of a triumphal arch for the first lady Prime Minister.

Literature: Brown, 1990, p. 206, fig. 31.

125 Robert Furber's *Twelve Months of Flowers*, 1730

Henry Fletcher (fl.1710–50) after Pieter Casteels (1684–1749)

Engraving

Dedication to 'His/Royal Highness/ Frederick/Prince of/Wales' and 'The/ Princess/Royal'. 'To their Royal Highness's Frederick Prince of Wales, the Princess Royal. To the Most Noble, Rt Honble and the other Generous/ Subscribers to these Twelve Months of Flowers. This Plate is humbly Dedicated, by their Most Obedient, and Oblidg'd/humble Servants. Robert Furber, Peter Cassteels, Henry Fletcher'

590 × 480mm (open) (23¼ × 18⅞in)

The National Trust (Bankes Collection), Kingston Lacy, Dorset

After so many designs for gardens and garden buildings, it may be appropriate to include, as a postscript, two pages from the earliest illustrated nurseryman's catalogue to appear in Britain: Robert Furber's *Twelve Months of Flowers*. First, it serves to commemorate the patrons (listed

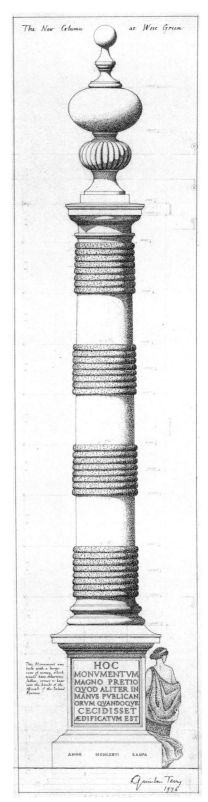

124

particular month, all the different varieties (including 25 American plants) actually formed part of Furber's stock. So, although he avoided offending his aristocratic clients by printing vulgar prices, the *Months* acted as an admirable advertisement for his business. It was followed in 1733 by a collection of 'several useful Catalogues of Fruit and Flowers' gathered together under the title *A Short Introduction to Gardening*.

Much work remains to be done on the species available at particular dates, and the influence this had on garden design. Meanwhile, Furber's list of clients – including Bowater Vernon of Hanbury, Lady Curzon of Kedleston and Henry Hoare of Stourhead, gives us an insight into one of the most creative periods in the whole history of British landscape gardening.

Literature: Harvey, 1972, pp. 14–15, frontispiece and plates 1–12.

here as subscribers) who made these landscape gardens possible; and, second, it suggests the enormous debt owed by them (and us) to generations of gifted botanists and horticulturists, who brought plants and seeds to these shores from all over the world.

Robert Furber was one of two particularly enterprising nurserymen, who purchased the majority of the rare plants from the famous collection of Henry Compton, Bishop of London, at Fulham Palace, after the latter's death in 1713. With the recent death of George London, the retirement of Henry Wise, and the preoccupation of Charles Bridgeman with pure garden

designs, Furber soon became the leading retailer of plants in the capital, with premises in Kensington Gore that were to become as famous as London and Wise's Brompton Park. In 1727 he produced *A Catalogue of English and Foreign Trees* and *A Catalogue of Fruit Trees* – the earliest printed nurseryman's (as opposed to seedsman's) lists known – and then, three years later, the *Twelve Months of Flowers*, containing thirteen hand-coloured engravings after pictures which he must specially have commissioned from the Flemish-born artist Pieter Casteels.

Despite the decorative effect of each plate, representing flowers supposed to bloom in that

Bibliography

Unless otherwise stated, books were published in London.

Binney, 1991: Marcus Binney, 'Wentworth Woodhouse, Yorks', *Country Life*, 24 January 1991, pp. 60–3

Bold, 1989: John Bold, *Gilbert White*, 1986

Brown, 1989: Jane Brown, *The Art and Architecture of English Gardens*, 1989

Burrell, 1983: Michael and Innis Burrell, *The Temple of British Worthies: An Illustrated Guide*, 1983

Carter, Goode and Laurie, 1982: George Carter, Patrick Goode and Kedrun Laurie, *Humphry Repton, Landscape Gardener* (exhibition catalogue), Norwich and London, 1982–3

Clarke, 1987: George Clarke, *Bridgeman's Stowe* (descriptive notes to the reprinted edition of Rigaud's engravings of Stowe, 1739), 1987

Clarke, 1990: ed. G. B. Clarke, 'Descriptions of Lord Cobham's Gardens at Stowe (1700–50)', Buckinghamshire Record Office, Vol. 26, 1990

Clay, 1941: Rotha Mary Clay, *Samuel Hieronymous Grimm*, 1941

Conner, 1979: Patrick Conner, *Oriental Architecture in the West*, 1979

Cornforth, 1967: John Cornforth, 'Saltram, Devon – I', *Country Life*, 27 April 1967, pp. 998–1001

Cornforth, 1979: John Cornforth, 'Dudmaston, Shropshire', *Country Life*, 8, 15 and 22 March 1979, pp. 634–7

Croft-Murray, 1970: Edward Croft-Murray, *Decorative Painting in England*, Vol. II, 1970, pp. 196–7

Crook, 1981: J. Mordaunt Crook, *William Burges and the High Victorian Dream*, 1981

Dixon Hunt, 1987: John Dixon Hunt, *William Kent – Landscape Garden Designer*, 1987

Dixon Hunt & de Jong, 1988: ed. John Dixon Hunt and Eric de Jong, 'The Anglo-Dutch Garden in the Age of William and Mary', *Journal of Garden History*, Vol. 8, April–September 1988

Du Prey, 1979: Pierre de la Ruffinière du Prey, 'John Soane, Philip Yorke and the Quest for Primitive Architecture', *National Trust Yearbook* 1979, pp. 28–38

Evans, 1972: Elspeth A. Evans, 'Jacques Rousseau; a Huguenot Decorative Artist at the Courts of Louis XIV and William III', *Proceedings of the Huguenot Society of London*, 1972

Fothergill, 1974: Brian Fothergill, *The Mitred Earl – An Eighteenth-Century Eccentric*, 1974

Friedman, 1984: Terry Friedman, *James Gibbs*, 1984

Gilpin, 1782: Rev. William Gilpin, *Observations on the River Wye, etc.* 1782

Gibbon, 1977: Michael Gibbon, 'Stowe, Buckinghamshire: the house and garden buildings and their designers', *Architectural History*, 1977, Vol. 20, pp. 31–44

Girouard, 1962: Mark Girouard, 'The Smythson Collection', *Architectural History*, 1962, Vol. 5

Godber, 1968: Joyce Godber, 'Marchioness Grey of Wrest Park', *Proceedings of the Bedfordshire Historical Record Society*, Vol. 47, 1968

Gowing and Clarke, 1983: C. N. Gowing and G. B. Clarke, *Drawings of Stowe by John Claude Nattes in the Buckinghamshire County Museum*, 1983

Gunnis, 1951: Rupert Gunnis, *Dictionary of British Sculptors 1660–1851*, 1951

Harris and Jackson-Stops, 1987: Leslie Harris and Gervase Jackson-Stops, 'Robert Adam and the Kedleston Landscape', *Country Life*, 5 March 1987, pp. 98–101

Harris, 1971: Eileen Harris, 'The Architecture of Thomas Wright', *Country Life*, 26 August, 2 and 9 September 1971, pp. 492–5, 546–50, 612–15

Harris, 1970: John Harris, *Sir William Chambers*, 1970

Harris, 1979: John Harris, *The Artist and the Country House*, 1979

Harvey, 1972: John Harvey, *Early Gardening Catalogues*, 1972

Hodges, 1977: Alison Hodges, 'A Victorian Gardener: Edward Milner', *Garden History*, Vol. 5, No. 3, November 1977

Hussey, 1953: Christopher Hussey, *The Life of Sir Edwin Lutyens*, 1953

Jackson-Stops, 1973: Gervase Jackson-Stops, 'A Formal Garden Re-formed', *Country Life*, 27 September 1973, pp. 864–6

Jackson-Stops, 1974: Gervase Jackson-Stops, 'The West Wycombe Landscape – I and II', *Country Life*, 20 and 27 June, 1974, pp. 1618–21 and 1682–5

Jackson-Stops, 1975: Gervase Jackson-Stops, 'A Thames-Side Parterre', *Country Life*, 9 October 1975, pp. 902–3

Jackson-Stops, 1976–7: Gervase Jackson-Stops, 'Formal Garden Designs for Cliveden', *National Trust Year Book* 1976–7, pp. 100–17

Jackson-Stops, 1977: Gervase Jackson-Stops, 'Rex Whistler at Plas Newydd', *Country Life*, 4 August 1977, pp. 286–9

Jackson-Stops, 1977: Gervase Jackson-Stops, 'The Cliveden Album: drawings by Archer, Leoni and Gibbs for the 1st Earl of Orkney', *Architectural History*, Vol. 19, 1976, pp. 5–16

Jackson-Stops, 1977a: Gervase Jackson-Stops, 'Cliveden, Buckinghamshire – I and II', *Country Life*, 24 February and 3 March 1977, pp. 438–41, pp. 498–501

Jackson-Stops, 1979: Gervase Jackson-Stops, 'The Park and Gardens at Wimpole – I', *Country Life*, 6 September 1979, pp. 658–61

Jackson-Stops, 1982: Gervase Jackson-Stops, *Nostell Priory* (The National Trust, 1978; revised edition 1982)

Jackson-Stops, 1983: Gervase Jackson-Stops, 'The Argory, Co. Armargh – II', *Country Life*, 7 July 1983, pp. 20–4

Lawson and Waterson, 1975–6: James Lawson and Merlin Waterson, 'Pritchard as Architect and Antiquary at Powis', *National Trust Year Book, 1975–6*, pp. 8–11

Leach, 1988: Peter Leach, *James Paine*, 1988

Lewis, 1831: S. Lewis, *Topographical Dictionary...*, Vol. 4, 1831

Mabey, 1986: Richard Mabey, *Gilbert White* 1986

Maddison, 1987: ed. John Maddison, *Blickling Hall* (The National Trust, 1987)

McCarthy, 1975: Michael McCarthy, 'John Chute's Drawings for The Vyne', *National Trust Yearbook 1975–6*

Mitchell, 1977–8: Anthony Mitchell, 'The Park and Garden at Dyrham', *National Trust Year Book 1977–8*, pp. 83–108

Newman & Maddison, 1987: John Newman and John Maddison, *Blickling Hall, Norfolk* (The National Trust, 1987)

Ottewill, 1989: David Ottewill, *The Edwardian Garden*, New Haven and London 1989

Pococke, 1888–9: ed. J. J. Cartwright, 'Dr. Richard Pococke's Travels through England', *Proceedings of the Camden Society*, 1888–9

Percy and Jackson-Stops, 1974: Victoria Percy and Gervase Jackson-Stops, 'The Travel Journals of the 1st Duchess of Northumberland', *Country Life*, 31 January, 7 and 14 February 1974, pp. 192–5, 250–2, 308–10

Robinson, 1989: John Martin Robinson, *Shugborough* (The National Trust, 1989)

Rorschach, 1983: Kimerly Rorschach, *The Early Georgian Landscape Garden* (catalogue of an exhibition at Yale Center for British Art), New Haven 1983

Rowan, 1988: Alastair Rowan, *Robert Adam* (Catalogue of Drawings in the Victoria and Albert Museum), 1988

Simo, 1988: Melanie Louise Simo, *Loudon and the Landscape*, 1988

Strong, 1979: Roy Strong, *The Renaissance Garden in England*, 1979

Stroud, 1975: Dorothy Stroud, *Capability Brown*, 1975

Stroud, 1976: Dorothy Stroud, 'The Gardens at Claremont', *National Trust Year Book 1975–6*, pp. 32–7

Tait, 1980: A. A. Tait, *The Landscape Garden in Scotland 1735–1835*, Edinburgh 1980

Taylor, etc., 1987: Judy Taylor, Joyce Irene Whalley, Anne Stevenson Hobbs, Elizabeth M. Battrick, *Beatrix Potter 1866–1943: The Artist and her World*, 1987

Venison, 1980: Tony Venison, 'Snowshill and the Baillie Scott Connection', *Country Life*, 17 April 1980, pp. 1178–80

Ware, 1738: ed. Isaac Ware, *The Four Books of Andrea Palladio's Architecture*, 1738 (Dover reprint, New York 1965)

Willis, 1977: Peter Willis, *Charles Bridgeman and the English Landscape Garden*, 1977

Woodbridge, 1970: Kenneth Woodbridge, *Landscape and Antiquity: Aspects of English Culture at Stourhead 1718–1838*, Oxford 1970

Woodbridge, 1982: Kenneth Woodbridge, *The Stourhead Landscape* (The National Trust, 1982)

London (Agnew), 1965: *English Pictures from National Trust Houses* (Agnew's, London, 1965)

Manchester, 1981: *The Order of the Day* (Whitworth Art Gallery, Manchester, 1981)

Norwich and London 1982–3: *Humphry Repton, Landscape Gardener, 1752–1818* (Sainsbury Centre for Visual Arts, University of East Anglia, Norwich, September–October 1982; Victoria and Albert Museum, London, December 1982–February 1983)

Index

Italic numbers refer to pages on which illustrations appear, **bold** numbers refer to catalogue entries